D1590261

INSIDE THE GAZE

The Society for Cinema Studies Translation Series

Peter Brunette, *George Mason University, Series Editor*

EDITORIAL BOARD:

Richard Abel, *Drake University*
Dudley Andrew, *University of Iowa*
Julianne Burton, *University of California, Santa Cruz*
Miriam Hansen, *University of Chicago*

FRANCESCO CASETTI

Inside the Gaze:
The Fiction Film and
Its Spectator

TRANSLATED BY NELL ANDREW WITH CHARLES O'BRIEN

PREFACE TO THE ENGLISH EDITION BY DUDLEY ANDREW

INTRODUCTION BY CHRISTIAN METZ

INDIANA UNIVERSITY PRESS

Bloomington and Indianapolis

This book is a publication of
Indiana University Press
601 North Morton Street
Bloomington, IN 47404-3797 USA

http://www.indiana.edu/~iupress

Telephone orders   800-842-6796
Fax orders   812-855-7931
Orders by e-mail   iuporder@indiana.edu

This translation copyright 1998 by Indiana University Press.
Published in Italian as *Dentro lo sguardo: il film e il suo spettatore*
(Milan: Bompiani, 1996).

In accordance with the author's preference, this translation was
prepared from the French edition, *D'un regard l'autre: le film et
son spectateur*, trans. Jean Chateauvert and Martine Joly (Lyon:
Presses Universitaires de Lyon, 1990), with reference to the
Italian edition.

All rights reserved

The paper used in this publication meets the minimum
requirements of American National Standard for Information
Sciences—Permanence of Paper for Printed Library
Materials, ANSI Z39.48-1984.

Manufactured in the United States of America

Library of Congress Cataloging-in-Publication Data

Casetti, Francesco.
    [Dentro lo sguardo. English]
    Inside the gaze : the fiction film and its spectator / by
Francesco Casetti ; translated by Nell Andrew with Charles O'Brien.
        p.   cm. — (The Society for Cinema Studies translation series)
    Includes index.
    ISBN 0-253-33443-8 (hardcover : alk. paper). — ISBN 0-253-21232-4
pbk. : alk. paper)
    1. Motion picture audiences.   2. Motion pictures—Influence.
3. Motion pictures—Semiotics.   I. Title.   II. Series.
PN1995.9.A8C3713   1998
302.23'43—dc21   98-34481

1 2 3 4 5   03 02 01 00 99 98

Contents

Preface to the English Edition

Dudley Andrew

In an introduction that is now, sadly, doubly touching, Christian Metz pays tribute to Francesco Casetti's work by situating it at the intersection of psychoanalytic and linguistic approaches to the cinema. Of course this is just where Metz would situate himself; indeed, as he notes, Casetti's effort points in a direction Metz assumed he would need to follow, and that resulted in his final book, bearing the most apt of titles: *L'Enonciation impersonnelle ou le site du film*. In effect Casetti helped bring Metz back to his home in semiotics and linguistics, after the Freudian excursions of *The Imaginary Signifier* and the unpublished opus on jokes. Metz's career likewise served as a model for Casetti, in its legendary generosity and amplitude first of all, and in the topics and method of investigation. One can only admire in these scholars the disciplined way they traverse in both directions the partly imaginary boundary of the screen.

Anglo-Americans will sense a different context than the rather purely "scientific" one that Metz details where positions are staked out, attacked, defended, and altered by newer ideas, seemingly outside the larger social environment that buys into them. Our film scholarship, tied rather explicitly to a constantly debated pedagogical mission, has been sensitive to the social consequences, as much as to the arguments, of ideas about films and how to study them. Thus the path for the study of cinematic enunciation in England and the USA was opened not so much by the fascinating claims of narratology (as laid out by Genette, Eco, and the others whom Metz mentions) as by the academic climate (admittedly floating over from the continent) that promoted the study of systems over individuals, and thus of enunciative mechanisms over authors. Enunciation theory helped bring about the death of the author by locating a film's principle of organization and address within the text rather than in the mind of an artist. When it came to studying the spectator, we see the same difference in tone. Metz's trenchantly Freudian essay "The Fiction Film and Its Spectator" is characteristic in analyzing the hypothetical film viewer that suited French and Italian scholarship. West of the English Channel, on the other hand, a concern for something like "real spectators" ultimately led to the proliferation of historical and cultural approaches that are with us today. These somewhat distinct contexts permit us to see why Casetti's book may have intercepted Italian and French debates in a productive way when it appeared in those countries in 1986 and 1990 respectively, but had it come out in English at that time, during the first euphoria of "reception studies," it would doubtless have been ignored.

Today, however, its reinsertion into film scholarship is far more promising and, I believe, absolutely salutary. For one thing, Casetti has always been conversant—and sympathetic—with the American turn of mind. Reading widely in English, teaching here on occasion, he came to appreciate the way film studies here responds to quite specific pedagogical functions on our college campuses. In fact, the version of "semio-pragmatics" that *Inside the Gaze* provides or leads to can be seen deftly to combine continental and Anglo-American work, in that it examines in detail those textual features that direct the experience anyone has of a film, while at the same time it pays attention to socio-cultural realities that activate a text in any given viewing of it. This makes Casetti doubly useful. Metz needs him to stand as the perfect interface between semiotics and psychoanalysis. We need him to anchor reception studies, to keep it from floating free of the flimsy breakwater that cinema studies keeps constructing so as to harbor its work; otherwise film scholarship may be in danger of entering the waters patrolled by sociology, or of just floundering in the vast sea of the anecdotal, the tendentious, and the merely "interesting."

While wary of the sense of security that his methodical approach extends, I nevertheless extol the clarity of Casetti's project. And I imagine the benefits that reading him will bring to our students. Not that they need emulate Casetti's highly European style or even follow up on his topics, as interesting as these are. What is more important—and what he models so splendidly for all of us—is the aspiration to articulate as cleanly as possible the factors entering into complex phenomena, in this case a phenomenon as amorphous as the experience of a film.

His method for doing so is traditional. Subordinating lesser to greater ideas, he produces an elegant tree of concepts. Detours there are, but always announced in advance and drawn upon, like a letter of credit, when the time comes. Casetti also makes judicious use of examples, analyzing brilliantly clear illustrations in a way that encourages his readers to come up with other examples on their own to test or confirm his points. In the era of cultural studies, we need to be reminded of the value of this kind of precise and progressive, rather than lateral, understanding. Casetti gives us a vocabulary that is learnable and teachable and that, over the course of five carefully structured chapters, ultimately renders a vision of cinematic vision itself. Metz aptly terms this method a "mise en scène" of ideas, an opera almost, where concepts become figures in a drama that every film plays out and that excites Casetti to no end. This is how he puts it: "The film offers itself to sight: it establishes its destination—and its destiny—as both an ultimate goal and a surface from which to spring." Casetti has learned how to specify the goal of cinematic discourse without constricting the spectator to a mere processor of pre-established codes. And he definitely shows us how to spring from a film like an acrobat, in whatever direction we choose. He renders semiotics dynamic, so that the terms "text" and "game" suggest genuine interaction and productive variability from the outset, not the injection of meaning into the spectator via codes.

Cinema studies has spread itself out to encompass many types of endeavors. But shouldn't everyone claiming to talk about film understand this primary interaction? Should we not all first become reasonably conditioned acrobats able to spring from texts in the most imaginative of ways? Understanding what is *Inside the Gaze* should be a sine qua non for anyone who really cares what the cinema has been or can be. We can thank Francesco Casetti for taking us so precisely, so insistently, and so deeply "inside."

Iowa City, June 1997

Crossing Over the Alps and the Pyrenees . . .

Christian Metz

I am delighted to write an introduction to the French and Spanish editions of Francesco Casetti's fine book, because this book, for me, is not simply an intellectual object, but has forced its way without warning into the personal development of my own work.

For some time now, the theme of filmic enunciation has been rattling around in my head. I wasn't alone in watching with great interest the various contributions that, sometimes happily, sometimes testily, nudged this issue toward the center of the network of discussions of our little cinematographic circle—a circle whose perimeter is fortunately overstepped from time to time.

Enunciation of this sort was first studied from a psychoanalytic perspective. It was in the 1970s, on the heels of issue 23 of the journal *Communications*, edited by Raymond Bellour, Thierry Kuntzel, and myself. The Freudian approach, while it concerns the film's text and its internal modes of "figuration," also had the additional effect—quite understandably—of making film theory more sensitive to the psychological position of the spectator. Here is the spectator, oscillating between belief and disbelief, between awareness and oblivion in front of the spectacle, between complete alertness and a state of reverie, a very particular reverie, piloted by real perceptions.

But we had to wait until the following decade, the 1980s, for filmic enunciation to be approached from a more formal, more "linguistic" (or more pragmatic), angle. Here again, the classic problem of the marks of enunciation was taken up. That is, the issue of perceptible traces—visible or audible in the cinema's case—left by enunciation along certain points of the enunciated (énoncé) during its emission. Cinematographic narratology has moved forward most notably with the work of Marc Vernet, André Gaudreault, François Jost, Edward Branigan, David Bordwell, André Gardies, and with contributions by the trio Lagny-Ropars-Sorlin. From narrative analysis one inevitably slides into the study of enunciation. Here I should repeat the names above (and I'm surely forgetting some), adding to the list Jean-Paul Simon, Dominique Château, Jacques Aumont, Jean-Paul Terrenoire, and Eliseo Veron (working with television), and the earlier analyses of Nick Browne on the "rhetoric" of the filmic text. The "semiopragmatic" project of Roger Odin, while distinct in principle, often crosses the same paths. In 1983, issue 38 of *Communications*, "Énonciation et cinéma," appeared, edited by Jean-Paul Simon and Marc Vernet.

And then, there are the Italians, of whom I have yet said nothing. Clearly, it is they who have influenced Francesco Casetti most directly, despite the voracious multilingual reading I know him to pursue. We should remember that the ball was set rolling by *The Role of the Reader* (*Lector in Fabula*), the work of that glorious, generous, and bearded Transalpine with whom we all are familiar. He introduced the idea that in some way (whether partial, ideal, anticipated, or whatever—and this is the heart of the problem) the reader or the spectator is not exterior to the text or film, but is "*within*." Soon after (and sometimes simultaneously) came the solidly argued contributions in the domain of film and television of Gianfranco Bettetini, notably *Tempo del senso* and *La conversazione audiovisiva*. This brings us to Casetti's entry upon the scene, or rather his "entry" into this particular issue, since his connections to film theory have been numerous, with some of his earlier publications directly anticipating the work we have before us.

Finally, to complete this nicely landscaped sketch, we should remember that "filmologues," at least those concerned with narrative, never lose sight of "literary" advances. And they are right, since throughout the centuries right up to our own, poetics has continually engaged problems of narration and enunciation. The theories of Käte Hamburger and those of Gérard Genette, which currently dominate the literary field (I have already spoken of Umberto Eco) are very often explicitly present in work on enunciation in cinema. Seymour Chatman, Francois Jost, and André Gaudreault combine the study of filmic narrative and literary narrative, thus giving body to a project of comparative narratology.

I do not mean to imply that narration and enunciation are one and the same thing. That would clearly be absurd. But in the history of this form of investigation, and certainly of late, various enunciative phenomena have been apprehended across multiple narrative *corpora*, so that while the objects of study may be distinct, such studies often intermingle.

And so, delineated with these rather cavalier strokes, this is the panorama that stood before me up until 1986, when I read the Italian edition of my friend Francesco's book. Before his book, I used to scan this panorama of narratology out of professional necessity but without energy. Certain elements were already in place, like scaffolding erected piece by piece by many laborers. It was generally agreed, for instance, through varied and sometimes picturesque vocabularies, that the very existence of the text implied an enunciator—the ideal subject of the discourse—an abstract entity distinct from the author. And symmetrically, there had to be an enunciatee, likewise a creature of the film, situated to the side of the spectator but not to be confused with him. With that, an entire game became possible. Here, the narrative can designate its own narrator, or by contrast, say nothing about it. Often it happens that the narrative ignores the spectator, carries on as though he or she didn't exist, while at other times, like those when the character looks into the camera, the narrative calls on the addressee in a manner that is undeniable. And so on.

In reading *Dentro lo sguardo*, I decided that my rather long period of leisurely incubation was over, and that I should tackle the study of filmic enunciation in a future work myself. Right off I'll confess that he upset my rhythm—reading Casetti transformed my rather vague interest into a definite determination. An (entirely legal) "doping" had occurred, a welcome alchemy which I have yet to fully understand. I must note that the book is marked by an exceptional stylistic energy, by uncommon intellectual dynamism. This is not to say that I agree with each of its lines. Such perfect complicity of views is not required for esteem, a fortunate thing, for if that were the case one would have esteem only for oneself. Style, technique, soundness and breadth of information, rigor and originality of approach count as much as what is crudely called substance. Besides, an introduction need not eclipse what it introduces, nor dip into the terrain of the book itself. I don't care to add to the troop of sponsors who present a work to you, taking their time with their own theories on materials dealt with by the work they feign to present—a calamitous and completely subordinate appendix. So let us allow his text to speak (I will try not to summarize it).

Above all let us listen closely to it, even if it comes to us in a language other than his original and must inevitably carry a certain loss of reality and of scriptural tension, despite the care taken in the translation.

If I were asked to define in a single phrase the contributions of Francesco Casetti in relation to their historical and geographical consequence, I would say that he is the first to have envisioned the elements necessary for formalizing the ensemble of film's enunciative apparatus, taken in its broadest sense. The specificity of his work, for me, lies in the combination of these three traits: a formalizing aim, a concern to "cover" everything, a deliberately synoptic view. These characteristics are particularly striking in the powerful and new chart that is proposed for the four cardinal points of cinematographic enunciation, corresponding to just this many different combinations between an ideal *I*, a *you*, and a *he/she*. It should be understood that the aim of the book is not to make an inventory of the enunciative constructions, with their numerous concrete forms and their slight variations, but to propose a conceptual frame, with examples to support it, that can accommodate them all. This is a courageous undertaking, and I am in a position to salute it without scruple, since, on this point, I chose the opposite, or more precisely, the complementary path.

My friend's book is, of course, a scientific book. No one would be mistaken in that, since it carries all the requisite characteristics. But it is also something else, something without which one could not understand its impact, its power to fill the spirit of the reader with a joyful and fertile saturation. Casetti's dexterity, his agility in moving concepts around and grouping them in little mounds that are just as soon undone in order to create other aggregates, his energetic romp through the shop of general theory: all this displays something akin to elation. This "forty-something" scholar is a young man, and he enjoys himself, even while working. You can feel the theatrical pleasure he takes in dramatizing the colossal body-to-body struggle between the textual approach and the structural one, between the spectator-decoder and the spectator-interlocutor, etc. Francesco Casetti has the gift—dare I add, very Italian?—in any case, he has the gift to be able to put theory on stage, to dress it up as imposing allegories in human form. At the same time, this man, reconciling *majestas* and *impetus*, directs his work like a Napoleonic cavalcade, never losing rhythm, permitting no slowdowns, never resting in one spot. Enunciation, abstraction, pragmatics, yes, but presented lean and trim, with the drum beating. Who would have thought?

Science, with Casetti, always comes wrapped in a thin film of poetry or reverie. From the outset he brings with him a joyous excitement, a kind of fever for thought, which if you compare his book to other specialized works, produces an accent and a style that are truly special, truly compelling. I was immediately aware of this and am convinced it can only come from real talent. He has a surprising aptitude for endowing scientific notions with a kind of personal and autonomous life, like characters in cartoon films. He always carries metaphors to the limit, to the point where we sometimes ask if he himself hasn't gotten carried away; a sentence then appears to reassure us, yet without preventing the figure from continuing its wild course. One of the parables that maintains itself throughout the entire book is that of two spectators: one is in reality sitting in the movie theater, while the other is actually a site within the film's own center, which it designates through its addresses and other marks. This second spectator—the enunciatee—does not exist. Casetti (of course) knows this and says it; nevertheless, by the power of his words, he still maintains at an arm's length the solid expectation, the enigmatic perspective—which he makes almost palpable—of a possible comparison of these two spectators, or an interface which would put them in contact, as though there were some superior entity of which these are the two faces. A good deal of the force of this work comes from such poetico-didactic fictions, from these *manners of speech* (as when we speak of table manners). These fictions might lead the reading astray if, not heeding other statements which prohibit it, we took them word for word. If they are well understood, they give theory's walls a fresh coat of paint.

I wish this bright-eyed and bushy-tailed little book good luck in its travels abroad, this book which captured in one fell swoop, through its singular spirit, a central place in the investigation of filmic enunciation, currently a major preoccupation among those of us whom films inspire to think, and who love both cinema and abstract thought.

Paris, February 1989

Author's Note to the
English Edition

I wrote this book a decade ago with two purposes in mind. On the one hand, I wanted to understand the ways in which a film pre-arranges its reception and pre-figures its spectator. In this sense I wanted to explore, beyond its metaphorical value, the idea largely shared in the Anglo-American debate of those years that a film "inscribes" or "posits" its spectator and guides that spectator along a "path." On the other hand, I wanted to re-locate this issue directly within semiotics. Although of obvious importance, the Anglo-American debate seemed so tied to an intricate theoretical framework that joined semiotics, psychoanalysis, and the critique of ideology that it was in danger of losing touch with the richness and complexity of the formal aspects of cinema. My hope was to understand the spectator via the film, but also to analyze films via their concrete formal procedures. The concept of cinematic enunciation seemed to offer an ideal theoretical framework for such a project.

In the years following the publication of this book in Italian, I continued working on enunciation, but I also tried to look at the spectator from the perspective of the actual, material mechanics of reception. In several studies, employing ethnographic and "life-story" methodology, I have engaged issues (such as gender) that were purposely kept in the background of *Inside the Gaze*. However, even in this newer phase of my research I continue paying great attention to the texts themselves. Indeed, I put my money on the conjunction of reception studies and textual analysis, comparing what the film does to the spectator and what the spectator does to the film. In so many reception studies the text simply disappears or becomes a completely indifferent object, whereas I insist that the text is crucial, if only because its presence is what turns a *social* situation into a *communicative* situation.

Specifically, my latest work has been on the notion of the "communicative pact." I am concerned here to see the text as a proposal that meets certain expectations, needs, and competencies of the spectator.

This meeting gives rise to many forms of negotiation: at the perceptual level we have textual cues, on the one hand, meeting interpretive procedures on the other; at the cultural level, we have textual meaning coming up against social interpretations. Within such a framework, texts manifest their full relevance as well as their richness and variety.

The American edition of this book allows me to recall with affection Christian Metz. Christian dedicated his 1987 seminar to enunciation and, because I was there that year, we discussed my book at length. He disagreed with certain points (especially deictics), but he too shared the need to go back to semiotics. Intellectual honesty and a real sense of friendship will remain the two great qualities of Christian's legacy.

Secondly, I want to thank Dudley Andrew. To him I owe the opportunity to have taught at the University of Iowa; the discussions there with him, with his colleagues such as Rick Altman, Steven Ungar and Lauren Rabinovitz, and with their students (not to mention my trip to Madison, Wisconsin where David Bordwell and I argued for two full days about enunciation, me finally giving up on account of an overdose of junk food, which Italian intellectuals aren't used to) . . . I count this midwestern experience among the very best in my life as a scholar.

November 1997

INSIDE THE GAZE

1　In Search of the Spectator

Spectator or Spectators?

A glance through the various texts written about the cinema will confirm that the spectator appears and functions as a nodal point located at the intersection of numerous complex and diverse paths. This individual is present as a witness to potential contradictions rather than as a subject of consensus, an object of doubt rather than a secure referent, a piece of a puzzle rather than a finished design. And while as critics we may confidently manipulate his or her outlines, the spectator ultimately exists as a rather cryptic figure.

In film criticism, for example, the spectator is considered above all as a given, an individual whose existence can be taken for granted and whose reality is self-evident. It seems that this circumstance (which, let us admit, is precisely what certain critical approaches challenge) finds its justification in the very laws that define the genre. The critic directly testifies to the fact of going to the movies, since it is this very act—often turned vocation—which authorizes the critic to provide information and judgment. The reader in turn furnishes flagrant proof of the spectator's experience, since it is most often the experience of having seen a film, or the desire to see one, which motivates an individual to read a review. All readers and critics qualify as either actual or potential spectators, at once a model and a testimony of a widespread social behavior. But indeed things are not always so simple. Promotional criticism, for example, aims to ensure the success of a film by anticipating a spectator who will submit to the film's propositions and orientations—that is, a spectator-to-be, not yet in existence. Evaluative criticism, on the other hand, plays upon the more personal relation to a film, favoring mood changes and heartfelt responses, summoning the idea of a secret ceremony for "those in the know." Finally, militant and engaged criticism transforms a film's vision into a life choice, posing the film as an act whose genesis and consequences must be evaluated. Despite their differences, however, these types of criticism show in principle no real variation concerning the notion that the spectator is nothing but a bit player. Here, the discussions emphasize the quality or significance of what is seen, rather than the manner in which the film offers itself to sight.

This critical orientation has antecedents—indeed roots—in film theory itself. The majority of texts, between the 1910s and the 1950s, which sought to define the essence of the cinema, evoke the spectator without question and treat his presence and bearing as self-evident. This was the case despite the emergence of theoretical perspectives which, had critics truly attended to them, might have reoriented such research. Thus for example, we have numerous writings on cinema as a popular art which insist on the action of the medium rather than on the variation of reception. Similarly, many theorists, for ethical or political reasons, have demanded that we construct typologies of films rather than question what it means to attend a show. Finally, many of the quarrels over the realistic or oneiric nature of the image accentuate particular forms of expression without analyzing the ways in which these different forms position a spectator. Even the most favorable circumstances fall short in one way or another; often present, the spectator still has yet to become a full-fledged agent.[1]

Within this context, however, certain distinct voices were heard raising essential questions that brought forth the indissoluble links between film and spectator. As early as 1916, Hugo Munsterberg not only analyzed the "mental processes" by which a film positions the viewer, but insisted as well upon the activity that the viewer must undertake so that the film can function (the spectator must attribute the criteria of reality to the image. This is criteria the film does not possess, but must appear to have).[2] Among the formalists, Boris Eichenbaum employed the notion of "inner speech" to explain how the succession of stimuli appearing on the screen locate their definition and relationship in the "spirit" of the film viewer (it is the spectator who unites the various shots into a whole scene by recognizing their common elements and filling the gaps between them).[3] In the mid-1930s Walter Benjamin suggested that an "age of mechanical reproduction" had modified both the nature of the work of art and the character of its beholder (rather than an initiate or a devotee engaged in a ritualized reception involving a participation beyond mere attendance, the spectator here engages in an act of visual consumption in which she is simultaneously present and separate).[4] During the 1950s, Edgar Morin defined cinema as a "symbiosis," a machine producing a procession that combines linguistic and psychic elements (the spectator, acting in accord with her particular affective needs and dispositions, strives to compensate for the apparent coldness of the images, thus revealing the depth of their action).[5] Although this list could and perhaps should include other names and examples, these few evocations suffice to show that even during the reign of a paradigm in which much was taken for granted, there existed an ongoing need to question and reevaluate a far from self-evident phenomenon. At the very heart of classical film theory were thinkers committed to studying the figure of the spectator, to exploring this figure's depth, and to defining its bearing.

Such commitment became yet more explicit with the film theory debates of the fifties and sixties, leading to a veritable revolution. "Essentialist" definitions were replaced by "systematic" investigations, the synthetic and global approach ceded place to inquiries defined within disciplines, and a tendency to borrow freely from various research fields surrendered to methodological rigor.[6] This new orientation produced a total reversal in the manner of conceptualizing the spectator. It transformed the spectator into an object of study, into someone, or something, apprehendable in the form of empirical facts and whose essential features were to be constructed as a function of research tools and objectives. The spectator, formerly a presupposed presence, now existed as an intended figure and a specific construction.

This transformation was far from insignificant; it upset old practices, changed the rules of the game, and completely redefined the field of research. It revealed, for example, that the "deviations" noted of certain earlier theorists might constitute ideal points of departure for a new research agenda. Of course these theorists could not entirely escape the ideology of their times (yielding in some cases to a temptation to discover the "secret" of cinema by reducing it to a supposedly exhaustive formula), but all the same they prefigure an attitude that would henceforth assert itself. This is particularly so in their insistence that the choice of perspective informs the analysis, indicating that nothing is self-evident, not even the state of being seated in the theater in front of the screen. A second consequence of the theoretical debates was a new interest in evaluating different approaches. Particularly significant was the discipline of "filmology," which was without question the first movement to rally toward these new research procedures, the first to describe film viewing as a complex phenomenon, and the most determined to discover film viewing's fundamental principles.[7] At the same time, there were types of criticism that generally preferred not to investigate what appeared to be an entirely banal activity. In short, this transition led to the appearance of two new phenomena. On the one hand, there was a disproportion in references to the spectator. In earlier writings such references were scattered throughout, though rarely in a fruitful way; now they appeared only in sparse texts, but in a quite pointed manner. Now, the spectator tended to figure only in works centered entirely on the issue of spectatorship. On the other hand, the identity of the spectator became multiple. In the past, the systematic manner in which the spectator was described suggested that at issue was a reality equivalent for everyone. However, the new awareness of the choices which underlie analysis—choices of both method and disciplinary field—led each researcher to pursue a specific type of investigation; each had his own object of study, and therefore his own spectator.

This latter phenomenon is of primary importance as it reveals, perhaps better than any other, the logic of the debate. To best grasp the contours of the new theoretical landscape, one only has to note the manner in which different disciplines approach the notion of the spectator. In psychology's view, attentive to issues of perception and cognition, the spectator is the pivot around which the filmic situation develops; in sociology's view, interested in interactions and behavior, the spectator is among the agents shaping the cinematographic institution; for psychoanalysis, attracted to operations analogous to those of dreamwork, fetishism, voyeurism, etc., the spectator is a component of the cinematic apparatus; for the discipline of economics, dedicated to charting a product's circulation, the spectator indicates the conjunction of a need and a commodity; for semiotics, focused on symbolic constructions and the flux of communication, the spectator is one of the poles of the "circuit of speech," and so on.[8] Despite its simple and obvious schematic character, this list is intended to stress that all approaches take a stance in relation to their object of study and that different perspectives evoke often contradictory visions. The lesson is clear to those willing to acknowledge it: caught between a newly recognized complexity and a fragmentation by differing approaches, the spectator appears henceforth as a plural figure.

But such a plurality—resulting, as noted, from various ways of defining the object of study—can be seen not only in the differences among disciplines but in the diversity of projects which can occur within a single field of research. It is not unusual that the awareness of working with a particular perspective leads to differentiation among approaches otherwise sharing the same roots. It has been the case, for example, within the discipline of semiotics, whose diversity of approaches merits a close examination.

From Decoder to Interlocutor

Semiotics can be understood as a theoretical domain divided into two parts, with its terrain of analysis likewise separated into two zones. On the one hand, the spectator can be thought of as a decoder: that is, as someone who deciphers an ensemble of images and sounds, a participant who aims to recover the meaning of representation, a transcriber who, at the end of a sequence, clearly translates a coded message.[9] On the other hand, the spectator can be understood as an interlocutor: that is, as someone to whom one can address the propositional structures and who can be expected to show signs of understanding, a subtle accomplice to the character that appears on the screen, a partner who can be given a task and who will carry it out in good faith.[10]

These two conceptualizations, quite distinct from one another in both basic characteristics and theoretical frames of reference, occupy a disputed terrain. To examine this more closely, the first model was established during the mid-1960s in the context of a semiotics of structuralist inspiration. Shaped by the dominant theories of the era, such as the self-sufficiency of the signifying object or the linearity of the communicative process, the decoder existed, however marginally, as a specific presence (though the issue of reception was acknowledged, it was considered secondary to the film itself, the true center of interest). The decoder was also assigned a precise but limited function (it was recognized that some tasks must fall to the circumstances of reception, but at the same time, they were assumed to have no influence on the transmission of the message).[11] Thus precisely when the long-neglected spectator was due to receive a certain credit, his profile and scope of activity were reduced. In effect, the spectator was seen merely to follow a pre-determined trajectory, registering only what was given, and to use pre-established codes for understanding the message addressed to him.[12] Here, ultimately, the concern is with a sort of prompter who, by so thoroughly participating in the representation, no longer exists independently of it.

The ensuing efforts to avoid just such a situation occurred in short order. Beginning in the early seventies, attempts to palliate the shortcomings inherent in the figure of the decoder became increasingly common and explicit. These were undertaken essentially in two forms. One involved a complex conceptualization of the state of reception, while the other entailed an analysis of the text itself for evidence of the reception process. One can certainly follow this duality, rich with hypotheses and cross-references, in literary theory. Consider the emergence of the idea that "to read is to rewrite" (the slogan of the journal *Tel Quel*,[13] and exemplified in the writings of Barthes,[14] Althusser, and Derrida), or the postulate that "to read is to interpret" (especially prevalent in Germany, in work inspired by hermeneutics and phenomenology).[15] In contrast, recall the appearance of the notion of the "implicit reader" (developed by critics like Wayne Booth, Wolfgang Iser, Seymour Chatman, Corti, etc.),[16] as well as numerous texts suggesting the concept of a virtual public (a theme derived from Yuri Lotman's work[17] and developed chiefly by narratologists).[18] The two approaches are also evident in writings on the cinema. Consider Christian Metz's *Language and Cinema*.[19] At the very moment where Metz proposes to reconstruct the architecture of film as faithfully and thoroughly as possible, he acknowledges the presence of plural readings, each one caught up in the specific system of "decoding principles" and thus determined by choice and personal orientations.[20] Recall also Raymond Bellour's *L'analyse du film*. While identifying signs within the camera movements of the metteur-en-scène's choices (conscious and unconscious), Bellour also perceives the anticipation (tacit or open) of a spectator destined to grasp these movements and their accompanying sounds.[21] Just as there is an insistence upon the activity and commitment demanded by a work, and an attempt to enact the very project that the work jealously controls, there is also a discovery of the possibility of legitimate counter-initiatives and an exhumation of the traces of a possible public, at last providing proof that the spectator, long waiting in the wings, does exist.[22]

The proof however, in addition to defining a particular role, introduced a new style of interpretation. Beyond their metaphorical suggestiveness, the works cited above, as with many others, invited us not only to notice and account for certain realities but also to recognize a new model of the spectator and to place it within a new theoretical field. The interlocutor was substituted for the decoder, and textual semiotics for structural semiotics. It is worth lingering on the mutation involved here. A good demonstration in terms of a general reflection can be found in Umberto Eco's *Lector in fabula*, in which this theoretical development appears with all the richness of ruptures, delays, and backward steps—in short, much less simply than in the condensed form presented here. For a reflection centered on the cinema, Gianfranco Bettetini's *Tempo del senso* is particularly useful.[23] This mutation operated on many varied levels, precisely because it put into question the object of study as much as the modalities of analysis. Consider for example, that to change the spectator's profile also alters the manner of conceptualizing her presence. If in the past the spectator had existed at the outskirts of representation—as an occasional participant or simple consumer—she was now seen as someone summoned to weave the threads of the intrigue. The spectator became both a true recipient, insofar as the story unfolds for her, and an obligatory reference point, since she is already inscribed within the fabric of the representation. Thus the concern was no longer with either a target to be hit or a subaltern who responds to the posed questions, but rather with a conscious partner who understands the incumbent tasks. Again, the change in the spectator's profile carried a simultaneous modification in the conceptualization of the mode of interaction with the film. If in the past it was assumed that to interpret images and sounds, one need only possess a code—that is, a repertoire of signs, a list of correspondences between signifiers and signifieds, and a table of rules of sign combination—it was now necessary to have mastered a knowledge of the situation in its ensemble, to be capable of appreciating the relevant choices, anticipating certain effects, grasping the particularities that emerge. In a word, what was needed was an open knowledge, with a syntax and lexicon akin to an encyclopedia.[24] This new analysis no longer relied on the notion of code, implying a rigid system applicable in only certain rare cases,[25] but rather on that of competence—that is, an ensemble of rules which, in its totality, restores the richness underlying a discourse's production and reception.[26] Finally, the change in the spectator's profile also changed her field of action: if what appears on the screen had formerly been understood as an ordered combination of elements and as a construction turned in on itself, it would henceforth be conceived as an organism which both submits to and influences its context. It was no longer the aim to distinguish structure, constitutive schema, various segments and sequences, but to identify a game, a strategy perfectly integrating all the elements and events. Moreover, a film was no longer discussed as a "work" or "message" but as a "text," a term closely associated with the theoretical literature which would come to shape present-day semiotics.[27] The notion of text, by virtue of its very etymology, also evoked the idea of a dynamic construction, of an open and complex organization, of an intended object.

There are those who noted that it was risky to apply this new theoretical orientation to the cinema, given the exisiting separation between the screen and the movie theater. In this way, it would be incorrect to speak in terms of interlocutor and text since the film does not actually gaze out before itself and because the one who does gaze exists outside the film. Such an objection is quite reasonable. It raises the issue of a situation which seems common to all the mass media, that of the distance—whether spatial or temporal—between the elements put into play. This distance implies a sort of reduction of the protagonists, an isolation which forces them to act in complete solitude.[28] In reality though, appearances couldn't be more duplicitous. The connections are far greater than they appear and the distances are rarely insuperable. Consider the case of film: far from being a self-contained universe, secure in its own autonomy and absolute sovereignty, film has a real intrinsic availability, well before it is consciously seized by any viewer. This is continually confirmed, even in the simplest moments of the viewing process: for example, when divisions are sutured and gaps filled with the collaboration of the spectator attending the show (think of the invisibility of the framelines which separate the individual photogrammes, or the illusion of the image's depth);[29] moments when information is ruled by the function of a system of expectations (in particular, phenomena such as suspense, narrative closure, etc.);[30] instances when all the possibilities of an image multiply even with the least bit of participation on the part of the spectator (recall the projection process and the identification put into play by virtually any narrative element);[31] and finally, moments when figures of substitution emerge which regulate access to the narrative (the simultaneously emblematic and functional aspect of numerous fictional characters).[32] But it is the cinematic apparatus itself which, beyond this or that particular operation, is organized as a snare ready to capture whoever enters its radius of activity. To exhibit a world—whether realistic or fantastic—presupposes the operation of the scopic drive.[33] To present a fragment of life—whether highly original or stereotypical—implies a response to fundamental needs.[34] So it is that a film continually proposes the existence of a locus where its own action converges or finds a double. The film continually directs outward the glances and voices which inhabit it—out toward someone whose existence it presupposes, or rather requires—with the hope of a response. The film, in sum, offers itself to sight: it establishes its destination—and its destiny—as both an ultimate goal and a surface from which to spring.[35]

The spectator accomplishes the same trajectory. To recognize this, we need only reverse the process. Far from advancing unequipped, and even prior to any personal response, the individual sitting in the theater contributes actively to the construction of what appears on the screen. This occurs, for example, when he puts together all sorts of scattered elements to construct a character or place (note how characters are constructed progressively or how a space takes shape through an accumulation of details),[36] when he frames the events in a way that endows them with a meaning (consider a genre's power to make the significance of an event relative),[37] when he passes through the visual field, retaining only what is essential and discarding the accessory (a gaze supple enough to fix upon one element while gliding over others),[38] when he fills the gaps in the narrative to give coherence to the intrigue (often that which is "unseen" serves to explain that which appears on the screen).[39] Thus the viewer seated in the theater lives with the film, and does so by finding the means to recognize himself in this or that motif, or more generally, by successfully placing himself within the scope of a reception continually subject to images and sounds.[40] The spectator, in sum, becomes engaged in the act of gazing, responding to the availability of the screen's world by assuming certain responsibilities according to the demands of a true vocation.

All this suggests an essential fact: to speak simultaneously of the interlocutor and the text is by no means paradoxical but a reference to the same phenomenon. Rather than opting for an eclectic research orientation, it involves choosing the most pertinent approach. It is to approach cinema in a manner superior to those that only envisage the spectator as simply consuming an object or responding to a stimulus.[41] It is finally to illuminate a whole series of mechanisms that, even if they act surreptitiously, assure more than anything else the functioning of the overall apparatus.

This methodological decision nevertheless introduces basic problems that must be approached in a synthetic manner.

Between the Symbolic Dimension and Concrete Reality

Let us consider the notions of text and interlocutor in a broad sense, as abstractions defined by their use within film studies. In this context, these two notions are fundamental to the articulation of at least two basic questions.

First there is the question of subjectivity in language. We have seen how the availability of a text exists not only in the process by which a sign can be offered to someone, but also in the need for someone to whom the sign is addressed.[42] What is actually involved in this ineluctable complicity? Beyond the various forms and degrees of implication suggested above, what is its profound nature? Responses seem to follow two parallel paths: the interlocutor can be conceived either as a partner the text locates at its very edge, where the signs give way to life, so to speak, or as a silhouette which the text creates within the interior of its own limits, on the page, canvas, or screen. In one case, the interlocutor appears as a creature of flesh and blood, while in the other, as a profoundly symbolic phenomenon. Which conceptualization should be supported? If one opts for the first, the task becomes one of examining the attitudes the text solicits and the behaviors it introduces—such as attention, judgment, pleasure, adhesion, etc. In a word, this choice gives proof that reading and visual perception are complex activities and not simply mirrors of that which has been already said, written, or shown. However even here something else exists—indeed must exist. There must be a plan, doubtless found between the lines, that foresees and underlies the outcome of the game; a plan inscribed within the text, perfectly coextensive to it, and thus constituting a model for the act of reception. Should we then change the optic and work in the depths of signs? To consider the interlocutor as a silhouette designed by the text offers certain advantages. It enables the discovery of a plot, which while latent is quite clear. This plot is manifest in suggestions or even in actual instructions, or still yet in the irreversible conversion from "wish to tell" into "make understand." It also allows a revelation of the various figures internal to the text: auditors perfectly described, spectators located within the scene, witnesses, spies. In short, all sorts of elements serve as veritable addressees internal to the narration. This approach allows us to closely follow the "implied reader," the image of the "public" elaborated within the text. However, in turn, even this path becomes insufficient: while it enables an investigation of the person developing at the center of the screen, it excludes consideration of the person existing beyond the screen's borders; while it places a trust in the indices and symbols appearing on the screen, it neglects and ultimately denies the possibility of their interacting with anyone; briefly, while this path lingers on emergent clues and manifest forces, it forgets the need for someone who knows how to engage with these in a way that makes the text's availability effective.

As the above formulation suggests, the choice between the two research agendas seems to lead to a kind of circularity: a commitment to one version of the spectator cannot be made without a confrontation with the other; a dedication to one research option cannot be made without taking account of the opposing possibility. Given this circumstance, one must accept that the text manifests the need for an interlocutor both as a participant in the game and as a guide to the reception process. Although quite distinct, the tasks of implicating an individual of flesh and blood and that of developing a symbolic construction will nonetheless interact.

The circularity here is reminiscent of Benveniste's manner of approaching the figure of the interlocutor. Here the pronoun *I* is both evidence of a concrete presence (the person who appropriates the virtuality of language) and a purely grammatical mark (signaling a discourse's "self-construction," its functioning),[43] both a sign available to the individual who actualizes the text and an autoreflective inscription within the text. Although Benveniste tries to distinguish clearly between them, it is their very superimposition that permits the emergence of subjectivity. It links the actual utilization of language to the appearance of the first person; or rather, it links the introduction into space of speech to a category that invests in and articulates what is said.[44] Moreover, what does the notion of the "subject" suggest if not both a source, the base of the elocution itself, and a theme, submitted to observation and reflection?[45]

In the event of a shift in attention from the locutor to the interlocutor, from the *I* to the *you*, the terms of the problem remain fundamentally the same. The concern now is with a subject situated "downstream" from the act of speech rather than "upstream," so to speak (even if such a formulation is perhaps founded on an optical illusion). This subject is able to reinforce its own basic characteristics since it seems to function both as the agency constructing the discourse (it does not actualize the language which would otherwise remain virtual, but instead enacts certain choices), and at the same time as the discourse's finality (even though at issue is not the imposition of a hierarchy but rather a directional movement). In sum, at hand once again is a partner who plays as much the role of the game's master (she literally subdues the text, takes control of it) as that of its victim (due to the attendant self-exposure, she undergoes a kind of subjugation). Thus the circularity among a concrete presence and a symbolic construction has correspondences elsewhere—in the locutor and especially in the notion of subjectivity as defined above. It is important however to inquire into how this circularity functions. Are current terminological distinctions, such as "empirical subject" and "ideal subject," sufficient for resolving the issues raised?[46] Or would it be preferable to treat the two levels as inextricably connected, and so emphasize their reciprocal outcomes? How does the text take the relation between interior and exterior for its own point of departure if it is unable to base the interlocutor solely internally or externally?

A second issue directly follows: which methodology to adopt? Again there are two alternatives. On the one hand, there is a generative approach that permits the delineation of the operations by which a text is constituted and the manner in which it defines its conditions of existence, one component of which is its recipient. On the other hand, there is an interpretive approach which attends to the acts performed by the recipient when approaching a text, and in particular the procedures required for unveiling, so to speak, the text's spirit and letter. Such a choice clearly involves a repetition of what we observed regarding the status of the interlocutor. That is, the definition of an object of study is linked to the chosen discipline. In any event, these two approaches are radically opposed to one another. In one case, the critic follows the progressive unfolding of a text—whether verbal, audio-visual, or pictorial—attending to both its deep structure and phenomenal surface, while at the same time defining the frame of the text's action. In the other case, the critic focuses on the individual who engages with a text, the reader or viewer, whose activity extends from recognizing signifiers to apprehending the work's overall significance. Consequently, in the first case, there is an investigation of the way in which the text constructs its interlocutor, while in the second case, of how the interlocutor constructs or reconstructs the text. In either case, the critic is confronted as much by signs as by concrete individuals. Nonetheless, the two approaches have intrinsic limits that are easy to identify. With respect to the first, the text has a power to impose itself on reality: the hypothetical interlocutor implied by the book, dialogue, film, etc. becomes a constraint in relation to an actual engagement with the page, spoken word, or image; expectation wears down in advance the moment of confrontation, to the point that the singularity of any particular act of consumption ultimately disappears. By contrast, in the second approach acts of reading and visual perception establish the reality of the text's structures; the act of discovery is superimposed on what is available to perception with the result that the text appears as a place deprived of true identity—a simple site of suggestion, or a system only capable of blocking overly aberrant interpretations.[47] Although certainly the two approaches do not always lead to the same results, they suggest the existence of a productive common ground. On the one hand, there is a realization of a succession of original effects, and on the other, an intersubjective confrontation that performs verification and other functions. To embrace one itinerary at the cost of the other, however, only occludes what we have already established, which is that one must choose between masking either the recipient's activity or the text's constraining structures.

It would be a mistake to imagine that reciprocal concessions might resolve this double evacuation. The two approaches must remain quite separate, not out of respect for different schools (today, in the domain of semiotics, the generative and interpretive models coincide with schools, represented respectively by Greimas and Eco) but out of fear of eclecticism.[48] To separate the two approaches is not necessarily to isolate them. On the contrary, the process of consciously working through specific hypotheses can lead each type of analysis to clarify its own limits. After acknowledging the two paths of investigation, there still remains the challenge of elaborating a system of oppositions, of specifying methods and objectives, implications and limits, possible overlappings or incompatibilities. Only by meeting this challenge will it be possible to judge the utility of the approaches and to determine their essential and constitutive borders.

A Research Hypothesis

Though the questions posed above will not be approached directly in the following pages, they will influence our choices to some degree. Following a precise itinerary, we will try to understand how the film constructs its spectator rather than the reverse, and we will focus on the text's operations rather than on the concrete circumstances of reception. From there, our aim will be to develop an understanding of three proposals: 1) that the film "designates" a spectator, 2) that it assigns this spectator a "place," and 3) that it sets the spectator upon a certain "course." We will demonstrate these metaphors, but so as to conserve their essential features, we will also examine successively: the manner in which the film identifies its interlocutor, either through simple allusions or open display; the manner in which it assigns this interlocutor a place from which to follow the proposed tasks, giving her a spatial position, of course, but also a cognitive and affective one; and finally the way in which the film causes the spectator to perform certain acts of recognition, leading her to identify not only the terms of the presentation but to recognize herself as the effective addressee. Thus, our analysis will center on the following three themes: the manifestation on the screen of the process of seeing oneself see, the spectator's mental and affective position, and the complicity maintained between the film and its potential partner. We will rely upon numerous concrete examples, chosen outright from the canon. Brief passages, complex scenes and, indeed, the unfolding of an entire intrigue will serve not only to illustrate certain problems but eventually to verify our hypotheses.

Thus, we will consider how the film constructs a spectator, assigns the spectator a place, sets him upon a certain course, and finally how all of these actions appear in specific examples. Again, within this investigation, an opposition of different approaches will seem to play a marginal role; marginal in appearance only, as the juxtaposition of approaches will indirectly help frame our research as well as theorize its results. The claim that the "inside" and "outside" of a text converge in order ultimately to annul the difference between them is thus entirely symptomatic. And it is with reference to this notion that we will conclude each stage of our inquiry.

This research agenda belongs to a disciplinary field that includes semiotics, linguistics, and even sociology, a field that falls under the heading of "pragmatics." Indeed, the task of investigating the way a film designates its spectator by structuring his presence, by organizing his activity—in a word, by the way it says *you*—involves focusing on precisely the relation between text and context at issue in pragmatics. The frame within which the film inscribes itself, its mode of address, its conditions of utilization, the practices it induces—are all essentially pragmatic concerns. But pragmatics here should not be reduced to a pure semantics (the text's meaning, or the meaning produced by a viewer) nor to a simple description of the different modes of address and their potential effects (a text's structures and the operations they elicit). It is precisely the awareness that a film's "inside" and "outside" are constantly interactive and capable of dissolving into one another that will keep us from such a reduction in the field of research.

An interstitial discipline whose precise contours remain in flux, pragmatics is all the same rich in intrinsic possibilities and openly suggestive.[49] As such it promises to provide a highly efficacious terrain for the research project proposed here. It is through pragmatics that we will pursue investigations concerning the questions "Who sees?" and "Who hears?" All of these investigations will be undertaken with the aim of understanding the functioning of a linguistic machine, an apparatus of representation, no matter how masked by apparent indifference and limpid transparency.

2   The Figure of the Spectator

A Look in the Eye

Let us begin by considering the openings of two films. The first is the long take at the start of Giuseppe De Santis's *Bitter Rice* (1949). A man in close-up, his face turned toward the camera, enumerates various facts on the cultivation of rice in northern Italy. Then a phrase is spoken: "This is Radio Turin!" The camera pulls back to reveal that, in fact, the voice comes from a loudspeaker mounted on the roof of a railroad car announcing the arrival of women pickers in a railroad switchyard. A panning shot reveals the station's expanse and the comings and goings of the pickers, while the voice from the speaker, now offscreen, presents an interview with a young woman. A further movement of the camera frames two men in discussion, in plan américain, their dialogue indicating that they are policemen in pursuit of a fugitive. Our second example is the opening shot of Bob Rafelson's *The King of Marvin Gardens* (1972). A man in close-up, looking into the camera, narrates a childhood story marked by long pauses, in a manner suggesting something between confession and an exploration of memory. Then, the man's movement toward offscreen, a blinking red light, and finally a cut to another shot reveal that, in fact, we are inside a radio studio, and the story he has just told in first person is now likely a fiction intended to hold the attention of a radio audience.

The significant feature of these examples (from two decidedly different films) is a direct address to a virtual spectator, a gaze and voice from the screen aimed at this individual as if to invite him to participate in the action. In other words, these examples both suggest a gesture of interpellation—that is, the recognition of someone, who in turn is expected to recognize himself as the immediate interlocutor. These particular examples operate via a look and a voice addressed to the camera, just as they might have involved an intertitle or other metanarrative announcement to address the individual following the narrative, rather than a character who lives within it.[1] A procedure of this sort is risky since it is traditionally considered both a source of incandescence and the transgression of a taboo. It constitutes incandescence because, in effect, whatever the motivations behind them, such moments of direct address have the power to literally illuminate a film's structures: first, they can reveal what is usually hidden (the camera and the work it accomplishes); second, they succeed in creating an opening to an irremediably "other" space, an offscreen space that can never become an on-screen space—namely, the space of the theater in which the film is projected; and finally, they tear apart the fabric of the fiction by provoking the emergence of a metalinguistic consciousness ("we are at the movies"), which by unveiling the game, destroys it.[2] As such, these moments forcibly exhibit what is ordinarily masked, and in this sense they are truly ardent. At the same time however, they entail transgressing a prohibition. Precisely in revealing a presupposition which has been and must remain silent, illegitimately attempting to invade a different space, and tearing apart a web that ought to stay intact, the look and voice addressed to the camera constitute an infraction of canonical proportions, an affront to the "proper" functioning of representation and filmic narrative. In this case more than in any other, an unforeseen development is thought to compromise the work's overall stability. In the end, such interpellation does not seem to fit the "normal" unfolding of cinematographic communication.

Nonetheless, this prohibition—and here things become complicated—is not effective in a uniform fashion. It varies, first of all, with respect to the form of the interpellation. For instance, a direct gaze into the camera carries a greater demand for attention than either an intertitle or an offscreen voice, both of which also aim to inform, solicit, or exhort.[3] Moreover, the prohibition varies as a function of a film's genre: while generally forbidden in adventure films, the direct look into the camera is relatively common in comedies and musicals.[4] The prohibition differs further according to the kind of discourse in the film: while prohibited in the fiction film, the look into the camera is allowed in the pedagogical film or in the home movie.[5] Finally, it varies as a function of the medium: the direct look prohibited in the cinema is permitted in television.[6] Indeed in certain cases, a violation of the prohibition becomes obligatory, as when the spectator must be convinced that it is precisely she being addressed or when the need for contact with the spectator exceeds the potential risks.

And so we face a minor enigma: concerning two films whose interpellation of the spectator could not be more emphatic, we propose, initially, that the operations involved are prohibited, and then, that the prohibition in question is by no means absolute. At the very moment of explicit contact between the movie screen and the inside of the theater, we discover that this contact is problematic, and doubly so. To resolve this question and to undertake the investigation proposed in the preceding chapter, we must begin by recognizing that in light of this apparent caprice, the explanations advanced so far are insufficient. We should try to understand if, when, and why the spectator is put into play, and under what conditions he or she is assigned a space of activity. It is not enough, however, to invoke an operation (of the camera) which the film is inclined to deny, a location (the theater) which the film tends to exclude, or a being (a seeing and hearing spectator) whom the film typically strives to conceal. On the contrary, to acquire even a preliminary understanding, it is necessary to refer to a domain far more complex, that of cinematographic enunciation.[7]

Cinematographic Enunciation

What is cinematographic enunciation? The term refers to an appropriation of the expressive possibilities of the cinema which give body and consistency to a film.[8] In other words, enunciation involves a conversion of a language into a discourse, a passage from an ensemble of simple virtualities to a concrete and specific object. At issue is the recognition of a concrete entity as a perceptible reality, an object localized to the degree that it is manifest in the world.[9] Note that this act (which has something inaugural about it, whether or not it is the "origin" in the proper sense) fixes the coordinates of a filmic discourse by adjusting them according to its own needs. Enunciation in fact constitutes the base upon which the persons, places, and times of a text are articulated, the ground zero (the "ego-hic-nunc," the who, where, and when) from which the text's various elements are organized. The persons, deriving from the enunciation's "who," can take the form of an I, you, he, or she; the places, deriving from the "where," can become a here, there, or elsewhere; and the time, deriving from the "when," a now, then, before, or after. We will continue to note throughout how a film takes control of these coordinates in a variable rather than fixed fashion. In any case, the existence and parameters of reference of a filmic discourse depend strictly upon the enunciation.

Among the axes just sketched, that of the people requires closer examination. This is necessary in part because an essential point is involved, given that this complex process seems above all to imply and promote a concept of subjectivity (notions such as appropriation and taking control suggest a subject), and also because the people provide the space where the spectator's destiny plays out (as well as that of her correspondent, typically labeled the "author"). Consider for one, that the enunciation, and the subject that it implies, never appear as such. Whether conceived as an instance of mediation assuring passage from virtuality to realization, or as the linguistic act which ensures the production of a discourse,[10] the enunciation can be seen only in the enunciated, or énoncé, which it presupposes (given that here the term énoncé designates any result of the enunciation: the film, sequence, shot, etc.).[11] The subject of the enunciation—whether reduced to either a simple operation (under the assumption that the process initiates itself) or to some empirical entity (an individual who initiates the process) is recognizable only through fragments, a series of indices internal to the film. In short, the act which initiates the game occurs openly, but always outside the field of play.[12] In return, there is always something in the énoncé which reveals and attests to the presence of the act.[13] There is, in effect, always an aspect to the énoncé which refers to the enunciation and its subject, an aspect which the film never wholly excludes: it is the gaze which broaches and organizes what is shown, the perspective which delineates and puts in order the visual field, the place from which one follows what comes into sight. In a word, there is the point of view from which things are observed, a point which provides the pivot around which to organize the images (and sounds), and which determines their coordinates and form.

We will note below the different facets of point of view, considering, for example, how point of view functions simultaneously as a locus of perception, knowledge, and belief. For the time being, let us attend to its fundamental significance as an indicator of the fact that a scene exists only because someone assumes a vision of it and in doing so, literally brings it to life.[14] At this point, however, we cross a new threshold. Point of view generally corresponds to either the camera's location during filming, or by contrast, the ideal position of an observer witnessing the scene projected on the screen. These alternatives have profound roots: before referring to either a technical installation or a hypothetical position, point of view emerges at the very moment when the enunciation undertakes its own énoncé as an object to be transmitted, by

The Figure of the Spectator 19

orienting the énoncé toward a point different from where it was constituted, and thus establishing within its very center an appropriation and an address. Or again it emerges at the moment where the enunciation is invested with a modality, thanks to which one can distinguish between "bringing the image to life" and "having the image brought to life," phenomena which correspond broadly to the act of showing and the act of seeing. In any case, what matters is that immediately a division arises, a polarity, a double activity, which leads the subject of the enunciation to separate into enunciator and enunciatee.[15] The point of view can then take both of these into account, distinguishing the often superimposed means of a film's self-construction and self-presentation. Of course, here we hope more precisely to define the enunciatee, both a target fixed by the énoncé and the moment when this énoncé delegates the interpretation. But first, we must pass through a third stage.

The subject of the enunciation can also exhibit itself openly, appearing as an explicit "guide" to the images and sounds. That is, in certain cases this subject, not content to act surreptitiously, will openly install itself in the énoncé. Such cases signal not only the constitution of a discourse under certain circumstances, but also the type of discourse and circumstances in question. They entail something comparable to the appearance of deictic marks. Though its capacity to refer to its enunciative situation is limited, a film exercises an effort in this regard, particularly during the opening and closing credit sequences. Thus, consciously or unconsciously, it accumulates numerous technical traces within its body—signs of the recording of image and sound, or instructions of explicit interpretation, as in cases of voice-over narration.[16] Moreover, the movements of the énoncé reproduce those of the enunciation. For example, the founding acts of appropriation and address translate in the text as instructions or injunctions which effectively dynamize the discourse. Or again, through a sort of openness or availability, the film accents its own points of departure and arrival, effectively introducing and enforcing a certain linearity.[17] Lastly, there is a vast domain of processes of figuration and thematization by means of which the enunciation can disguise itself and merge into one or another of the film's elements. Think of the many ways in which a film can incarnate a linguistic operation, often quite literally: the omnipresent glances, the staging of spectacles, voyeurs and spies, phantoms and doubles, actions imitating the behavior of the camera, anthropomorphic camera movements, etc. In all these incarnations, the subject of the enunciation seems to search for motifs where it can develop, as if wanting to become a whole and autonomous being through the film, rather than a reality identifiable only through its traces.[18]

Our critical landscape is becoming increasingly rich and complicated. Focusing on certain common trajectories and outcomes within this complexity enables an understanding of the specifics of certain operations. First, it is clear that if the journey described above is followed to its end, then a correspondence or intimacy will develop between the enunciation and the énoncé. In effect, this is an énoncé which traverses its own enunciation prior to controlling anything else, identifying its paths and mechanisms (an enunciative énoncé). This is complementary to the enunciation which attempts to appear within the very énoncé which presupposes it (the enunciated enunciation). There is always an unbridgeable zone between the two terms of the relation— what appears of the enunciation is never anything but the énoncé—but this particular configuration involves a situation in which the first term seems to merge completely into the second. Consider, for example, certain appeals to the spectator, which by insisting on the role of the enunciator, reveal and emphasize an address. But again there are other ways of presenting this. On the one hand, the journey may remain incomplete. In this case, the marks of enunciation stay suspended, and the discourse unfolds without acknowledging the gesture that constitutes it; it is as if the discourse's constitution alone testifies to the processes which gave it shape and substance (such is the case with the classical cinema). On the other hand, the journey can achieve completion, but in an excessive fashion. Here, the marks of enunciation become invisible insofar as the narrative completely reabsorbs them, submitting them to its logic and integrating them within its universe (a blatant example is the metacinematic "film-within-a-film"). In both cases, the body of the film keeps a secret, so to speak, either because its presuppositions are passed over in silence, or because its indices are excessively disguised. We must now offer an account different from the one proposed above, when the énoncé no longer calls attention to itself but instead becomes preoccupied with its own "contents" (enuncive énoncé), and the enunciation no longer aims to pose as a protagonist, so to speak, but instead retires docilely into the wings (receding enunciation).[19]

Such an opposition brings to mind other antinomies. There is, for instance, the platonic dualism of diegesis and mimesis, or the Jamesian distinction between telling and showing. Both distinguish a text in which the "author" intervenes from a text that aims to faithfully mirror reality. Consider the quite relevant distinction between "discours" and "histoire," or that between commentary and narrative.[20] These distinctions involve an opposition between a saying that manifests its own parameters of reference (the who, where, and when of the act that initiates it) and a saying that functions as if independent of any such determinations. They distinguish thus between representations that reveal their own enunciative situation and those that have neither the will nor the need to do so. We need not analyze here the degree of correspondence between these binarisms and those listed above. However, it shows the need for the elaboration of relatively varied solutions, and that through articulations of this type we can estimate the effective value of each element of the enunciation. Consider again the case of the enunciatee. The enunciatee's presence is obvious both when a film speaks openly of itself or when it concentrates on narrative (that is, in cases of either commentary or "pure" narrative, to employ the terminology proposed above), but when a concurrence of different forms exists in the same film (in other words, in cases involving an alternation between the poles of commentary and narrative), it must be derived from a process of confrontation.[21] Nevertheless, whatever the solutions obtained and methods adopted, a film will always have an enunciatee. Whether manifest or implicit, the enunciatee provides a kind of frame deriving from the enunciation and accompanying the text throughout its development, a thread that cannot but be woven into the fabric. This now suggests a *role* (a term that indicates the enunciatee's active nature, its capacity both to act on the text and to take control of that which acts on the text). Once the film has defined its parameters and structures, and we have moved beyond our current horizon, it is a role upon which a *body* will be grafted, in an encounter that will initiate what is commonly referred to as an act of communication.[22]

An Enunciated Enunciation

This lengthy digression has been intended to outline the premises of enunciation, to indicate the enunciatee's existence, its presence within the énoncé, its availability in a space divided between narrative and commentary or between a receding enunciation and an enunciated enunciation, and finally this enunciatee's availability as a role destined to connect with a body. We can now return to our point of departure:

two opening sequences of films involving a direct address to the spectator, an interpellation, a questioning of someone in order to make him either appear on the screen or be captured in the film, and finally, the taboos that hinder this appeal in varied and capricious ways. Perhaps we now have the tools needed to disentangle this knot. Concerning the frame defined earlier, the look into the camera, and particularly the act of interpellation, would in effect strongly suggest a case of enunciated enunciation. Not only does it indicate the site where the coordinates that situate a film through its enunciation are inscribed, but also where these coordinates become explicit signs and carriers. More precisely, the gesture of turning toward someone who then becomes a discernible target introduces a destination. Perhaps this applies only to the precise instant when the gaze into the camera is unleashed and not to any subsequent moment. Nevertheless, such an instant inevitably influences the film's parameters to the point of conditioning the development of the narration. We will return to this point, little by little, in our examples.

On the one hand, it is evident that the two film sequences described above present a case in which the enunciatee accedes to a sort of equilibrated plenitude, appearing in the énoncé in the form of an obvious destination but without betraying its identity. That is, the enunciatee emerges as its traces, perhaps not identifiable as a figure, can be clearly distinguished on the line established by a gaze extending beyond the screen, and into the field which faces it—into a space which is certainly complete but not at all delimited, and in which the enunciatee can function for what it is, a simple point of view. At the same time, the two sequences provide examples of commentary rather than narrative. It is as if these sequences, in order to complete the stages of a dialogue—and thus reach the decisive moment when the enunciation's who, when, and where are established—immediately put their cards on the table and establish the *I* and *you*. On the other hand, such a characterization soon appears provisional, not because the cinema is incapable of following certain paths to the end, but because the paths suggested in our two examples imply a change in goal. Such a reorientation was foreseeable from the beginning, from the moment when the characters in the two films, in medium close-up, tell their stories into the camera. Public events or private, giving a report or recalling a memory: these deliberate acts provoke a hesitation, requiring the viewer to verify whether what is occurring concerns the film or something else. The suspicion is confirmed when the characters are shown speaking into microphones: upon discovering that something other than a filmic enunciation is at issue, the viewer is led to inquire about the identity of the actual addressee. The question is thus not only "What kind of story is it?" but "Am I the one being spoken to?" Finally, a few slight modifications turn the doubt into certainty: sidelong glances that transform off-screen space into diegetic space (a traversable space, ready to be entered); a final camera movement which frames the characters in plan américain, a movement wholly impregnated with the world of the fiction (manifest in the two police officers); and a diction whose rhythm and hesitations suggest a narrative situation (the recording of a radio broadcast). Following these modifications, the enunciation tends to become surreptitious, each element of the mise-en-scène now plays a role in establishing the story, and the overall form becomes that of pure narrative. But the gaze and words addressed to the camera were by no means inconsequential. No countershot reveals the one toward whom the characters turned.[23] Even if lacking precise contours, it remains always possible to presume the existence of a living being, a point of view, the sign of an enunciatee. The instant of direct address thus serves as an indelible reference point throughout the film's duration. It indicates henceforth the existence of a free zone reserved for an encounter with the individual who, sitting in the theater and attending to what appears on the screen, guarantees the possibility of connection.

The lesson to be drawn from the two film beginnings is clear: by assuming the function of someone who opens a discourse, someone who performs a dedication, by offering a gesture of complicity that recalls the rules of the game, these introductory moments seem to declare, "It is you that I am addressing." In effect, they make us aware of what is important. They show that the enunciation defines the film's coordinates (and the *you* who emerges draws its identity from this initiating gesture). They show that the énoncé gathers the traces of the enunciation along the directional line of its outward gesture (and the *you* can then accede to a privileged position, with the dedication dominating the text as a whole). They show that the rhythm of the narration can blend the enunciation's traces into an énoncé (and the *you* then becomes a simple character, while the gesture of dedication performs the function of a first chapter, and the story's frame becomes the story of the framework). At the same time, however, they also show that there is always a precise point that offers itself to sight. Whether manifest or submerged, obvious or concealed, this point marks the place where an enunciatee is acknowledged and installed, where a role joins a body and thus defines the behavior and profile of that figure known as the spectator.

Interpellation: Form and Taboo

Armed with this lesson, we can now move straight to the second aspect of the problem posed above, the prohibition against the direct look into the camera and other forms of interpellation. Consider this taboo within the viewpoint provided by our project. If the look into the camera and toward the spectator is a case of an enunciated enunciation, why does the filmic text typically avoid or eliminate it? We can perhaps formulate a response by analyzing two additional film examples. These examples illustrate a binarism suggested by cinema's historical evolution, given that one concerns an early experiment in filmic narration and the other a quite radical attempt to demonstrate cinema's role as a fiction-producing machine. Because they are well known they will not require a detailed description.

The first comes from Edwin S. Porter's *The Great Train Robbery* (1903). At the film's end, after the assault on the train and the subsequent arrest or killing of the outlaws, the bandit leader, his eyes fixed on the spectator, raises his gun and fires. (The shot in question has been placed at either end, so this moment might also occur at the film's beginning, even prior to the start of the narrative).[24] The second example comes from Jean-Luc Godard's *Wind from the East* (1969). A young man, first in close-up and then medium shot, faces the camera, praising the place from which he speaks and inviting the spectator to come and join him there. Meanwhile, an off-screen voice also addressed to the spectator mimics the young man's words in an ironic tone, underscoring the absurdity of the invitation.

How are these two examples structured? Immediately apparent is the phenomenon we have encountered previously, the alternation and superimposition of commentary and narrative. Both examples entail once again a situation where the representation, through an explicit gesture of complicity, refers briefly to its fundamental parameters before pursuing its own process of development. Here, however, the alternation between acknowledgment and discretion develops in two different manners. In *The Great Train Robbery*, the look into the camera produces a shock, associated with a gunshot likewise intended to "hit" the spectator. At the same time, though, the camera shot in which this event occurs could not be more marginal. Not only is it unrelated to the narrative, but it is situated outside the borders of the text, to the point of occurring either at the film's beginning or end, as if it were simply an arbitrary supplement. The contrast between such a spectacular means of making contact with the spectator and the marginality of the site of the encounter is certainly perplexing. It does, however, permit a recognition of the rather basic fact that in a cinema which chooses a narrative form, any face-to-face meeting with the spectator tends to be subordinated to less direct kinds of encounters. In the case of this example, the intent is to get the attention of the individual watching the film and to remind this individual of her status as spectator—an intent expressed in an absolutely radical fashion by the conjunction of the gaze and a gunshot. Following such a moment, however, the look into the camera will be circumscribed and finally subordinated to gazes completely internal to the fiction. The gazes between the characters, which occur either within the depth of a single shot or between one shot and another, also have the capacity to attract the viewer's attention. Moreover, they are far more adept at circulating that attention within the "magic realm" of the fiction. Thus when the fictional apparatus is strongly tested, certain emotions will block this displacement, permitting the enunciatee to establish only a silent presence afterward.

The situation proposed by the extract from *Wind from the East* is entirely different. Here the look into the camera is made obvious—but only in order to be subjected to criticism or derision. Its intent and effect are attenuated by means of another procedure of interpellation, that of the off-screen voice. Observe the mechanism involved here. On the one hand, a character, eyes turned toward the spectator, speaks of his screen world (a space defined by virtually any kind of landscape) and of those facing him (the theater in which the film is projected and all those who fill it). There is thus an explicit attempt to initiate a dialogue that will end the isolation of the participants and assure them an "authentic" meeting. On the other hand, an off-screen voice, superimposed upon the character's discourse, defines the character by commenting upon his statements, as if to emphasize the weakness of both the character's claims and his degree of authority, while at the same time questioning his good faith (the character is a "seducer," the voice tells us, comparable to all those film heroes who only reveal themselves in order to more effectively subjugate the spectator). The situation is thus one in which an attempt at dialogue remains stillborn, due to the double failing of not taking things far enough and not obeying the constraints imposed by reality. Confronted with these facts it becomes easy to distinguish the different forces operative in our example. The look into the camera, which constitutes something like the action's center of gravity, is also the carrier of a failed promise. It introduces a procedure foreign to traditional fiction with the aim of overturning fiction's rules. But at the same time it is accused by the voice of a complicity with the surviving fictional ancien regime, the voice which claims to be the only one capable of a truly different discourse. At issue is thus not liberation from the narrative universe but an attempt, by means of a gaze, to exhibit the mise-en-scène. It occurs, however, at the risk of becoming an object of parody and accusation and thus returns to the same rank as what it had criticized. This involves a very clear interpellation, but which according to its own terms, holds the potential to become complicitous with the narrative.

Context

Our observations on the extracts from *The Great Train Robbery* and *Wind from the East* show how a procedure, regardless of how well it illuminates the enunciation's motivations, can assume different values. In the case of the first extract, it constitutes a "shock" motif that ultimately runs aground outside the text's limits, whereas in the second, it assumes a metatextual function that eventually becomes the object of a critique. Both cases, however, involve the same terrain, that of cinematographic narration. Perceived as a goal to be attained as much as a constraint from which to be liberated, narration appears in both cases as an encounter to which we must attend, simultaneously a landmark and a possible impediment. This permits the recognition that there is always a second frame within which each of a film's moments is recorded. We have already examined the system of person, place, and time fixed by the enunciation, a system that might be called the "enunciative frame." In addition, we can now recognize an "environment" made up of the whole of the text as well as all the ancillary texts—cinematographic but also literary, pictorial, and so on—which adhere to their own distinctive norms and rules of behavior. Thus we have a tripartite "environment" which includes énoncés in the form of sequences (the cotextual component), a broader ensemble of discourses (the transtextual component), and the rules of elaboration applicable to all (the institutional component).[25] The environment is represented here in particular by narrativity, by the story told in a particular film, the ensemble of existing stories, and the rules of story construction. While this is the case in the examples analyzed above, which relate to issues of narrative, other examples could just as easily suggest the relevance of a different "environment."

Both the enunciative frame and now this second frame, with its triple articulation, belong under the heading of "context." Both define what "surrounds" a collection of images and sounds. The first designates a circumscribed structure (though progressively extendable), while the second refers to a more general domain (an "intertext," strictly speaking). This difference of size and bearing suggests the need for a prudent approach. If the first context determines parameters at the level of person, time, and place, so does the second, but insofar as to project these parameters onto a relatively larger horizon; if the first context defines a space of operation, the second takes such a space into account only by integrating it within a larger totality. The differences between the two types of context may seem quite significant, but the compatibilities in the end are more decisive. Each example cited above, defined by its own enunciative structure, must appear coherent in relation to both the frame established by the text as well as the genre and rules which govern it. Coherence here involves not simple consistency but, on the contrary, the capacity to adapt.[26] Thus an image, sound, shot, sequence, etc., will appear acceptable if, in addition to being grammatical on the syntactic level and congruent on the semantic level, they are "appropriate" to the parameters of the text's general frame, what we are calling the pragmatic level.[27]

Context and appropriateness: these concepts suggest the basis for the internal variations of our examples as well as the taboo concerning certain procedures of interpellation. Consider the problem of the taboo. The look into the camera is forbidden whenever the intrigue's unfolding and the film's genre must maintain a "narrative" form (as in the case of an "adventure film" in which the regime of absolute fiction and the transparency of the diegesis require masking all marks of enunciation). On the other hand, the look into the camera is recommended in the case of pure commentary (as in filmed declarations, where the self-construction of the film is quite evident). It would likewise be

28 *Inside the Gaze*

authorized in narratives which are open to commentary (as in the musical comedy, whose fictional regime includes an overtly metatextual component).[28] Lastly, it is optional in films that refer to themselves by speaking of something else (as in documentaries, where what is represented is the visible conquest of representation).[29] The taboo is thus not absolute but, on the contrary, relative to the frame of reference. It concerns not the look into the camera itself but rather this look's capacity for insertion into a larger frame.[30] Moreover, the same observations could be extended beyond procedures of interpellation to include specifically diegetic elements, such as the play of characters, decor, and other aspects of the mise-en-scène. While dissimilar to the situation of interpellation, when related to a context, these elements likewise concern problems of appropriateness that involve a scale of values.

We proposed that the variations within our examples had the same roots as the taboo. In fact, it is again the perception of incoherence between the look into the camera and the status of the narration that provokes a passage from the level of commentary to that of narrative. Due to incompatibility with its frame of activity, the enunciated enunciation is masked to the profit of a diegeticized enunciation. Such a movement involves two aspects. The first concerns the values that can be attributed to this act: the composition of the frame of reference permits an interpretation of the look at the spectator, and its subsequent eviction, as the repression of a still-open possibility, or rather as a test of practicable alternatives. Such is the case in the examples from *The Great Train Robbery* and *Wind from the East*. In the latter, with the cinematographic narration on the point of asserting itself, the fact that a too-obvious sign of complicity has been kept apart indicates the renunciation of impracticable forms of implication. In the former, where the cinematographic narration seems to have reached its end, to propose this kind of operation signifies a demand for acceleration and radical change. Thus the same procedure can acquire different meanings, depending upon the horizon on which it is projected and the place where it is found.[31] The second aspect concerns the manner in which one rejects what is considered inappropriate. Again, the specificity of the context can permit either rapid recuperation or ultimate overflow. In the example from *The Great Train Robbery*, that the direct gaze is held at the text's margin (literally, at either the beginning or end of the film) neutralizes its effects.[32] In *Wind from the East*, the look into the camera is accompanied by a more emphatic verbal interpellation. This runs the

The Figure of the Spectator 29

risk, clearly intentional, of turning the film into something other than narrative, perhaps so that it can ultimately become all the more narrative. Given these two films, we can see that the quality and power of a single operation—the look into the camera—can develop differently depending upon the force field within which it is inscribed.

Context and appropriateness: the *you* seemingly implied by the film henceforth acquires a rather complex identity, rather than offering a simple gesture of complicity. The notions of context and appropriateness suggest precise rules, numerous possible types of confrontations, and the evaluation of options and prudent compromises. There is often a cost (as in our examples, marginality or irony), but also a profit: the enunciatee can always emerge, even if only for a moment, without exposure to real mortal danger.

A Few Questions

The general outline of our project is now evident. Three points are particularly compelling: the idea that the enunciation fixes a film's coordinates, defining its points of constitution and address; the idea that the énoncé chooses between two extreme solutions, self-confession (commentary) and utter discretion (narrative); and finally, the idea that an intertextual frame functions as a kind of background within which each of a film's fragments acquires both a place and a distinctive identity and weight. At this point, the problem of the spectator becomes more particular, defined now as a problem of a mark, within the film's interior, that indicates an invitation to see and to hear. We are also concerned with the degree to which the mark is obvious in the course of the narration, and of the mark's appropriateness in relation to what surrounds both it and the film as a whole.

The examples analyzed above now appear to involve aspects that require more precise description. First, there is an obvious difference in treatment between the traces of the enunciator and those of the enunciatee. In our examples, the enunciator is manifest in the act of someone giving the news, throwing a glance, or telling a story; the enunciatee, on the contrary, is situated offscreen, a condition which is entirely symptomatic. This dissymmetry confirms the existence of several levels of figurativization concerning the marks of enunciation. These include traces which simply recall the presence of a presupposition (the énoncé refers to the enunciation by the sole fact of being an énoncé);

there are traces that function by metonymy (signs of the filmic process that indicate, by revealing the conditions of their fabrication, that the images and sounds are constructed); there are traces that work at the level of composition and rhythm (like certain types of lighting or montage that in themselves suggest the idea of the film's "self-construction" and "self-offering"); there are traces which follow a path of symbolization (certain recurrent insertions—mirror, window, eye—which function as obedient metaphors of the forces ruling the text); there are traces modeled on elements of the fiction (like certain canonical behaviors—informing, hearing, seeing, observing—which mark the progression of the film through the action of its protagonists), etc. We will reserve the terms "enunciator" and "enunciatee" for abstract and implicit instances in the text, which can be rendered explicit only by means of a hyperphrastic formulation, such as, "*I* say and I make *you* understand that . . ." or "*I* show and I make *you* see that . . ."[33] Conversely, we will reserve the terms "narrator" and "narratee" for figures that mark the full and complete emergence of the enunciation's motivations within the énoncé, to the point of acquiring a sort of exemplary and autonomous life, as for example, in the case of characters who tell a story they are in the process of living, or in contrast, characters within the intrigue who offer themselves as the addressees of the narration.[34] Once this distinction is made (between an I and you that act silently and an I and you who act as protagonists), there remains the task of defining the potential differences in degree of figurativization, and in a more general manner, the effect induced by the emergence of the film's governing factors.

Secondly, the examples analyzed above juxtapose an interpellation by voice and an interpellation by gaze. In *Wind from the East* the two even oppose one another. Such a layering of textual operations can have important consequences. It can, for example, recall the old polemic concerning the difference between the visible and the verbal. Often manifest in film theory, this difference suggests a variety of other distinctions, between the perceptible and the intelligible, the concrete and the abstract, sensory impressions and logical thought, and the currently popular distinction between what connects with the emotions, such as the world's beauty revealed on the screen, and what appeals to rationality, like the narrative with its combination of actions and semantic models.[35] Such a confrontation also suggests certain diametrically opposed visions of the cinema, like the aspiration for a "pure cinema" in which the image guarantees a truth greater than the supposed precision of verbal language, or like that of the "film essay," in which the imposition of a rational structure is assumed to be an account of the world better than a direct representation.[36] But most of all, this opposition between the visible and the verbal enables an identification of the now common juxtaposition between point of view and voice: with it, one can distinguish within the text between the one who filters the events through his gaze and the one who relates them verbally; that is, between the one who sees and the one who speaks.[37] Here our examples suggest two different principles of organization: one, linked to the gaze, necessarily probes the space before it and attempts to put things in perspective; the other, connected to the word, suggests and reveals the facts, and thus assumes responsibility for the narration. In order precisely to oppose this last alternative, it is necessary to relativize any divergence between visual and auditory kinds of facts. Often, as here, they only represent two paths of access to the énoncé for the subject of the enunciation: this inevitably functions as the point from which things are shown, but it is manifest either as the apparent origin of vision, or else the origin of the word. In other words, at issue are two different manners of demonstrating the agent who has taken possession of the world in order to exhibit it,[38] making this agent appear as either an observer or a speaker. Here we have the same basic principle (which legitimates the énoncé as an énoncé) and two complementary forms of figurativization (the eye and the mouth). Thus instead of interpreting the questions "who sees?" and "who speaks?" as opposed to one another, it would be preferable to ask first, "What is the enunciation?" and then, "Who manifests it?" It also no longer seems possible to place point of view and the voice at the same level; it is better to consider point of view as a more general condition because of its complexity as a mark of enunciation, and the voice associated with a gaze as a more particular case, given that it already functions as a place of figurativization. Having now reduced the difference between the verbal and visual, we must still decide whether they are ultimately interchangeable or whether each type of production, each form of contact, entails specific consequences.

Third, our examples (particularly *Wind from the East*) tend to use an opposition of "good" and "bad" interpellations, right and wrong, a truth and a lie. Such a tension reveals what seems to be a fundamental rivalry between two enunciations engaged in a struggle for dominance.

But point of view, the textual structure which refers to the film's "self-construction" and "self-offering," always acts in a plural fashion: besides being a site of division, it acquires a multiple identity throughout the course of a film's narration, due to the proliferation of framings, camera angles, sources of narrative information, etc. Fundamentally, we need to demonstrate a multiplicity of filmed moments and conditions of recording, an inevitable imbrication of points of view, even though these can achieve a harmony within the frame of a complex project. And so, in our examples the line separating the different enunciative marks is situated on a particular terrain, that of the "aptness" of the trace. We can then determine in what respect one element can reveal better than another a film's "self-construction" and "self-offering," or how a single element can suggest a film's overall project. In other words, which, among the points of view in question, can legitimately achieve dominance?

Narrators and Narratees

We will respond to these questions by analyzing two new examples. The first involves only a simple presence: the voice that accompanies the closing credits of Orson Welles's *The Magnificent Ambersons* (1942) and concludes the enumeration of names by saying: "My name is Orson Welles." In this name so distinctly spoken, this interpellation which becomes an appellation, is the obvious presence of an author conscious of his rights and responsibilities; yet it also makes us aware of the manipulations throughout a film's narration, and their implications. The question, if you will, concerns the author's wish not only to "sign" his work but also to unveil the work's process of construction. In effect, the character who appears on the screen, through the intermediary of this voice, inevitably incarnates the logic organizing the film's images and sounds. By claiming responsibility for this filmic project, this character establishes itself as, on the one hand, a "sign" or "emblem" of the principles which the text obeys, and on the other, a "direct source" of information and "immediate regulator" of their circulation. Briefly, the character puts himself at the service of the enunciator, becomes the narrator, and thereby dominates the entire narrative.

In *The Magnificent Ambersons*, Welles-as-character is the one who accomplishes this act. But other characters could have easily done so.

Consider, in general, the many ways in which a film harbors all sorts of declarations of intention, the reminders and foreshadowing which punctuate the narration, and the variety of characters who play the role of "data banks." In such cases, the film makes its project explicit and permits the spectator to recognize the paths of the images and sounds as much as to enter into the life of a subject. Here, in typical fashion, Welles-as-character fulfills his function as narrator as openly as possible: he recites the casting and the list of technicians and thus directly testifies to the film's "self-construction." In doing so, he establishes himself as the "center" around which the other elements are organized. His position as presenter ideally allows him to command the other characters' actions, to the point of confiding to a "surrogate" the task of elucidating the story's moral. And so, Lucy Morgan, a veritable stand-in for the narrator, tells Eugene (and thus the viewer) the story of the Indian chief Vendonah, thereby providing the significance of the film's entire intrigue. A story of two warring families involving numerous parallel situations, *The Magnificent Ambersons* establishes an interweaving of delegations so dense that virtually any of the characters is able to assume the responsibility of guiding the narration. This perpetual shifting of the speaker, however, ultimately renders any truth unstable: in this regard it is symptomatic that names also undergo certain shifts, as is the case during the recounting of the legend of the Indian chief, when "Lomo Nasha" becomes "Mola Hana," and so forth.

Let us consider a second example, also drawn from Wellesian filmography. In *F for Fake* (1975), Welles actually appears, often turning toward the spectator,[39] and personally tells the story.[40] Welles promises that for the next hour he will speak nothing but the truth. In the course of the film, Welles relates the cases of several art forgers, particularly the story of Oja Kodar's grandfather, who forged certain of Picasso's paintings and later had them authenticated by Picasso himself, who professed to be an admirer of the forger's work. Welles subsequently confesses that the hour he alluded to at the film's beginning had ended seventeen minutes before. Thus, this story of forgers and liars, disguises and masks—this story which, irony or paradox, has been presented in the guise of *cinéma vérité*[41]—shows a profound shift, a drift from its course. For at least seventeen minutes, the character appearing on the screen has done nothing to help us grasp the principle of the text's construction, nor has he allowed the spectator to identify with any particular character. For at least seventeen minutes, the narrating voice has been an obstacle to the recognition of either the one responsible for the narration or the one intended as its recipient. In other words, in this duplicitous story, the appearance of the proper name, instead of facilitating a relation with either the enunciator or enunciatee, eventually leads to fraud.

What are we to make of all this? The situation is all the more perplexing given that the same person (and the same name, Orson Welles) openly decrees the rules of the game in order then to transgress them. This situation recalls numerous moments in the typical fiction film, when an author who speaks through the characters comes into conflict with a character who insists upon speaking in her own name. In either case, at issue is both an affirmation of the film's guiding principle and an attempt to delineate a space which is in some sense independent. In this context, the apparently illogical displacement which occurs in *F for Fake* is understandable as radicalizing the fundamental fracture that traverses such films (including, in a latent fashion, *The Magnificent Ambersons*) whenever figures vie with one another, each with a different influence on the plot. Involved here is thus an interrogation concerning truth and falsehood, carried out by the very characters represented, through the complex analysis of their possibilities and degrees of intervention within the representation.

Formulating the problem in this way, beyond enabling an understanding of the Wellesian "sense of humor," allows us to recognize the implications with regard to filmic enunciation. Let us take a closer look.

First point: there are different kinds of characters organizing what appears on the screen—differences in voice, gaze, and gesture. There are thus different types of narrators. We have already discussed those who, hovering above or at the story's margin, qualify as faithful incarnations of the agent which organizes the film's images and sounds. We must now add narrators implied by the story, who function as the origin of a representation which matters to them but perhaps not at all to the one organizing the text as a whole. The same can be said of the narratees. It is precisely the position of both in relation to the story which first defines their degree of responsibility: "metadiegetic" or "extradiegetic" narrators and narratees, in principle, indicate the logic of the narration more than do their "diegetic" or "infradiegetic" counterparts.[42] These latter ultimately personify a "second" point of view at the interior of the mise-en-scène—"second" in the sense of alternative and subordinate. Although they imitate and depend upon the enuncia-tor and enunciatee, they do not serve as full delegate: as soon as the film establishes them and gives them room, it seems ready to abandon them to their own fate.

Second point: the differences between the two levels involve many elements. Again, in principle, the first level is situated outside or above the narrated story while the second is situated within it. Thus the rela-tion between these two levels suggests the opposition between com-mentary and narrative. Moreover, as suggested above, what do the first type of narrator and narratee relate and witness if not the unfolding of the film in front of our eyes? And what does the second type of nar-rator and narratee tell and hear if not their own personal story of which the film becomes a simple carrier? Besides the nature of its implication within the narrative, there are other elements of difference: in the first case the action follows the path of metonymy, while in the second, that of metaphor; in the first case it is coherent and unified, while in the second, plural and fragmented; and in the first case it tends to be all-encompassing, while in the second, to be encompassed itself, etc.

Third point: this distinction confirms once again that the basic dif-ferences in no way concern the filmic text's "truth," but rather its status. That is, the two types of narrators and narratees define not the repre-sentation's degree of factual authenticity but simply the type of relation the images and sounds maintain with the agents they presuppose (that is, the enunciator and enunciatee are not manifest, beyond any figura-tivization, except when the filmic text suggests a hyperphrase of the type "*I* gaze, and I make *you* see that . . ."). Such a relation, depending on its mode of realization, indicates the degree of faith it should be accorded. Any displacement of a role acts mainly upon the film's basic organization rather than on the quality of the representation. And cor-respondingly, a narration's degree of acceptability[43] depends on the sys-tem underlying the representation rather than the representation itself. In other words, Welles-as-character seems to pass without interruption from the position of absolute master to that of a fictional element, and back to the initial position. If the viewer doubts for a moment what this character says, it is neither because the character has violated the logic or morality of the story nor because the latter is unsustainable; rather it is because the film doubles its own levels, separates them, and moves from one to the other. More precisely, it multiplies points of view, which it then differentiates and superimposes. First we must make a sort of ideal division of the field of observation, defining the entire frame of each behavior, with its hierarchies and references; only through this can we precisely locate the perception that corresponds to the reality of events, or in contrast, put these events in question, even refuse them.

Fourth point: Although separable and by inclination opposed to one another, the two types of narrators and narratees will always find a means to unite, for it is through this reciprocal engagement that their true identity emerges. They undertake two fundamental types of relation: *coordination*, in which the members of the two couples cohabit (as is the case in an interaction between two characters in which one relates an event while the other explains how to understand it, or when one recapitulates what has so far occurred while the other offers a personal response); or *subordination*, when members of the first couple introduce those of the second (such is the case when a voice-over narration gives a character the capacity to tell his own version of events or when a character, in recalling an earlier event, reveals the insincerity of previous witnesses). These procedures could be described in a more precise manner with reference to the concepts of engagement and disengagement.[44] But, even according to the relatively basic terms proposed above, it is clear that the establishment of the different roles, and thus of a film's different levels of narration, is punctuated by highly productive rites—in the literal sense of the term.

Fifth point: the links between these varied presences transform the filmic text into a site filled with echoes, appeals, exchanges: in a word, into a fully "dialogical" set of relations.[45] It is useless to expect an absolute homogeneity. Points of view orient themselves toward one another, enter into articulations and disperse, often with the result of decentering the lines of force that support the film. As such, much more than a gesture, glance, or voice is needed to develop the consciousness a film has regarding its own coordinates.[46] Moreover, doesn't a film reveal its identity and indicate the manner in which it is to be understood through certain symptomatic gestures, as well as through the actions of its principal protagonist? Not only through explicitly designating the placement of the camera, but also through the nature of the mise-en-scène? Not only through direct interpellations, but also through exemplary narrative situations? Each of a film's signs functions as an opening allowing the film to reflect itself.

Let us stop for a moment. Through a name (Welles) we have rediscovered the same markings as in our preceding analyses: the enunciation's "self-construction" and "self-offering," the different rules characteristic of the énoncé, the short circuits produced by interpellation, the weight of the context, and so on. Moreover, we have been able to analyze in the most detailed fashion the relevant points of articulation. We can now propose a synthesis in a schema (figure 1).

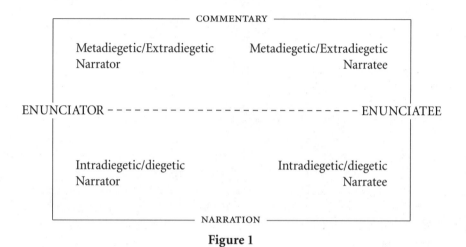

Figure 1

At the schema's far edges are the enunciation's constitutive elements—respectively the enunciator and enunciatee, which are abstract instances, representable only through the emergence of a hyperphrastic formulation along the lines of "I tell you and I show you that . . ." At the schema's interior are the narrator and narratee, figurativizations at the level of the abstract instances at the surface of the text. These indicate the *I* and the *you* who speak and display themselves. At the top are the metadiegetic and extradiegetic narrator and narratee, whose position above or at the side of the story allows them to organize the text's fundamental presuppositions (or, what amounts to the same thing, to allow these presuppositions to become effective). At the bottom, the intradiegetic and diegetic narrator and narratee accomplish a task which gives them a certain autonomy, appearing as ordinary characters, simple elements of the diegesis. Finally, at the schema's upper and lower extremes are the two basic contextual structures, commentary and narrative. In this schema, the positions which most interest us, vision and hearing, are clearly defined.

Once again it is time to move forward. In our example, the proper name is not only the ultimate pivot which organizes the filmic discourse, but an indicator of an expansion, not only a key to the constitution of roles, but an opportunity to attach these to bodies. It is in this direction that we will now advance.

To Enunciate, To Communicate

The opening and closing titles of most films display two series of distinct elements. The first involves pointing out the artistic and technical rubrics (the formulation may vary—for example, "director," "a film directed by," "a film by," etc.), the list of the principal characters (sometimes replaced by a succession of close-ups of the actors or of medallions representing them), written statements (of the type, "Any similarities with actual, existing persons or events is purely coincidental . . ."), the presentation of key narrative actions (which often function as veritable prologues or epilogues), musical accompaniment (generally symptomatic of the film's genre), and finally, the film's title. All are indications that a spectacle is beginning or ending, and all refer to the particular spectacle before us and to no other.[47] In contrast, the second series mentions the names of the director, the story's author, production and post-production technicians, certain expressions of gratitude ("We wish to thank . . ."), and so forth. All these are indications that there is something weighing upon the spectacle but which appears on the screen only indirectly, if at all: the personnel who have produced the spectacle, the occasions that determine it, the materials that constitute it. Thus, the succession of names listed in the credits—presumably read by the viewer—suggest a decidedly ambivalent operation. On the one hand, they trace a border that circumscribes the properties of the film, designating an "interior" and characterized as such. On the other hand, they convert this border into a bridge to an "exterior," a reality that exists outside the film but is nonetheless relevant to it. It is not unusual that a film's opening and closing sequences, together with the list of names that constitute the credits, serve as transparent metaphors illustrating this dual identity. Consider, for example, the many opening scenes involving locations where strangers enter unexpectedly: campsites, expedition parties about to depart, or enclosed private properties and untrodden paths. A good example can be found in the first and last images of Welles's *Citizen Kane* (1941) in which the gate and protective fence which surrounds Xanadu (bearing a monogram of the character who gives the film its title),[48] along with the "No Trespassing" placard, signal that the story will attempt to penetrate an individual's life and, unsuccessfully, break through to his secret.[49]

This juxtaposition of an "interior" and an "exterior" may suggest the dialectic between cinema and reality, raising the familiar issue of the referentiality of the sign. But here the difference between interior and exterior produces not a systematic confrontation between what appears on the screen and what actually exists in the world, but instead an analysis of the sometimes surreptitious confrontation between a character who makes the narrative advance by participating in it and an individual who constructs or appropriates a representation, making it one of the stakes in a game. In other words, the list of names which serves as the film's "frame" or "proscenium"[50] and which coincides with the beginning and end of the screening, the lowering and raising of the house lights, elicits a reflection on the relation between those who act "during" a text—the subjects of the enunciation whose marks and traces constitute the essential lines of force of a developing process— and those who act "via" a text—the empirical subjects who wish to express themselves and to understand, to act and interact.[51] This list of names incites us to reflect on precisely the links that connect "roles," an enunciator and enunciatee, and "bodies," a sender and receiver.

So far we have insisted on the film's capacity to "offer itself" apropos of a spectator, leaving aside the issue of this spectator's concrete presence and capacity to receive it. We now reach a point at which it becomes necessary to elaborate this second dimension of our project. Immediately questions arise: above all, why should we call this a "second" dimension? Our trajectory, in effect, can be accomplished in either of two ways. Put simply, if the emphasis is on roles, as it is here, then the moment when a text determines its *I* and *you* becomes not only an initiating gesture but the major activity of the text. This moment founds, or at the very least determines, each successive development, and carries the responsibility of actualizing what has been already decided. If, in contrast, we reverse our critical path, we must assign principal responsibility to the body. The body then founds and determines a film's coordinates, and is responsible for reflecting the conditions of existence within the text. Clearly, to speak of our investigation in terms of "first" and "second" stages can be misleading. At one stage, we favor a symbolic geography (no doubt with difficulty understanding how such a geography could ever become real and yet remain symbolic), while at the other, we deal with concrete forces (surely with difficulty conceiving how these forces flow into what often betrays them). Once we recognize the existence of these two contrasting itineraries (implying two apparently irreconcilable research agendas), it becomes necessary to conclude that at hand is an essentially "reversible" trajectory.[52] Such a conclusion arises not from a love for compromise but rather from a respect for the integrity of our theoretical frame. A text finds its own realization in a continual coming-and-going, through which roles and bodies support and adapt to one another, pursuing each other in turn. The inextricable and inevitable complicities between telling what is and being what is told can perhaps give an idea of the perpetual pendulum-like movement involved here.[53] Once again, certain sequences from *Citizen Kane* can provide helpful examples. A single name, "Rosebud," appearing in both the film's prologue and epilogue, performs different and speculative functions. At the film's opening, it provokes an interrogation, and from there projects the viewer into the very heart of the representation. At the film's end, it is offered as a personal confidence and thus reintegrates the viewer into her own skin. Though the passage back and forth over the threshold may sustain the mystery, even thicken it, and though the utterance of the magical word provides no great relief, the repetition of the name is far from useless.[54]

Second question: in what sense can we speak here of a body? How does a body enter into relation with a role? It should be said at the outset that the use of the term "body" is not intended to imply a reference to a purely "empirical" reality, to a domain of raw facticity. It alludes rather to a structural relation, whose contours differ from those implied by the elements examined so far, but whose intervention is entirely indispensable and decisive. We once again approach the issue from the perspective of the spectator. When a film elaborates a point basic to its own construction and from which it demands a response, when, most fundamentally, the film institutes its own destination, it is not expecting to encounter an absolute stranger. Between the interlocutor anticipated by the images and sounds and the interlocutor whose gaze intersects with the gazes coming from the screen—a process and a behavior, respectively—there is certainly a difference involved, though by no means a total one. The basic commonality between the two derives from the fact that a body is at once the support and the reserve of a role. A "support" above all: the lines of force by which a filmic text establishes and defines its fundamental articulation must acquire support from something or someone in order to transform certain hypotheses into actual operations as well as to stabilize rather variable actions. In other words, an effective presence is needed to adjust the lines of conduct and to organize the perpetually fleeting points of view around a fixed point. In this sense, a body facing a role is like a photographic plate that reveals an image's precise contours, and at the same time freezes the movement into a canonical pose. This body is like a surface that becomes engraved and brings action to a standstill. But the body is also a "reserve." The plate is also a palimpsest whose superimposed inscriptions bear the traces of preceding inscriptions, each trace serving as an occasion of memory. In effect, the text's lines of force, rather than encountering inert presences, draw sustenance and information from something or someone; they meet with the receptacle of a competence.[55] In this sense, a body confronted with a role is like a ledger listing an account's debits and credits, like one who endorses a loan, capable of interrupting expenditures if the account is overdrawn, or of raising the amount if the interest is promptly paid. A support and a reserve: it thus becomes clear why the functional rather than the material dimension prevails. The close "complementarity" between body and role pushes each to influence the other, to the point of perfectly coordinating their respective though discontinuous movements.[56] Again *Citizen Kane* provides a perfect example. During the closing credits there are presentations in close-up of all the principal actors in character, with the exception of Kane/Welles, who is signaled only through a simple subtitle, printed moreover in a small font at the very end of the list of secondary characters. The mise-en-scène and its creator are treated no better, appearing only under the last title, among a list of names.[57] Nevertheless, the body of this author and actor, avoiding an overly visible manifestation, fills the text with its presence, providing the foundation for a succession of disguises and masquerades (consider the young Welles's narcissistic complacency in personifying Kane near death), always nourishing the mystery (a curious coincidence between a nearly clandestine process of filming and the story of a man whose secret we search to discover). The discretion manifest at the film's beginning and end is only a paradox destined to clarify that the origin of the images and sounds, and with it the ideal destination of the film text, are indebted to the existence of concrete shifters.

These questions and tentative responses should have clarified some of the main issues we are up against. The interaction of the role and the body implies a two-way circulation as opposed to a single prescribed trajectory, and two distinct spaces rather than incompatible characters. More precisely, this binarism determines two reversible and complementary domains, that of *enunciation* and that of *communication*. While the role is engaged in the conversion of a language into a discourse, the body concentrates on the interaction between individuals. While the role establishes clear lines of force and constructions, the body displays the practices and energies. While the role illuminates a field of relations, the body illuminates premises and effects. At issue are two domains that conceal neither their convergent interests nor their willingness to share pertinence and responsibility. On the one hand, they make clear, implicitly at least, that there is no enunciation outside of a communicative goal and that one cannot communicate without producing an énoncé.[58] On the other hand, they provide a recognition that the constitution of the text as such is by no means reducible to the stages of its construction.

An awareness of the existence of these two zones, simultaneously adjacent and juxtaposed, allows a clarification of a number of problems that fall within the frame of our study.[59] In particular, it encourages an elaboration of the notions of context and appropriateness introduced above. As always, the problem is to understand why the interpellation both invokes and denies certain values, why it can be considered both "taboo" and perfectly acceptable. So far, we have insisted on the coherence that this procedure must maintain in relation to its context, a fidelity that responds to both the fundamental options (commentary or narrative) and the reliability of the more general coordinates (the enunciators and enunciatees, with their respective figurativizations). The entrance of communication clearly complicates the game. Above all it gives a new dimension to the references: the text discovers an environment which is not only linguistic but made up of personal behaviors, relations with others, and affective dispositions. These elements are structural not so much because they account for fundamental processes but because they refer to canonical circumstances. They are determinant not because they preside over the succession of signs but rather because they define the very conditions of the success of an exchange. Here the context becomes a "situation of discourse."[60] Secondly, the introduction of considerations of communication displaces the constraints we face: the text is asked to account not only for its own unfolding but for an imbrication of different intentions, a superimposition of goals, a totality of fixed objectives. In particular, it is asked to control the exhaustive whole of the deixis, the legitimacy of the text's illocutionary dimension, and the practicality of the perlocutionary. In this context, appropriateness entails an "adaptation" to the order of things.[61] If their essential nature is to be discovered, the procedures of interpellation must submit to the verification that comes from such an adaptation. Gazes must be able to enter the space of the theater, voices to reach understanding ears, writings to find attentive readers, and filmic propositions to become effectuated acts. In sum, the enunciated enunciations must die during the process of communication in order to truly live.

It should be clear that this applies to everything that organizes and constrains a representation: a curious term that signifies both the birth of a semiotic object and the social rite involved in the consumption of the mise-en-scène.[62] Nonetheless, moments of looks into the camera, titles addressing the viewer, voice-over narrations, or again, credits at the film's beginning and end are exemplary; they are moments that lay the cards on the table and offer a game to those who want to play it. The credit sequences are particularly instructive: placed at each extremity of the film, and reproduced on posters and advertisements at the entry to the movie house, they function, in a most obvious manner, as an elastic border between two universes, between an interior seeking to escape its limits and an exterior wanting to penetrate into the discourse of the film. Once again, there is a confrontation and conjunction between roles and bodies, between two entities that make the text at once the terrain of sport and the stakes in the game.

And so, on the hypothetical finale supplied by a mechanical piano or the contemplation of today's movie posters, we conclude the first grand stage of our investigation. We began at the moment when a text, through the "ego-hic-nunc" of its enunciation, establishes the parameters that organize and define its distinct universe. We now stop at the moment when the text, offering itself to the world and discovering itself there as one object among others, enters into a process of communication. It is a brief journey, yet perhaps longer than might have been expected, a journey which could have been completed in any number of directions, right-side-out or reversed, a journey whose arrivals and departures function reciprocally. And as in any other voyage, we continue to advance.

3   The Place of the Spectator

The Four Gazes

The look into the camera, voice-over narration, and credit sequences have enabled us to inquire into how a film defines its own parameters, puts these parameters in perspective, and makes them a space accessible to the viewer. Even more precisely, it has shown how a film constitutes an enunciatee, how this enunciatee becomes manifest in the text through a series of figurativizations, and finally, how the enunciatee, in the form of a role, encounters a body with the result of encompassing, in all its plenitude, a spectator. Our progress, however, is still somewhat haphazard, with several intercrossing trails and many ways to reach the same end. We must enlarge the field of observation if we wish to comprehend the various possible scenarios and to explore in depth the way in which throughout a film, and from one film to another, a *you* is suggested.

Let us begin with a new example, the first sequence from *The Kid from Spain* (1932), directed by Leo McCarey. The sequence opens with a young girl who is just waking. Turning toward the camera, she begins to recite a children's rhyme. It becomes clear that the room is a dormitory that houses a group of young girls. One after another, the girls look into the camera and toward each other, continuing the rhyme until it becomes a song. The musical rhythm initiates a geometric dance that involves a movement out of the dormitory, down a spiral staircase, and toward a swimming pool. A downward tracking shot frames the bodies in the pool, where they form a completely abstract design. Outside the pool, near a slide, the young girls dry themselves and change clothes behind translucent screens. When the camera attempts to go around the screens, the young girls flee, casting glances at it. Finally the headmistress enters and imposes order. Exhibiting the liberty characteristic of a particular genre (the musical comedy), an époque (the early years of sound cinema), and a form of choreography (Busby Berkeley's), this sequence displays surprising modalities. Rather than simply encouraging the emergence of an enunciatee—that is, emphasizing and manifesting its presence—the sequence seems committed to exploring the different places an enunciatee can occupy and the variety of actions it can perform.

To comprehend what this involves, it is necessary to return to the notion of *point of view*. The gaze which shapes the scene unites and brings forth what is shown, who is showing, and who is being shown. The latter clearly do not refer to individual persons, but to principles of textual construction, *operators* that define the film's "self-construction" and "self-offering." One might dub them *subjects* the way we speak of "logical subjects."[1] They are also equivalent respectively to the enunciator, the enunciatee, and the discourse through which these operate. That is, they correspond to the gesture of appropriation that enables one to see, the gesture of address that offers something to sight, and the thing (or person) which is seen. Again, at issue are not individual persons but "logical operators" that a film can represent only through personification, in the form of an *I*, a *you*, and a *she, he,* or *it*. To avoid ambiguity, it is best to consider the three elements of this triad as designating abstract categories that derive from the filmic text's fundamental articulation, rather than from the momentarily implied reality. For instance, the *you* put in place by a look into the camera refers not to a particular person among all those who watch the film, but rather to the fact of the film's act of self-offering. It does not address this or that actual individual, but rather the very possibility of a spectator, a possibility actualized during each encounter between a role and a concrete body. Similarly, recall that here are traces derived from the filmic text's constitutive mechanisms, relations that only the enunciation could have initiated, but once opened remain always available. The actualization of a *you* is not possible solely within the terrain of the cinema, peopled by pure virtualities.[2] Within the realm of film, it can occur only as something born from the conversion of a language into a discourse; and the discourse, precisely through its intrinsic destination, guarantees that an itinerary of this type will never fail. Here are terms that indicate both a film's accessibility and its underlying parameters. Such a conjunction between generality and necessity reveals perfect solidarity between these elements. The possibility and even obligation that these elements always exist means that they never appear in isolation from one another. Even if one wishes to distribute them on several fronts, it would be a mistake to consider them independently of the relation that unites them. Though the enunciator and enunciatee refer to a gaze, and the énoncé corresponds to the space of a scene, there can be no gaze without a scene, nor scene without a gaze.[3] The notion of point of view is thus a site of confluence where the point from which one observes, the point through which one shows, and the point which is seen inevitably connect.[4] What plays the determinant role is not the obligatory presence of this or that element in itself, but the *form* of the relation the elements undertake with one another, and by consequence, the *position* a given element assumes within the ensemble. In other words, an element's weight depends less on its pure and simple prominence than on the nature of its development or on its capacity to master the complexity of its context.

With these observations, we can construct a typology of a film's recurrent propositional structures, defined through the different perspectives offered to the enunciatee. First, consider a case where there is a fundamental equilibrium among the elements. The opening shots of *The Kid from Spain* are a good example. It aims, with a composition of full-face framing, to provide an immediate recording of the facts, as if to seize the essence of an action without revealing the labor of observation and examination that produced it. More precisely, think of those moments when we see that the young women look and speak to each other, while we are unable to see the gazes upon them. Here the enunciator and enunciatee exist at a level of perfect equality, finding support in a point of view which reveals only what it cannot hide: the énoncé. Facing a self-evident *he*, *she*, or *it* are an *I* and a *you* which are understood without being explicitly present. The enunciatee must assume the position of a *witness*. It is the one led to watch, the one permitted to see, but the mandate is never made explicit and the accomplishment of the task never interferes with the events.[5] If this enunciatee wants to make a deposition, it can do so only outside the diegesis, in another story in which it is the protagonist. Classical "grammars" list this case under the general rubric of "objective" framings or anonymous shots ("nobody's shot"), indicating that the gaze engendering them belongs to no one.[6] But again, the "no one" in question is equivalent to the potentiality of everyone.[7]

The second case, already familiar to us, is that of interpellation in its diverse forms. In the example from *The Kid from Spain*, interpellation occurs in the shots where the young women directly address the camera. These looks destabilize the relation set up in the preceding shots: the enunciator and enunciatee are established within the énoncé but in an unequal manner, where the énoncé "pays off" one or the other. Note that this example involves a character who, as if she were the one responsible for the film, interpellates the one to whom the film is addressed. Someone gazes (the spectator), and sees someone else (the character) gazing and seeing in return. But here the character shows itself to someone who, while gazing and seeing, remains unseen. The elements of the riddle are as follows: an *I* (who gazes and sees) confronts, to the point of coinciding with, a *she* (who makes herself seen, but who also gazes toward the he who is intended to gaze), while a *you* (destined to gaze and be gazed at without ever being seen) enters the game without assuming any precise form. This is what produces an unequal disposition between enunciator and enunciatee. Both openly display themselves but the first is figurativized in a character identified through action (the act of gazing) and objective (to ensnare the film's viewer), while the second is presented simply for what it is—an "ideal" point of view. It is in this sense that the énoncé "pays off" the enunciator, by exhibiting what is ordinarily simply presupposed, laying claim to the enunciator at the very interior of the image, and giving the latter the status of narrator (a narrator either located within the diegesis or capable of being located there). These dynamics are proper not only to looks into the camera (or, as noted, to voice-over narration or certain kinds of titles). They also come into play when, for example in *The Kid from Spain*, the young women take off their bathing costumes behind the screens, and a general pandemonium results as the camera tries to surprise them in the process. In this passage, the *I* merges not into the *she* of a character, but into the *she* of the énoncé in general. The presupposition encompasses all that lies within its scope by projecting and reflecting itself into its own space. The screen within the screen (the screen which shields the girls), the shadows within shadows (the silhouettes behind the screens) aim to unite metalanguage,[8] designation, and interpellation within a structure that expresses something like the statement "this is for you; it comes from the cinema, that is, from me."[9] In the subsequent shot, the young women who flee in front of the camera and throw glances which are at the same time furious and provocative confirm this syncretism: if an *I* can engage with a scene's entire space, there is all the more reason to accept that it can do so with a single component. But let us attend to our central concern, the enunciatee. In each of the variants examined here, the enunciatee performs the classical function of the *aside*. More or less a reprise of the usage proper to theater, the author uses a character (who lives both for him and thanks to him) to inform not the character's co-equals on the stage, but the audience (who then becomes an accomplice).[10] Here also we have a situation in which someone *participates* in the game while remaining *apart* from it. Note that traditional cinematic "grammars" rarely take up this case, either because it involves a prohibition, as we have said, or because it typically entails a "subjective view" which constitutes a configuration in itself.

The "subjective view," in effect, differs profoundly from the preceding case: though it involves a display of gazes, the purpose is entirely different. Lines of force are asserted, but directed toward other poles. If we examine the structure in question, it is clear that it prefigures two components corresponding on the syntactic plane to two frames or to two different sides of the same frame. One represents a character who gazes, the other represents what is seen through the character's eyes.[11] The first moment of such a structure (in which we see a character who gazes) can be interpreted as, "I gaze and make you gaze at the one who gazes," and the second moment (where we see through the character's eyes) as "I am making him see what I make you see." A displacement occurs from a "we see it, you and I," to a "you, and she, see what I show you."[12] As a result, the conjunction no longer occurs between character and enunciator, but rather between character and enunciatee in a syncretism achieved through a single act (I make both you and her gaze), as a juxtaposition of two shots or two "objective" moments neither of which, taken separately, are capable of revealing either the enunciator or the enunciatee. The final configuration no longer says "you and I, we gaze" as in the case of an "objective view," nor even "she and I, we gaze at you" as in situations of interpellation, but instead, "I make you gaze, you equally as her," which is obviously something else. The third configuration, in which the enunciatee assumes the position of a *character*, is not directly exhibited during the opening of *The Kid from Spain*.[13] It might have been had the camera movement which aims to surprise the young women dressing behind the screen been followed by a countershot attributing this mischievous gaze to a character. The absence of such a countershot requires one particular interpretation and confirms that what distinguishes our second example from the third depends on the presence or absence of perhaps only one or two basic structural elements. The procedure is nonetheless quite common, even causing radical experiments[14] and rather distinctive aesthetic proposals.[15]

On the other hand, *The Kid from Spain* illustrates a fourth case in the characteristic passage involving an upward craning of the camera above the young women, producing an abstract image in the swimming pool. What motivates this rather paradoxical crane shot? It seems to embody the structure of an "objective view," such as, "I gaze at something and make you gaze, too." But the contortions that occur at the level of the camera angle upset the very equilibrium essential to an objective view—we move from an angle corresponding to ordinary human vision to an impossible aerial perspective, with the result that the horizontal mutates into a perpendicular. The activity of the enunciator and enunciatee are foregrounded, imposed in an obvious manner at the end of the sequence: "I am the one who gazes and who makes you gaze." Such an accentuation has precise implications. Besides the strange effect, it not only displays certain founding presuppositions (there is someone who gazes), but determines the sense of a relation (if you see, it is thanks to me). In other words, the enunciator and enunciatee announce their complicity with each other. To progress from this condition to a syncretism requires only a single step. The enunciator can initiate an exchange of roles with the enunciatee simply by proposing that such a possibility exists, that in fact the two are basically equivalent: "what you see, thanks to me, is that I alone am able to see: thus *we see*." The effect of such a conjunction is very pronounced in the sensation produced by a shot like that described above, a sensation of detachment from any contingency, of domination of the visual field, of the capacity to fabricate reality, in a word, of sharing the camera's omnipotence. In sum, along with the "as though he were me" of interpellation and the "as though he were you" of the "subjective view," it is necessary to add the "as though you were me." Traditional grammars have labeled framings like that in our example as "impossible objective views." And we might find use for this term if it refers not only to the impossibility of finding a character to whom to attribute the view (which can involve an interruption of the narration) but also to the impossibility of the scene appearing without the gaze of an enunciator or enunciatee; without this gaze, the scene's self-offering could not occur, particularly in a case like the above, in which there is an alibi neither of reality nor of naturalness.

A Gaze without Effect, A Gaze without Intention

Let us stop here and ask what can now be said about our typology. Recall, first, that this typology derives from an analysis of the opening sequence of *The Kid from Spain*. The example is perhaps not well known, but it proves very useful because of the variety of forms it brings together within a relatively brief passage. We could easily generate our four cases from the sequence, though we cannot claim to have produced a complete and exhaustive table.

This typology can revise certain categories still in use today, particularly the classifications of traditional grammars that are based upon a proper question ("Who gazes at whom?") but that fail to reach all of the possible conclusions. On the one hand, in their preoccupation with the "origin" of the gaze, they appeal to both a single criterion (that the shot be attributable to someone's "eyes") and a partial criterion (forgetting that there is always someone gazing, even if this individual is unnarrativized). On the other hand, as to the concept of the shot, they posit a technical unity rather than a textual one (remember, at least *two* elements in combination are needed for a "subjective view"; and the type of construction involved can be identified only through the verification of any repetitions, substitutions, anaphora, cataphora, etc.).[16] Our intention is not to reject these established categories, but to rethink them.

Finally, recall that our typology responds to a precise project. It is, in effect, born from the idea that one can distinguish the coordinates established by the enunciation through an analysis of how the filmic text varies as a function of what activates it and interacts with it. We have quite naturally focused on the addressee, noting that this addressee performs respectively the function of a witness (in which a *you* is affirmed in the face of an *I*, as in the "objective view"), an aside (in which a *you* is indicated through an *I* combined with a *he*, as in interpellation), a character (in which a *you* combined with a *he* faces an *I*, as in the "subjective view") and the camera (a *you* combined with an *I*, as in the "impossible objective view"). All these functions are ultimately of capital importance for their part in defining the essential properties of these configurations—canonical configurations in many respects. In this context, our four cases acquire consequences much more important than those identified so far. Even before declaring the direction of the filmic discourse's address, they can help us specify the mechanisms which permit the emergence of what is generally called a "subject," as well as the blind spots that this subject might meet.

Consider, for example, the case of interpellation. It is clear that here a *you* appears only insofar as it responds to the appeal of an *I*. At the same time, this *I* is quite paradoxical, merging into a *he* that gazes out with no guarantee of actually seeing anything, addressing an off-screen space which can never actually be made visible. Here is someone who is seen but whose own view is blocked and whose gaze ultimately reaches nowhere. The enunciator, the very moment it attempts to become figurativized within the énoncé, discovers a void, a blank space, a zone of suspension. Let us consider another configuration, the "subjective view": here, a *you* merges into a *he* and both see only what they are permitted to see. What appears in view exists only because someone shows it, not because of any attempt to uncover it. Facing an enunciator who functions as the absolute shifter, the enunciatee can't help but have thoughts about its own capacity for action; the sensation of being inscribed within the diegesis encourages a suspicion that everything has been decided in advance. The comparison between the two cases is then easy: in a case of interpellation, the enunciator, however much it appears to master the game, produces a gaze apparently *without effect*. In the "subjective view," the enunciatee, however much it seems directly engaged in the game, produces a gaze seemingly *without intention*.

The above remarks suggest at least two conclusions. On the one hand, it is easy to perceive the limits of our two configurations' pivot points. The points of syncretism—the *we* and *you*, respectively—constitute the explicit point of articulation between the enunciation and the énoncé. They also mark the blind spot where the potentiality of vision is annulled. That is, in the filmic text, too, the emergence of subjectivity risks subjugation. Between the frame's edge and the off-screen, it only takes a blink of the eye to rediscover or lose oneself.[17] On the other hand, it is also easy to clearly understand the configurations' strong points and the logic governing the relation between the characters and the different forces put into play. A reexamination of the two situations clearly shows that the character in cases of interpellation does not actually see (that is, the character gazes without seeing what he gazes at: a gaze without effect) while the character in the "subjective view" does not gaze (that is, the character sees only what he is shown: a gaze without intention). This suggests that the *he* in cases of interpellation (who functions as narrator) calls attention to an *I* enunciator (through gazing) while opposing a *you* enunciatee and its figurativizations (who are not made to gaze). And the *he* in the "subjective view" (who operates as narratee) summons a *you* enunciatee (by seeing) while opposing the *I* enunciator and its figurativizations (by not gazing). Now a sort of "logical square" appears that permits us to map the terms other than in simple linear form (figure 2):[18]

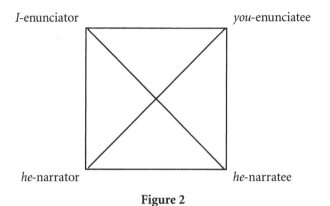

I-enunciator   *you*-enunciatee

he-narrator   *he*-narratee

Figure 2

The corners of the square belong to the *I*-enunciator, the *you*-enunciatee, the *he*-narrator, and the *he*-narratee, respectively. Each is systematically linked to the others through different types of relations. These are relations of contrariety (enunciator versus enunciatee, or narrator versus narratee), and opposition (enunciatee versus narrator, a true non-enunciatee as it is a character not required to gaze; or enunciator versus narratee, a non-enunciator, a character who does not gaze). And they are relations of complementarity (enunciatee and narratee, a character who functions as the enunciatee's correspondent and incarnation; or enunciator and narrator). Moreover, the sides of the square link characters (the *I* and *you* of the upper level) who oppose certain non-persons (the two types of *he* of the lower level). They also link subjects in the proper sense of the term (the *I* and *he*-narrator of the left-hand side) who oppose the anti-subjects (the *you* and the *he*-narratee of the right-hand side). This "logical square" underlies the system implied in our configurations. By manipulating this square's components—uniting, separating, and displacing—numerous filmic figures can be revealed in their essential logic and form, in particular those concerning acts of vision and hearing.[19]

The Gazes and Filmic Construction

Let us linger on this schema and on the four configurations that have guided our inquiry. We proposed that the various views ("objective," "impossible objective," "subjective") as well as instances of interpellation are all ways to activate the audio-visual discourse, particularly with respect to its address. They are various ways of saying *you* that are relayed during the course of the narration, framing the film's propositions. In addition, they commonly perform a more specific task. Instead of referring to one another, they illuminate the text's overall orientation by anchoring the flux of images and sounds to a single point. Here, we are dealing with blocked and blocking structures rather than changes of orientation. Based on what we have said above, we can consider elements of this type as true "operators of context," as factors that designate and determine the environment in which a text or textual fragment hopes to inscribe itself.[20]

It is easy to find examples of this "emblematic" aspect of the four configurations. What comes to mind first are certain passages which, behind simple figures of style, act as true indicators of the film's fundamental system. Think in particular of the frontal shots involving depth of field in William Wyler's most impressive scenes: Frank's entrance into the drugstore and Homer's marriage in *The Best Years of Our Lives* (1946), and the death of Horace in *The Little Foxes* (1941).[21] We have already proposed that such "objective" shots amounted to a kind of "neutral" writing, adhering to a theatrical conception of mise-en-scène while perfectly conforming to canons of cinematographic realism, assigning meaning to the represented action while respecting the spectator's liberty.[22] On the other hand, what has yet to be sufficiently examined is how such a neutrality results from a particular enunciative journey, one which has been able to impose itself in place of other possible solutions. In effect, these frontal and deep-staged shots, like any "objective" shot, depend upon a particular treatment of the basic filmic components. In offering a self-sustaining vision, they refer only to the gaze from which they originate and the one summoned to consume them. The world on the screen appears as factual by having suppressed the presuppositions of its own elaboration and readability. Here the image can construct and offer itself only through such a suppression. This means that only the upper portion of our square is mobilized: in effect, the filmic énoncé, as an object already endowed with its own principles of organization and interpretability, puts in play an enunciator and enunciatee, but without figurativizing the actions of this enunciator and enunciatee in any way. The visual field is abundantly full of elements whose placement clearly denotes the point of view according to which they have been assembled and organized, but no character fulfills the function of true scopic subject, no element represents the *you* or the *I* who have produced the scene.[23] It is precisely such a placement which justifies the complex characteristics referred to above: in a frame which exhausts itself in its own formation, there are different competing possibilities as to the coordinates. There is either the realist dimension (which derives from the facts evident in the representation) or the theatrical (which involves the meaning produced by figuration), either a narrative functionality (nourished by pure diegesis) or the liberty on the part of the one called upon to see (invited, indeed summoned, to explore the world presented on the screen). It is the insistence with which a given configuration is used that transforms its defining marks into common traits. Because they coincide with the principal dramatic knots, because they carry a programmatic value, these framings, when employed systematically, have an influence that extends to the film as a whole.[24] Thus, an "objective" shot assumes a responsibility and duty that lasts throughout the narration. On the one hand, it signals the formula governing the operation of the audio-visual discourse, but on the other, it blocks any revelation of the nature of the formula itself.

Without a doubt, this type of operation appears in its most concrete form at the topological level: what is constructed and maintained is a space in which all the elements are clearly placed, yet without anyone appearing to benefit from them. This is a space in which the composition of the visible surface is elaborated to the maximum, without anyone's gaze determining precise zones or trajectories, a space, in sum, that we might appropriately call *anonymous*. But what interests us most is the slope of the destination: what is affirmed is an intelligence ready to act but not to show itself; an ideal spectator elicited and implied by all of the details of a scene entirely open to her, but hidden in relation to this scene; a *witness*, we have proposed, who tries to find her place and, once having done so, will not abandon it.

The Place of the Spectator 55

Our second example contains the marks of production rather than those of style, and illustrates the "impossible objective view" rather than the "simple objective view." However, here once again, we find an enunciative trace and its capacity to guide the entire process. Passages like this turn entirely upon an unforeseen and unforeseeable expansion of the visual field. Consider, for instance, the backward tracking shot in *Gone with the Wind* (1939) which isolates Scarlet O'Hara in the midst of her land by producing her silhouette against the horizon. Also in the same film, think of the moving crane shot that literally loses the heroine in the city of Atlanta, strewn with dead and wounded bodies. Beyond the events depicted, what characterizes such moments? These camera movements which alter the shot compositions are not intended to clarify the narrative content, but rather to inflate the affective quality. They clearly indicate the presence of the point of view from which they have been fabricated and in relation to which the event has been organized. Such a transformation of the image exceeds simple narrative utility to the point of exhibitionism and links the scene both to what has produced it and to the one who will receive it. As a result, the enunciator and enunciatee find their figurativization in, respectively, the (explicit) manner in which the énoncé displays its technical components, and the (brazen) way in which it demands to be deciphered. A film's "self-construction" and "self-offering," usually tacit presuppositions, become declared principles here due to a form of writing which, turning in upon itself, rises up and expands. As in all impossible objective shots, our square is completed with its two inferior summits thanks to an emphasis on certain aspects of the cinematography, like choice of framing and the means used to carry it out, all perceptible and revealing signs of the logic animating the process.

It is this fundamental structure which allows certain particular marks to appear: a spectacle is born from the importance of the camera as a direct guarantee of how the universe on the screen is constructed and defined, more than from an accumulation of marvels. Hyperrealism is based not so much on careful and slightly abstract scenography as on the operation's ability to find the elements within itself for orienting the audio-visual discourse. Any impression of extravagance and overabundance results less from the nature of the materials staged for the camera than from the task of the technical apparatus to present itself as the origin and finality of its own functioning, much in the manner of a "bachelor machine."[25] But it is moreover the maintenance of this basic structure that transforms these characteristics into fixed points of articulation. This can be confirmed, on the one hand, by the privileged placement of the shots cited above (particularly the traveling shot of Tara, which coincides with the action's apogee, or rather, the moment of "moral" expression), and on the other, by the invited guests who traverse a number of shots. For example, other procedures can perform the same task as the camera movements analyzed above: limiting the analysis to just the play of color, one might mention the overly red sky in a frontal establishing shot, which cannot be caused by the burning of Atlanta alone. Such a shot exceeds the typical "ground zero" of the "objective" configuration and becomes an "impossible objective" shot in which the mise-en-scène is unusually emphatic.[26] The vocation of the cinematographic apparatus to become a character within the enunciative process is confirmed in a diffuse fashion; and what one first sees emerge is shown to be profoundly rooted in the film.

An important consequence of this is that the film's ideal addressee is assigned a stable place. There had been much attention directed to the addressee inscribed in the film's images and sounds. Summoned to confront a traversable and transformable space, this spectator was invited to respond by using her legs—so to speak—rather than with a simple gaze, as in *The Best Years of Our Lives*. Forced to submit to incongruous camera angles, this spectator is led to identify with a machine in operation rather than with a detached and exterior eye. In the face of such a confirmation, the implied spectator can consider her role as certain. From here on, she can resolutely expect to find a correspondent in the technical performance (and no longer as a suppressed presupposition, for ultimately the enunciatee is figurativized in explicit traits). This spectator can deliberately plan to occupy the position of a "practical" subject (rather than merely a "contemplative" subject, the game is now guided by something more complex than simple framing). She can solidly prepare to follow what the camera movements lead her to follow. The spectator recognizes that such is her place and that she may remain there with security.

A third example to consider is from a musical comedy, Busby Berkeley's *Babes on Broadway* (1941). It requires a detailed description because its significant traits emerge not only through the passage's general enunciative procedures but through its very composition. The sequence featuring the song "Hoe Down" begins with a lowered stage curtain and an orchestra conductor, his back turned, directing the musicians to begin playing. The curtain opens to reveal a rustic decor. At screen right is a small group of country musicians. At left is Judy Garland, who sits on a bale of hay, singing. The camera tracks in to frame her gazing into the camera in medium close-up. In the following shot, Garland springs up and enters the room to dance with the young people who make up the audience. The orchestra has disappeared, leaving only a few musicians in the foreground who appear in the crowd. The dance continues, couples form and separate. Each time a couple enters the foreground and looks into the camera, a brusque panning movement directs attention to someone else. A few shots later, we see that the room is surrounded by barriers creating a dance floor in whose center a dancer enters to improvise a tap dance. At the end of his performance, in medium close-up, the dancer gazes into the camera. There is another cut, and now the camera advances, causing the collapse of the barriers, one after the other. The dance continues until there is a cut to a new shot in medium close-up, of Judy Garland and Mickey Rooney, who gaze toward the camera. Cut: a rapid ballet atop the overturned barriers brings the protagonists to the foreground, their gaze once again directed into the camera.

This new example clearly shows an insistent use of interpellation: at least five times the characters turn directly toward the movie audience which faces them; at least five times (conforming to a montage structure of an "A/B/A/B/A" pattern) a long shot is followed by a close-up where a character directly addresses the viewer. In each case, what is astonishing is the way in which this "alternating" montage involves a slight perversion. Whenever a new "A/B" segment begins, an element is modified in relation to the preceding segment. While the beginning of the first segment suggests that the spectacle will begin within the confines of the stage, the long shot at the beginning of the second segment shows the actors mixing with the audience. It would be reasonable to conclude that this is a momentary invasion of the theater space; but a new long shot, at the beginning of the third segment, makes it clear that the dancers have made this their new performance space. The barriers that define the space of the tap dance are now visible, but at the beginning of the fourth segment, these barriers are literally knocked down. The two protagonists can be seen only with difficulty, but at the beginning of the fifth segment, the entire theater becomes visible. Thus the gaze into the camera concluding each "A/B" couplet signals both the end of one scenographic module and the beginning of a new one. Better yet, given that the glances into the camera announce a new curtain-raising, a transcendence of the barriers that define the mise-en-scène, or the possibility of an extension into the space of the theater, these glances seem to accompany a permanent alteration of the space of action. It is almost as if the site of the singing and dancing were continually absorbing the space facing it, as if the place from which the spectacle is seen were directly welcoming the performers, as if, ultimately, the stage and audience space are conflated to the point of becoming one and the same.

The superimposition of these two traditionally separate spaces, however, is more than the guiding thread of a brilliant choreography: it is the very mirror of an enunciative configuration which punctuates and supports the narration. What, in effect, constitutes an interpellation? The key factor is clearly an opening directed toward the film's spectator (a gaze into the camera, as is the case here, or perhaps a voice-over, a subtitle, or comparable device) which brings an "incandescence" to the parameters supporting the audio-visual discourse, and moreover, suggests a double movement. On the one hand, the system governing the cinematographic representation is highly self-conscious: the progression of images and sounds occurs in the form of a direct intervention, a gesture of invitation or confidence from one pair of eyes to another. The film's "self-construction" is figurativized in various rather obvious ways. It is not by chance if, in our example, after each glance into the camera, the character then enters the place from which she has just been seen—Judy Garland, after gazing directly into the spectator's eyes, appears at the foot of the stage. Likewise, the tap dancer ends up off the dance floor, and Mickey Rooney appears on the opposite side of the barriers. The itineraries of the characters correspond to their enunciative roles, from implicit presupposition to implication in the first person.[27] In sum, the stage can be extended outward because of the precedent set by the enunciation, which has become explicitly manifest in the énoncé. More precisely, it can extend because the enunciator has already tried to prolong itself as a permanent narrator. On the other hand, the gaze into the camera, here as elsewhere a sign of total complicity, gives the film's "self-offering" a particular character. While it suppresses a figurativization, something we have touched upon elsewhere, it does enable us to determine a point of vision and hearing which exists within the space facing the screen, the irremediable off-screen space that no shot can ever saturate.[28] Nevertheless, the gaze into the camera implies a space which is perfectly available, pried open by the glance of an eye, and ready to be filled, even with communication as the ulterior frame.[29] If only the enunciator finds a direct representation in the interpellation (completing only the upper left part of our square), then the enunciatee also has the means to announce itself through a well-calculated absence, existing as a reservoir of possible approaches and intention. It is again not by chance that the on-screen audience for "Hoe Down" dances with Judy Garland after she has gazed at them, that this audience joins the tap dancer after he has glanced at them, or that this dancer gives his arm to Mickey Rooney following his gaze. These actions all illustrate the condition of the film's ideal addressee. Elicited as a possible partner, this addressee is brusquely converted into an accomplice who is asked to approach and be implicated in the action. Here, the spectator who appears within the representation, and the spectator outside who has been constructed to unify the film's images and sounds, find the means to acknowledge and prove one another's existence and status. Moreover, it is the very moment when this operation begins, not when the enunciator is personified but rather when the "aside" occurs, that becomes decisive. Because the film addresses the room in which it is being projected, it can then be brought inside. By turning toward the public, it becomes possible to engage with this public. In short, by offering the position of *you*, the distance is reduced in a single blow.

It now becomes clear how profoundly interpellation marks the sequence. By modeling the fundamental roles to which the diverse presences put in play adhere, an interpellation dictates a line of conduct whose consequences are progressively described by the "objective" shots, with their successive topological variations. Given the effects that a configuration can have on marks of style or production, it then becomes evident how it can engender the metaphor of uniting stage and audience, presented here in rather literal form. Such a metaphor characterizes the "Hoe Down" sequence which, like other musical numbers in the film and ultimately all musical comedies, is traditionally founded upon the reversibility between performance and reception and the circularity between spectacle and life. It is thus filled with looks into the camera, glances to the spectator, confidences, and so on. In this sense, instances of interpellation are truly indicative of a cinematographic genre,[30] as much through the frequency of their occurrence as through their capacity to suggest the "philosophy" involved. They initiate a particular enunciative journey (again, with a spectator's *aside*) and impose this journey with all its consequences.

Our fourth example, which involves the "subjective view," the last of the canonical configurations, aims to show how the establishment of the enunciation can influence the film's very framework to the point of making the story a sort of mirror of the film's own criteria. After an example that displayed marks of style, production, and metaphor, our new example, the opening of Alfred Hitchcock's *Vertigo* (1958), centers on an intrigue. A police lieutenant, Scott Ferguson, pursues a thief across the roofs of a San Francisco neighborhood. He slips and is hanging from a gutter. In terror, the man, in medium-close shot, sees the void beneath him. A long shot, punctuated by a zoom backward, reveals the abyss. This is followed by a shot of the roofs of the city, then a medium-close shot of Scott, a long shot corresponding to Scott's vision, a shot of the roofs, and then back to Scott's face. Meanwhile, an officer who was accompanying Scott approaches to help him. In close-up, Scott sees the approaching officer suddenly lose his balance. Then the following succession of shots: a new close-up of Scott, a long shot of the falling policeman, a close-up of Scott who gazes below, and finally a long shot showing the policeman's body on the ground.

In this example, the subjective shots follow quite rapidly. Through Scott's eyes, we see the void above which he is suspended, the policeman who tries to help, the policeman's silhouette while falling, and finally his corpse on the ground.[31] Of course the use of this procedure, and particularly in this form, serves to accent the episode's dramatic aspect, but it also makes the police lieutenant more than the simple protagonist of an ordinary adventure. Consider what, in effect, a subjective shot involves. By showing images seen through a character's eyes, the film depicts the point of view from which it is understood, rendering explicit its "self-offering" and figurativizing its own destination.[32] As opposed to the preceding example, this subjective shot concerns the opposite side of our square: while the enunciator remains a tacit presupposition, the enunciatee becomes confused with a component of the énoncé, acquiring the function of observer, and transforming into a narratee. A result is that the presumed spectator of the film merges into a character, adopting the latter's perceptive faculties, movements, and attitudes. Scott incarnates precisely this entry into the diegesis of the point toward which the film extends, that point of conjunction between an ideal *you* and a visible reality. However, Scott plays his role so literally that he never abandons it: initially summoned to stand in for the individual sitting in the movie theater, Scott will come to personify all that individual's characteristics during the course of the narration, to the point of offering a complete portrait.

Now in the first part of the story, the lieutenant might seem to function as a model for a "critical" spectator. His aim, in effect, is to discover why the young woman, Madeleine, identifies with her great-grandmother and to protect her from the danger and seduction of such an obsession. Naturally, Scott falls into the trap: while trying to convince Madeleine that she is a real person and not the incarnation of an ancestor, he falls in love with her. Moreover, he does so without knowing that he is dealing with a sort of fantasy. This woman is not, as she pretends to be, the wife of a friend but someone playing a role. Scott then becomes like a spectator completely taken in by the fiction, by a reality which appears actual but, on the contrary, is only a representation. In the course of the story, he radicalizes his own hallucination. He meets Judy Barton and recognizes in her something of Madeleine. Following her, he transforms her little by little, to the point of dressing and making her up in the image of what he had lost. He even goes as far as to embrace her, believing that he is embracing her double. From here on, for Scott, the only thing that counts is appearance and its capacity to embody a desire. He is so profoundly possessed by the mise-en-scène that he makes it into a total and exclusive universe. He is like a cinema spectator whose involvement is so intense that he can convert life into the cinema, but never the reverse.[33] Of course, the trompe-l'oeil's effect does not last indefinitely, and even the purest effort of the imagination cannot withstand an accumulation of evidence. Scott discovers the truth (Judy Barton is the same woman as played Madeleine) and so he awakens for good. The price, however, is heavy; the reconquering of his self-mastery comes either from the disappearance of Madeleine, a dream, or of Judy Barton, who twice has supported this dream. What ultimately takes precedence is the representation and the apparatus which has supported it: the fictional character and the actress playing the role dramatically leave the scene. At this point the spectator can again become a "critic" in the most complete sense, reestablishing mastery by stopping the play of his imagination and what had nourished it. In sum, the spectator can achieve self-mastery by putting an end to the film.

Such is the story of *Vertigo* considered in light of the subjective shots of the film's beginning. The gaze from above engenders the hero's nervousness (his fear of the void) but also defines his role at the enunciative level (that of narratee). It announces the nature of his character (obsessional) but also fixes his destiny (he will be called upon to organize the images and sounds throughout the story).[34] Consider again that the principal consequences of this occur at the level of topology. The most certain effect is that the framing acquires an explicit point of reference or, if one prefers, that the directing lines, even the hypothetical ones,[35] are related to a point of observation which is itself visible within the frame. In short, a lived space is constructed and maintained. But what is still most interesting here concerns the address which the film institutes and imposes: the *you* enters the field, assumes the guise of a character and becomes a spectator within the narrative's interior. By figurativizing its own "self-offering," the text creates the occasion for a precise and stable meeting. The film knows its addressee and wholly gives it life.

The Geography of the Spectator

Again, it is only natural that while attempting to define the form taken by the *you*, we have been led to speak of the modalization of space. The coincidence is manifest in our four configurations: the objective shot reveals, to a spectator considered to be a simple witness, an anonymous space rich with detail but deprived of a seeing subject; the impossible objective shot reveals a literally unforeseeable space, both the product and limit of a technical performance, to a spectator in solidarity with the camera; interpellation, which implies a spectator through an *aside*, suggests a reversible space potentially available to a character appearing within the diegesis; and finally, the subjective shot shows, to a spectator become character, a lived, interior space, marked by the character's physical and psychological interaction. This encounter has real legitimacy. The enunciation, in effect, gives a kind of life to the discourse, and defines the profile of those who claim to operate the énoncé as well as the contours of the énoncé's proposed world. From its "zero mark," the enunciation organizes in a single gesture the subjects implicated in the text (the articulation of the "ego") as well as the spaces that the text assumes and exposes (the articulation of the "hic"). In this sense, the kinship between the ideal addressee and the geography of the visible is rooted in the initiating act of the game.

One can describe this encounter with even greater precision. Still within the frame of the enunciation, let us reexamine point of view and the way in which it produces both the point from which the gaze departs and the point seized by the gaze, its way of releasing both a gaze and a scene. Beyond marking the scene's "self-construction" and "self-offering," such a gaze can also put the scene at a distance to be considered in itself, as a reality already constituted, an object to be considered in terms of its manner of existing as much as its content. In the same way, an enunciatee is affirmed in the face of an enunciator: the *you* implied by the énoncé is not only the opposite of the *I* but also the aim of the discourse, a well-delimited set of relations ready to be seized. It is in this manner that the function of the observer emerges: when a *you* arrives in the énoncé, it sees a discourse already seen, a discourse belonging to someone else. It is on a similar basis that a destination is born. However, if the gaze—the "receptive" gaze, that is—can seize the scene in all its autonomy and availability, it can also play on the distance which exists between this scene as an analyzable object, and itself as a moment of analysis. It can distance itself and consider the diegesis in its totality or move in close enough to isolate particular fragments. It can place itself downstream and consider the diegesis an accomplished fact or accompany the scene, following its evolution step by step. It can approach it head on and consider it a homogeneous surface or it can be oblique, emphasizing this or that component. This involves what we call a process of aspectualization: from a point of reception, an ideal eye modulates what it has been led to examine, as a function of its own attitude and goals. According to a determined perspective, it organizes what appears before it.[36]

These "aspects" operate at different levels. First, there is the level of the *dimension* attributed to a reality that is progressively unveiled. As indicated earlier, what is framed (that is, literally put into the frame) can be perceived either as something complete or as something fragmented. The former is obvious in panoramic shots, or in medium shots which feature a gaze whose scope is global. The latter, apparent in the case of the close-up or insert, involves a gaze which perceives the scene as fragmented. One might conclude that considerations of aspectualization determine the scales of the cinema's different shots—from the distant long shot to the extreme close-up. The second level at which aspectualization operates is that of the *order* governing the scene, which can appear either centered or dispersed. In the first case, the gaze privileges a space, concentrating its attention on a precise point. In a word, it gives hierarchy to the elements that figure in the frame. In the second case, the gaze freely traverses the scene nonpreferentially, with uniform attention. The difference between the presence or absence of focalization suggests the alternative involved here.[37] The third level is that of the *limits* attributed to the framed reality, which can be seen as either complete or incomplete. In the case of the former, the gaze cuts out a perfectly finished and autonomous portion of the world and thus isolates a self-sufficient scene. In the case of the latter, the gaze acknowledges the cutting and framing imposed by the camera and thus aims to enlarge the scene beyond the frame, extending it into an offscreen world, an active though perhaps implicit space.[38] Finally, there is the level of the *status* of what is seen, which can be approached either directly or indirectly. In the first case, the gaze seizes the scene as an observable and already formed concrete object; in the second case, it seizes the scene at the same moment as the gesture which constitutes it and, as a consequence, filters it through the motivations, conditions, and objectives which have presided over it. It is largely in this alternative that we find the emergence of the metadiscursive dimension—such as an explicit citation or self-citation.

Clearly, the process of aspectualization dominates an entire series of very important phenomena. Although there are other possibilities, the four levels identified above—dimension, order, limits, and status—are enough to define the basic problem. The gaze, which is at the origin of the scene, can also endow the scene with a certain independence and thereby suggest that it be seized according to a certain optic. The screen world, formed by the film, can also appear as an already complete reality and thus available under this or that aspect. Precisely here, a direct link is established between the act of reception and the form of the film's space. On the one hand, the ideal eye, through the act of organizing both the narrative event and its representation, confirms that the *you* instituted by the film is not just the antagonist of the game's initiator, a simple anti-subject, but also its prolongation and extension. Through this *you*, the *I* is able to see itself seen so that "self-offering" is truly superimposed upon "self-construction." On the other hand, the ideal eye, by encountering a reality that appears already constituted and autonomous, models this reality as a function of its own behavior. It then pulls forth a surface either dense or fragmented, richly composed or lacking solidity, finished or unfinished, smooth or striated.

The Place of the Spectator 65

The result of the meeting of a gaze and a scene is an authentic *geography* integrating the representation as well as its addressee.

At the beginning of our project we located the "position" of each element within a play of relations; now we see this play reflected in a topology: to be in a relation is inevitably to place and to place oneself. And it is exactly in the name of this double operation, inherent in each "position," that we can conclude by developing what our examples have shown us. Through an enunciative configuration which holds for the entire film, these latter construct and situate a *you*, then simultaneously *expose* and *dispose* this *you*. Thus, in the objective configuration, a spectator who functions as an effective but silent witness (a truly hidden spectator) faces a space that, in general, refuses marked terms, a *neutral* space. In the impossible objective configuration, a spectator embodied in the camera (and thus a mobile spectator) encounters a space traversable in even the most extreme respects, an authentically *modulatable* space. In interpellation, where the spectator is implicated but held at a distance from the action (the *aside* keeping the spectator at the scene's margin), a space is displayed at the heart of which there is radical opposition of the on-screen and offscreen fields, of the visible and invisible, a space unlike the preceding ones, founded on a *dissymmetry*. Lastly, a spectator in the subjective configuration, whose perception passes through a character's eyes (thus a spectator within the on-screen field), meets a space, also not homogenous, but this time because of a powerful degree of focalization; here is a space which exhibits itself with an explicit attention, which offers itself as effectively seen and appears, in a word, *expropriated*.

Seeing, Believing, Knowing:
The Complexity of Point of View

Only just completed, the above analysis leaves open a number of questions. We have observed the structuration of the four enunciative configurations, their capacity to dominate the entire film, and also their role in articulating subjects and spaces. Now is it possible to identify the rules and syntax that organize these configurations? Is it possible to enlarge the list of procedures that allow a single event to direct the text in which it appears? Is it possible, finally, to define in all its aspects the relation between a role and the "place" in which it acts?

We might respond to these questions through an example in "negative," so to speak: the opening sequence of Fritz Lang's *Fury* (1936). The sequence begins with the image of a store window behind which is a music stand holding a sheet of paper bearing the words "The Fall Bride." The camera moves laterally, somewhat uncertainly, to reveal a wedding gown. Then in a slight retreat, again lateral, it frames a new window featuring a bedroom display. In the foreground, in front of the display, stand a man and woman, their backs to the camera. A straight cut to a frontal medium shot of the two characters shows them looking at something before them. This is followed by a cut to a long shot of the bedroom. After yet a third cut the man and woman, again in medium shot but this time from the back, exchange replies and exit frame left. The scene ends with a plan américain of the two characters leaving the window, led by the camera.

A notable feature of this passage is the apparent linearity of its unfolding: an objective shot situates the event, a subjective shot emphasizes a couple and its center of interest, and two new objective shots describe the behavior of characters who are likely to become the film's protagonists. Nevertheless, the first shot involves a slight hesitation: given the manner in which it is held (the camera's height, angle, and movement suggest a human gaze) the shot could signal a subjective configuration if it were then completed by the presentation of a character located in the position from which things are seen. But in fact, the two gazing characters appear in a place such that it excludes the possibility that the point of view in question is theirs—they stand before the second window, occupying the same visual field presumably reserved for what they see. Nevertheless, the first hypothesis is so powerful that the subsequent denial comes as a real surprise; in a sense, the objective configuration at the scene's beginning constitutes a "falsely subjective" configuration.

This sort of unkept promise (or momentarily unkept, given that it is not until the second or third shot that a true subjective configuration takes shape), this rather paradoxical structure is precisely what leads to its description as an example in "negative": what appears is a play of differences rather than a direct proposal. However, its indications are no less fruitful, and deserve close study.

First, as with any "failed" act, this example involves an unforeseen superimposition of a law and a transgression. There are, in effect, a certain number of obligations that each configuration must respect as a condition of existence.[39] In the case of the subjective configuration, there is the necessity of depicting both a portion of reality as well as the one who perceives this reality in a way that stabilizes the bi-univocal relation between revelation and perception.[40] At the syntactic level, this means that the construction of subjectivity requires both a gesture from someone who acts (an agent) to someone acted upon (a patient) and a display of the action which links them (a process).[41] In practice, this rule can be actualized in two ways. The most minimal case requires the presence of two distinct elements within the same shot, one offering a literal visual field and the other referring metonymically to the person seeing (this includes hands or feet which intrude from off-screen, or the sounds of breathing, footsteps, etc.). More commonly, though, it involves an articulation of two different shots, one showing what is seen and the other the one who sees, the two linked spatio-temporally[42] and joined edge to edge.[43] It is uniquely due to the coordination of these two elements that the images and sounds can imitate their own act of "self-offering." Someone will appear on the screen in order to receive what appears; at the heart of the film, there will be someone who represents the film's destination. Rather, this structure, and it alone, allows the subjective configuration's expressly chosen enunciative strategy to reach its end through the simultaneous constitution of an effective and diegetic observer.

Consider here that the other configurations are also governed by constraints directly linked to the different situations put in play. Interpellation, which claims to represent someone or something who incarnates the logic of the discourse, must use the emergence of a self-reflective mark rather than an agent/patient structure.[44] The objective configuration, which relies upon an entirely implicit enunciator and enunciatee, must avoid the manifestation on the axis of the screen/theater of gestures that might evoke acts of showing or seeing.[45] The impossible objective configuration, which gives the enunciator and enunciatee the obvious technical nature of an exercise, must organize a space and time totally submissive to the camera. Clearly all of these rules merit more detailed consideration. But here, what is important is that they are in operation and that no configuration functions without them.

Secondly, the "falsely subjective" configuration with which *Fury* opens announces a principle of construction easily verified in the course of the film. This configuration, in effect, institutes a particular journey. It seems to involve a certain goal shot, behaving like a subjective shot, which is then abandoned by the sudden introduction of a slightly abnormal objective shot. It thus recognizes itself in a vocation that it hastens to mask. Hence there is sort of tension between the "will to be" of an intention and the "being" of actual facts, a tension that, again, reappears several times in the film. Recall, for example, the zeal with which Catherine mends her fiancé's white raincoat with blue thread, thereby making the rent in the fabric that much more visible; or Joe's desire to appear elegant when he sends the young woman a note on which he has written "momento" instead of "memento," and so reveals his lack of culture. These examples establish the good faith of the characters, but also the reality of their behavior. These small errors ultimately turn out to be positive as they facilitate the resolution of the drama. Along the lines of expression, recall the early long shot during the assault on the prison in which a camera movement—in front, corresponding to the advance of the crowd—seems to represent the vision of the people, whereas the excessively high angle of the framing prevents such an attribution. Again, here is an imperfect subjective configuration, a gaze which seems ready to enter the scene but then refuses to do so. At the level of both the actions represented and the modes of representation, these lapses confirm an opposition between the declaration of intention and actual reality, established by the film's first shot. However, they also indicate that the correspondences between one occurrence and the text as a whole can come about in more than one way. So far we have emphasized that a configuration can find its reply in a strategy; for example, now that reply can also be found in the introduction of dissymmetry or analogous structures, in the introduction of variants, etc. Though these characteristics could be schematized with greater precision, what is important here is that the enunciative configurations can be imposed throughout a film in all sorts of ways, and willingly so.

Thirdly, the "falsely subjective" configuration that opens *Fury* offers an improved understanding of the notion of the spectator's "place." The opening presents not only the transgression of a syntactic rule or of a symptom ready to reappear, but also the emergence of a constantly present possibility—seeing things "from the inside." Of course this involves no more than a hypothesis, ultimately rejected, but it is not without consequence. How can this relation between the "might be" of hypothesis and the "being" of verification be established? It is problematic that the first shot of *Fury* is not a subjective shot, but appears to be one:

The Place of the Spectator 69

while it does not reproduce precisely what the characters see, it still suggests something of their manner of experiencing the world. This something is the sensation of direct contact, a trace of curiosity, a mental attitude of availability and interest—in sum, those aspects that in their relation to the world are complementary to the gaze. In our example, a character within the diegesis represents this relation to the world, but when approached in a more general manner, it becomes clear that point of view follows not only the signs of perception in the proper sense of the term, but also those of a particular way of apprehending or adhering to things. It is simultaneously a geometric point from which the world is seen, the point from which things are apprehended, and a point from which one decides whether or not to believe what one is facing. We have not just one, but three realities: the first concerns scopic activity in the strict sense (perceptive point of view), the second the cognitive process (informational point of view), and the third the degree of faith (epistemic or emotive point of view).[46] Note that this triple reality operates through the same mechanisms as aspectualization: point of view is the indicator of the scene's "self-construction" and "self-offering," and thus of the presence of the enunciator and enunciatee as extreme poles between which the scene is organized. The point of view also has the power to take the scene as an object placed before it, and to consider itself as the exterior addressee permitting the articulation of its different levels of activity. Point of view thus joins together seeing, knowing, and the relation between what is seen and what is known. It is a manner of placing oneself "upstream" and a manipulation of the distances which explain this plurality of dimensions.

At issue is thus an articulation of different activities, but also of their modes. Each configuration reserves a particular destiny for the three components of point of view. Briefly, the different situations can be schematized as follows (and as always from the spectator's perspective): the objective configuration entails an exhaustive seeing which invests the scene with the slightest detail, a diegetic knowing centered on the information coming from the story, and a solid believing, putting none of the represented facts into doubt; the impossible objective configuration unites a total seeing (which by coinciding with the eye of the camera is set to pass beyond the limits of the frame), a metadiscursive knowing bearing as much on what the scene shows as on what the scene's conditions of existence reveal, and an absolute believing, which is able to speculate on the degree of certitude of the facts; interpellation

	Seeing	Knowing	Believing
Objective	Exhaustive	Diegetic	Solid
Impossible Objective	Total	Metadiscursive	Absolute
Interpellation	Partial	Discursive	Relative
Subjective	Limited	Intradiegetic	Transitory

Table 1

connects a partial seeing, fed by instructions coming from the diegesis ("gaze at me"), a discursive knowing preoccupied most with the relations between addressee and addressor and the enunciative frame itself, and a relative believing, attached only to the guarantees offered by the screen; finally, the subjective configuration approaches a limited seeing linked to a character's vision, an intradiegetic knowing touching lightly on the lived experience of a character, and a transitory believing destined to last as long as the character's credibility. Of course these definitions are only preliminary, but it is clear that to define the various modes of seeing we need to account for the "scope" of vision (exhaustive, total, partial, limited). To define the different modes of knowing requires specifying the level of the text at which information acts (diegetic, metadiscursive, discursive, and intradiegetic). And to define the different modes of believing entails accounting for the "value" of the confidence (solid, absolute, relative, transitory).

We can put these observations into a table (table 1). While this table certainly requires elaboration, even in its current state it successfully indicates the basic articulations concerning point of view in film.

Seeing, Knowing, Believing: Some Diffractions

We have just stated that point of view comprises three dimensions. While these dimensions can be "in phase," mutually reinforcing one another, they can also exist in a state of opposition. That is, what the film might affirm at the level of perception it can deny at those of knowledge and epistemology. This is precisely what happens in the opening shot from *Fury*: because the gaze which frames the objects in the shop window does not correspond to the gaze of the man and

The Place of the Spectator 71

woman, the shot is not subjective, but because the mode in which the diegetic world is apprehended and the status given to that world suggest the experience and indecision of the two characters, it could be. (Consider the nearly human rhythm with which narrative information is presented and the fortuitous nature of the objects' appearance, both suggested by a camera movement revealing the objects one by one, almost with difficulty.) And so this opening shot, while not entailing a subjective seeing, implies a subjective believing and knowing. Such a dissymmetry is more common than it might seem, appearing often, especially in more attenuated form. In particular, it can be found whenever there is a conflict between the fear of implication and the pleasure of domination. The fear derives from the impression that following events from within the diegesis runs the risk of an excessive self-exposure or submission, and the pleasure comes from the fact that being at a scene's center offers a privileged position, an advantage which yields a profit. Lang's films often insist on these two poles: as for risk, recall the many characters who pay for having cast an excessive gaze (like the child in *Moonfleet*, who becomes the protagonist of a miserable adventure for having seen what should have remained hidden), or those characters who become obsessed by what they have observed (like the professor in *The Woman in the Window*, literally seduced by the portrait of a woman); with respect to power, it is enough to recall those characters for whom the gaze is an instrument of domination (like the two versions of *Dr. Mabuse*, masters of hypnosis and closed-circuit television, respectively).[47] But beyond Lang, the cinema in general recalls the tension between fear and pleasure. The documentary, for instance, elicits the emotion that comes from witnessing an event, the dramatic comedy welcomes the spectator in the manner of a discrete host, the adventure film provokes the thrill of directly experienced exploits, the pornographic film appeals to the viewer's voyeurism, and so on. And certainly the subjective configuration, more than any other, offers a potential for such effects. In the fantastic or horror film, fear on the one hand, and exaltation on the other, can arise suddenly due to subjective shots representing the vision of the creature or monster.[48] In such cases the fear of being "with" the monster alternates with the exaltation of "being" the monster. The subjective configuration both aggravates and relates the extremes. To render the situation more supple (and also more current), one can then effect a displacement of the perceptual level and directly engage not the characters' gaze but their belief and knowledge. Such is the case at the beginning of *Fury*.[49] There is a compromise, certainly, insofar as any failed act is a compromise; there is also a transitory moment, given that the following shot will precisely reproduce Joe and Catherine's vision; but it is above all an invaluable indication of how to represent a scene seen from both the exterior and interior.

We can now conclude, at least provisionally, that the series of questions posed above is closed. We began by posing the problem of the different places a film's implied spectator can occupy, places determined above all by the type of relation that the enunciatee undertakes with the enunciator and énoncé. Through an examination of the different types of possible relations, we identified four common textual configurations (the objective configuration, the impossible objective configuration, interpellation, and the subjective configuration), each deriving from a specific pragmatic frame and obeying precise syntactic rules. But above all, we illuminated the principal importance of the process of aspectualization: namely, an ideal eye ready to take into account that which is represented as well as the act of representing in order to hold on to this or that of its aspects. This process has shown that the *you* instituted by the film is not only the antagonist of the one directing the game but also its prolongation (the *you* provides a point from which the enunciator can see itself), and complement (this *you* serves as the point at which the film's "self-construction" finds a conclusion in a "self-offering"). Likewise, the process of aspectualization shows that the spectator's place depends on the system of relations established between the diverse constitutive elements, which then translates into a concrete positioning within the space of the scene. In addition to these considerations, we finally approach two other problems. The first is that of point of view, a phrase that designates not only the point from which one sees, the point that one shows, and the point that one sees, but also acts of perceiving, knowing, and believing. The second problem is that of the functions assumed by the four canonical configurations (again, objective, impossible objective, interpellation, and subjective). Beyond articulating the surface of the text, they often serve as a guide to the film whose criteria and orientations they determine.

Our analysis of *Fury* involved an exclusive focus on one particular configuration, the subjective configuration. This is also at the center of our new example: the beginning of Luis Buñuel's *El* (1952), an analysis of which will allow us to reexamine the themes raised so far and to specify what is behind them.

The Subjective Configuration

El begins with a series of frontal compositions, primarily in medium or medium-long shots, presenting the unfolding of a religious ceremony of the washing of feet. The treatment resembles that of numerous documentaries in which "objective" camera angles show what happens without signaling any fundamental filmic coordinates, positioning the addressee as a simple witness. The result is a perfectly transparent diegesis suggesting a pure and simple statement of facts: something is happening right there in front of you.

But this seemingly neutral development is suddenly ruptured. The camera pushes forward to frame the priest in a medium-close shot lowering the foot he has just washed. There follows a similar framing of a child from the choir closing his eyes. After a few medium-long shots of the ceremony, there is a reappearance of the shot of the priest, who lowers another foot, followed this time by a medium-close shot of a man observing the scene and slowly turning his head. Linked to this gesture, a camera movement reveals in close-up the feet of the faithful. The movement then returns to a particular pair of feet, elegantly booted, and after slowly climbing up the length of her body, concludes by revealing the face of a very beautiful woman. In this way, the objective register of the sequence suddenly converts into one inscribed with subjectivity: someone at the heart of the action registers what is happening. More precisely, this character serves as the point where the images and sounds converge, linking his gaze to the different shots, and filtering through his eyes the spectator's vision of the events. Francisco, the character in question, is the true pivot of this change for at least two reasons. First, he seems willing to see, in contrast to other characters who refuse and reject this role: Francisco continues to gaze at the priest washing the foot, whereas the choirboy lowers his eyes. Second, Francisco's vision involves both attention and desire: his gaze on the feminine foot is rendered through a camera movement as hesitant as it is obstinate—quite unlike the linear and descriptive movement which precedes the shot of the choirboy—and which renders almost obvious his effort to discover and his wish to possess. This desire is conveyed by a traveling shot, instead of a more logical panning movement, as if to show the materialization of a mental attitude rather than an actual physical movement. These two traits—the eyes kept open and the tendency beyond strict perception—make Francisco a true scopic subject, a place of convergence for the capacities of attention and profound interest, for fidelity to the facts and personal curiosity. In this sense, Francisco is the true figurativization of the enunciatee, the point towards which the images and sounds flow and from which they can expect an eventual impulse in return. Henceforth, this character is at the center of the scene in full light. At one and the same time, the film has found both a protagonist and the means to bring out the coordinates that regulate it from its point of reception.

However, a new series of shots introduces another variation. The man in medium-close shot, now framed slightly differently, gazes ahead. The woman, also in medium close-up, first lowers her eyes and then lifts them to gaze at him with a determined air. There is a cut back to the man's face, a cut to the woman again closing her eyes, and the man turns away his head. Above all, this new passage signals that a previously exclusive gaze has been replaced by an exchange of gazes. Francisco is no longer the only one who sees; the woman, Gloria, now also has this capacity. And in fact, each character is placed under the gaze of the other: while Gloria continues to be framed from Francisco's point of view, he abandons the medium-close shot in order to coincide with her point of view. On the other hand—second variation—an effect of this face-to-face encounter is to reify the gazes, to transform them into pure action. After a closer examination, it becomes apparent that what occurs is less a process of seeing and being seen than an interlacing of the gazes of two powerful "heroes." Here is a face-to-face exchange involving a spatial organization wholly independent of the actual to-and-fro exchange of the characters' gazes, to the point that Francisco can occupy a shot immediately following one in which Gloria appears with closed eyes. That is, rather than a superimposition of subjectivities, what occurs is an ordinary shot/countershot. The doubling of the two observers, Francisco and Gloria, allows them to merge perfectly into the diegesis, to the point of becoming presences without depth. The result is a neutralization of the scene despite the presence of potential subjects and an insertion of the coordinates of the film into the reality that it represents. The ultimate consequence is a return to an objective unfolding, one involving only witnesses outside the diegesis, though now with perhaps greater consciousness.

Let us consider the last part of the sequence. After a direct cut, a medium shot travels back from the altar and the ceremony's participants to cross the church threshold and become a long shot with a slight downward plunge. But again, the framing modifies the ordinary scale of the shots. In effect, the preceding motif is flattened into a background that now absorbs it. This occurs not simply because Francisco and Gloria have dissolved into the crowd, and with them their face-to-face exchange, but because a space marked by an exchange of glances between a man and woman is replaced by a space dominated by a different kind of point of view, one beyond any character's subjectivity (the slightly plunging angle) and endowed with a special mobility (the traveling shot that passes beyond the threshold of the church). In short, the objective configuration at the film's beginning cedes place to an impossible objective configuration with the camera affirming, "I am here" and "I am seeing," signaling the filmic discourse's points of departure and arrival. Under shelter of the sequence's final fade-out, the cinema visibly takes the game in hand. Thanks to a mechanical eye, an *I* and even more, a *you*, come to define the parameters of the representation.

We observe this opening sequence with particular care, not only because it directly raises the question of the gaze (as does another film's prologue and an entire career: the eye-cutting passage in *Un chien andalou*) but because it does so in a most exemplary fashion by its very progression. The sequence's structure is relatively clear: following a moment during which the gaze is absent, there is an entry into the field of someone who happens to see (Francisco) and who is then put under the gaze of someone else (Gloria), and then finally under a different gaze altogether (that of the camera). At the same time, we move from a short instant of dispersion to a scene centered on a man, which is then recentered, due to the appearance of a woman, and finally decentered by the perceptible intervention of the cinema. The textual constructions involved in this development are, respectively, a quasi-documentary objective configuration, a subjective configuration ready to nourish the diegesis, a more structured objective configuration, and an impossible objective configuration. The successive positions assumed by the enunciatee are those of an anonymous witness, a character present in the field, a now conscious witness, and finally, the camera. It is easy then to recognize the different journeys as well as the support they take from the second moment in the operation, when Francisco's attention, under the appearance of an anodyne gesture, actually bends the diegesis and signals its reception from the interior. Such a global project, once again with its lines of development and points of emphasis, is highly instructive, signaling that beyond simple intrigue, it is the film's rhythm that is truly pregnant. Clearly, this extract can reveal much of real interest. And between the lines, it tells us at least three stories.

The first story concerns the appearance and then disappearance of the marks indicating the film's "self-construction," and even more, its "self-offering." During the passage featuring the subjective configuration, Francisco proves through his gaze that the images and sounds have a destination and inscribes this destination by the fact that he is the target of it. But the shot/countershot and the backward tracking shot transform the acts of seeing and hearing into implicit behaviors or attribute them to the cinema in general. In other words, at first the enunciative roles become manifest in all their plenitude ("there is someone who sees along with you, and you see him seeing"), then they move to the margins and act in perfect silence ("there is no longer anyone who sees for you, and your seeing no longer sees itself"). This recalls certain operations encountered earlier regarding the gaze into the camera. The direct gaze also tried to reveal the film's parameters before being reabsorbed into a perfect diegesis, and it, too, testified to the presence of a "complete" subject ("I gaze") before ceding place to an énoncé dotted with simple traces of enunciation. Thus, the opening sequence of *El* confirms in the most obvious manner that the subjective configuration, like interpellation, its opposite in many respects, is an effective though delicate construction.[50] It establishes the rhythm of the commentary, but at the same time, is defenseless in the face of the narrative.

The causes of this hesitation cannot be understood solely within the issue of appropriateness: when the traces of the enunciated enunciation are effaced, it is not just due to writing, as narration, which will readily pass silently over that which manifests it. As we have already shown, the fact is that the subjective configuration embodies a gaze lacking true intention. The character who sees, with all the hesitations and difficulties that such an act demands, effectively lacks the capacity to choose or direct his gaze. In the end, this character grasps only what his or her counter-field makes visible, inscribing his or her action in an obligatory face-to-face. Rather than simply gazing, the character is made to see. Likewise, an abusive use of the subjective configuration can provoke losing the of power of this very act. Here the failure of certain experiments in "total" subjectivity[51] is highly revealing. The perfect imitation of the addressee's perception (where the character and spectator are placed at the same level; what is seen by one is also seen by the other) enables a film to fully enact its "self-offering." At the same time, by defining the represented world according to an overly exclusive point of view, thereby limiting the film's "natural extension" and questioning its very capacity for domination, this configuration prevents the film from developing what it tells. In other words, the technique of filtering everything through the eyes of a character allows an exaltation of the act of seeing but sacrifices the scope and autonomy of what is seen. Despite these considerations, however, the subjective configuration has proven undeniably useful. It encourages the frame to shape itself according to an explicit gaze, even if thereby assimilating it to one action among others. It permits the staging of an observer, however provisional. And in this way it animates a scene's space, turning it into a place of representation rather than simply a represented place. It protects the point of view before reintroducing it into the diegesis. The beginning of *El*, as if aiming to remind us of something we have already observed, tries to show us how a configuration can be both provisional and of an extraordinary force.

The second story that our example suggests centers on the apparent source of the subjective configuration—that is, Francisco. Our example presents Francisco as a character who agrees to see, in contrast to the choirboy, but also as a character whose gaze engages with two other gazes which surprise and interrupt his. After having noticed Gloria, Francisco in turn is observed; one moment he incarnates the camera's objective, in the next the camera turns to frame Francisco, distancing him. The sequences which follow will develop this alternative: on the one hand, they describe the behavior of a man who cannot bear that others lay their eyes on him or on his property;[52] on the other hand, they oppose the character's vision of facts and that of the film, to the point of making them diverge.[53] Why, exactly, does the film's progression insist so much on this "battle of the gazes," and what does such an insistence signify?[54]

Note above all the opposition between Francisco and Gloria, which seems intended to represent a difference in the status of vision. Whereas Francisco must open his eyes in order to see, Gloria can see through closed eyes.[55] Whereas Francisco is captivated by details (feet), Gloria goes directly to what defines a person's identity (the face). Whereas

Francisco is enchanted by what he sees, Gloria exhibits a balance between curiosity and discretion. Finally, the man approaches reality by submitting to it (he is positioned precisely as the one to whom things are shown in the subjective configuration); the woman, however, experiences things by dominating them (not only is she capable—in the shot/countershot—of "objectivizing" a relation born independently of her, but later—in a long flashback—she will be capable of revealing a reality beyond appearances). Thus the man adopts the gaze of a "spectator" whereas the woman adopts that of an "author." The opposition here between the two characters mirrors that between two roles. On the one hand, there is someone who knows only how to see (a narratee), and on the other, someone who wants to gaze (a narrator); someone who acts on behalf of the enunciatee, and someone who serves the enunciator.[56] In this sense, Francisco's defeat (should we really call it a defeat?) appears determined not only by his membership in the bourgeoisie or by his male pride,[57] but also by the place he occupies at the level of the enunciation. The one who incarnates the *you* that the film addresses must take into account the *I* which activates the film. As the point of reception, he cannot claim absolute authority.

Similarly, the second opposition, between Francisco and the camera, presents a case of two different types of gazes. Instead of an opposition between two juxtaposed figurativizations of the enunciatee and enunciator, we have two superimposed levels of the énoncé and the enunciation. The division this time concerns two orders of reality, at once separate and closely linked—the film as constructed and offered, and the act of construction and of offering. The scenario is once again quite clear: Francisco offers to play the role of guide for the spectator's gaze, while the camera frames him as an element of the intrigue. Francisco takes control of the film's images (what he sees appears directly on the screen), while the camera ridicules his vision (due to the paroxysm of the crisis of man, a new subjective configuration will appear, but this time totally hallucinatory). Francisco declares his readiness to look reality in the face, while the camera will eventually show him from behind in a posture of renunciation, perhaps even abdication. Here is a character who, after having tried to occupy the place of the cinematic apparatus, is finally returned to the interior of the frame and imprisoned there; a glance of an eye aiming to be determinant and a gaze that is able to define the limits of the scene. The dissolve in the opening sequence well defines the terms of the problem: from a subjective configuration in which the function of the *you*[58] is assumed by a diegetic element, to an impossible objective configuration, in which the function of the *you* is assumed by the cinematographic apparatus itself (that is, a point of view participating in the action is linked to the point of view that dominates it, without ever detaching from it).[59] After the prologue, the parable of *El* goes on to confirm and radicalize these points of rupture. Francisco's defeat thus appears provoked by a second factor: he who lives within the diegesis cannot forget that which has given him life. The representation must never deny the act that produced it.

The meaning of this double opposition that engages *El*'s main character from the first moments now becomes clear. It is precisely Francisco's dream of being the only protagonist which pushes him to struggle against the other characters in the scene (like Gloria, a figurativization of the enunciator) and other instances in the filmic discourse (like the camera, the trace of a presupposition without which there would be neither images nor sounds). The illusion of a complete domination effectively collapses in face of the affirmation that new factors are needed and that there are other ways of proceeding. And so one experiences, in Francisco's place, the defeat of an exclusive vision which momentarily filled the entire screen. Even this gaze must connect to other gazes within the scene.

The need for this process of connecting has a double meaning (*El* provides an example concerning the destination, but the same applies to any enunciative component).[60] First, it indicates once again the limits of any subjective configuration. In effect, the gaze constructed by the film and attributed to a character loses certain of its characteristic traits precisely because of this double reference. We have already noted the degree to which this configuration appears empty of any intention on the part of a character because it is linked to a counter-field determined by the text. We can now add that the intention is no longer adapted to the text, because the text articulates itself precisely on the character. Beyond *El*, there are also cases where a change in focus, a chromatic alteration, or a moment of blackness, etc., reproduces a character's visual response. These images permit the film to display the fact that it is seen, but because of their provisional character, they also show that the film can escape the constraints and see better than the character. Exact representation of what a character perceives allows the film to exhibit its own "being seen." The fugitive aspect of this perception reveals through the images that frame it that the film can enact its "self-construction" and "self-offering," without any hesitation. In other words, when a subjective configuration puts in scene an internal recipient and gives him certain responsibilities, it does not provide him with unlimited credit. This recipient will accomplish more when, renouncing the role of soloist, he rejoins a place prepared for several. If our character wishes to have real influence, he must, for better or worse, reintegrate into the ensemble of the orchestra.

Beyond the subjective configuration, however, this need for connecting gazes recalls the structure of any address. Consider particularly the case of the observer. His construction depends upon a distancing of the represented events (and of that event which is the representation itself), as well as their reorganization as a function of a precise optic. Moreover, in a manipulation of this sort, the interlacing of gazes becomes essential, enabling a recognition of both the singularity of the action and the background against which the action develops. An entire network of gazes enables a definition of both the specificity of the chosen point of view and the ensemble of eventual perspectives.[61] In this respect, the observer is doubly "situated": on the one hand, his spatial position determines the entire look of what appears, and on the other, this very position is the result of a play of alternations and reciprocities.

In the structure of an address and in the functioning of a subjective configuration, the obligation of connecting is manifest and imposed. Nonetheless, Francisco will decline the invitation. An eccentric character and hesitant to decenter himself, he will try to travel the path alone, only to finish, like any narcissist, by finding death in the mirror—or, should we say, on the screen?

We now reach the third story told by the opening sequence of *El*. So far, we have considered Francisco as a mark of reception. In the subjective configuration where we are led to see someone, a character mimes the situation of reception. Francisco is able to take on this role because of the effective split between the one who sees and what is seen. The succession of shots (a close-up of the man's face, then an insert of the woman's feet) produces a veritable break between the subject who perceives the supposed object and the object perceived which, at that particular moment, lies outside the field. Certainly this is an entirely normal alternation; all subjective configurations require two distinct elements for their construction, one indicating the origin of the gaze and the other its point of arrival.[62] It also has a singular utility, enabling a judgment on either the character who is in the field ("it is because he is seeing that things appear this way"), or on the content of the vision ("if things appear this way, it is because that is the way they are").[63] But above all, this alternation is symptomatic; the face-to-face encounter between the one charged with seeing and the result of such an act precisely recalls the juxtaposition of the gaze that grasps the scene from the exterior and thus brings it to life, with the scene that claims a gaze and implicates it as a function of the decoupage. The face-to-face between an eye and something seen suggests that the spectator (precisely the one to whom the address is directed) represents two very distinct things: a concrete given, a receiver who acts "on" the film "from the exterior," and an abstract instance, a "self-offering" to vision and hearing originating "from the interior" and "at the initiative" of the film.

The role Francisco assumes participates in exactly this dynamic. It indicates a destination because of the movement on the screen from someone who sees, to something seen (so that its presence is double—both in the close-up of the face, the gaze's origin, and in the insert of the feet, what the gaze encompasses). But it also marks a destination because of the cut separating the subject who sees from the object seen (its presence is thus divided into either a pure sensory organ or the simple effect of an act of perception). It follows that the construction of a *you* capable of mutating into a character (again, a task reserved specifically for the subjective configuration) leads not just to a confrontation between different forces weighing upon the shot, but also to the distinction of a fracture weighing upon the visible and leading to the awareness of a dimension that "transcends" the images and sounds. The addressee placed in the scene constitutes not only the point at which all the threads of the representation are joined, but a figure maintained at a distance from his center of interest (if only through framing), and thus the sign of the distance (much more clear) separating the one seated in the movie theater from the action on the screen. In sum, to the necessary aspect of connecting gazes one must now add the discovery of a fleeting aspect. The place of the point of reception thus crosses a radical "elsewhere."

The same tension appears when the cinema runs through the schema in reverse, through the bias either of observers who do not take advantage of the available opportunities or the bias of certain visions which remain mysterious to those who attempt to decipher them. Such displacements are not rare. For instance, even if the discussion is limited to Buñuel, one can cite the two pilgrims of *The Milky Way* who never understand the meaning of the events they witness or the woman of *That Obscure Object of Desire* who has two different faces.[64] In any case, in their failure as much as in any ultimate success, these displacements confirm that the display of a "spectatorial" moment, in its very structure, inevitably refers to those beyond the film's limits, necessarily containing within itself its own supersession and negation. An inevitable conclusion is that in this case as in our sequence, the act of seeing amounts to a voyage within the confines of the film. It is a play of differences, a challenge to absence.

Such are the stories related in the prologue of *El*, read between the lines of an intrigue that seemingly concerns a man's lovestruck response to the feet of a beautiful, unknown woman. Three secret stories: not many given the reflections which they have inspired (and leaving aside that prologue from a different film, in which an eyeball is cut for having contemplated the moon, an event which tells us of the potential for reproducing reality as well as the need to go further, to blindness, or love at first sight). Three allegories: the first concerns the fragility of the enunciated enunciation, ready to cede place to pure narrative; the second involves the play of relations to which an observer submits, forced to confront both the one playing the role of "author" and the existence of an abstract instance; the third, finally, concerns the split which defines the point of reception, suspended between a hypothesis offered by the film and an ineluctable out-of-field. The three stories, perfectly self-reflective, develop in conjunction with the sequence's unfolding and justify its movements. At the same time, they reveal the nature of both a representation, especially when a subjective configuration is involved, and a point of reception, manifest through a character's behavior. Here an act of seeing is offered to a gaze, and *your* seeing is proposed as a model narrative. Moreover, within the weave of a rather obvious plot, does not each story hope to find itself? Behind its own literality, does not each story enact its own "self-offering"? "You understand what I mean, dear spectator. . . ."

4 The Spectator's Journey

Simulated Enunciation

Houses of mirrors, winks, Russian dolls: often a film opens out upon a moment that will suddenly double it, either because the images and sounds provoke additional significations or because what is shown reveals the reality backstage. Particularly important among such moments are the film-within-a-film and the flashback. With these common devices a representation is superimposed on another representation, a frame is inscribed within another frame, a discourse is brought into relation with another discourse; in short, articulations occur that allow the world depicted on the screen to include, or to depend upon, another parallel world.

We can define the essential features of this type of construction by means of two relatively famous examples from *Citizen Kane*. First is the scene featuring the newsreel *News on the March*, and second, the visualization of events recounted in Thatcher's diary. Given their canonical status, these examples do not require a detailed description.[1] The first example presents a rather clear case of the film-within-a-film. It begins in a manner that is both decidedly emphatic (the music and titles produce a true marker) and clearly indicative of what will follow (the titles *"News on the March"* and "Obituary" announce the subsequent tone and theme).[2] It is something that both signals its own irruption into the field and anticipates its own development. Following this introduction is a heterogeneous series of shots—exotic decors, statues, animals in cages, Italian gardens, etc.—superimposed over a mysterious bit of verse: "In Xanadu did Kubla Khan / A stately pleasure dome decree . . ."[3] Here is a fully elaborated film, displaying the difficulty of presenting a discourse, but also showing the will to tell a story.[4] Passages follow, concerning the death of a man and retrospectively illustrating various aspects and contradictions of his life—Kane at the height of power, and then confined to a wheelchair; Kane branded a communist by his former guardian, then denounced as a fascist by a labor leader, and so on. Intertitles punctuate the visuals, as much to identify what we see ("In Xanadu last week / was held 1940's biggest / strangest funeral")[5] as to specify its significance ("Few private lives / were more public").[6] The game begins from here, and a world is composed before our eyes. Continuously from the beginning of the newsreel, an off-screen voice organizes and explains what is shown. Here, an agent shapes the discourse, and while piecing together the events, will directly address a willing spectator.

What is the purpose of this set of procedures? They reveal the status of what is exhibited. They mark the existence of a film, a film which shows itself for what it is, and which addresses anyone who wishes to receive it. But suddenly there is a crack, a rupture. Exactly at the moment when the title "The End" appears, the image suddenly shifts on its axis and is shown to be projected on a screen. As if in a recoil,[7] there appears a group of people who have also been following what we have just seen and who speak of it, unsatisfied and discontented. This theatrical flourish provokes a double surprise at least. On the one hand, it introduces an abrupt change in direction, with immediate effects. Whereas the representation had initially designated its "self-construction" through the emphatic opening of *News on the March*, with titles and voice-over narration, it now situates its activity within another representation. This new representation is less marked than the first (one need only compare the credits of *Citizen Kane* and those of *News on the March* to conclude that the framing discourse is clearly more evasive than the interior discourse) and also very conscious of its nature (consider that the journalists are backlit and filmed in front of a blank screen rendering only the essentials: simple shadows, pure silhouettes). On the other hand, a distance is introduced: the representation can now show into whose hands it falls; and rather than to us, the viewers of *Citizen Kane*, it had already given itself to some other held in reserve until now, to a group of characters suddenly gathered together within the scene who discuss *News on the March* with an awareness of purpose. In one sense, the images and sounds complete their trajectory, while in another, they set off in a new direction: a double potential that modifies and complicates the game. As a result, this new consideration of the film's "self-construction" and "self-offering" reposits into their proper place both the object offered to the gaze and the subjects called upon to see.

Here our example ends. By following it step by step we have been able to mark its arrangements, as well as characterize its basic structures and implicit construction. What strategies does the film-within-a-film use to establish itself? Let us reconsider the situation in terms of enunciation. The first question to arise concerns the coordinates that the film manifests through its constitutive gesture. The operation is essentially structured between four poles. First is an instance which guides the images and sounds by situating itself at the point of articulation between a pure virtuality (to be able to film the world) and its realization (the world as it has been filmed);[8] this, briefly, is what activates *Citizen Kane* in its ensemble. Next is a series of givens which figurativize this instance, imitating its procedures and trajectories. These are moments which, once represented, seem to account for that which has determined the representation, forces which indicate the existence of a backstage realm. These are not simply symptoms, but signs that work together to direct an appeal to someone (the *I* who controls the game) and to affirm the self (the *I*, in the guise of a *he* or *she*, who forms the voices and characters of the story). Such signs are especially evident in elements like the credits, intertitles, and voice-over narration which, showing the "self-construction" of *News on the March*, refer to the "self-construction" of *Citizen Kane*. There is a destination inscribed within the very presence of the images and sounds, a target seemingly exterior to the film but which in reality is integral to it, serving as the ideal point toward which the film's operations are directed. These operations aim toward an outcome and eventual response, implying a destination that corresponds to the reception foreseen and proposed by *Citizen Kane*. Finally, someone or something figurativizes this destination, certain elements within the intrigue which, once represented, serve as signs of the representation's "self-offering." These function as confidants, recipients of a spectacle, voyeurs, like the group of characters in *Citizen Kane* who have viewed *News on the March*. Such are the four poles put into play. We already know them well: they correspond to the figures of enunciator, narrator, enunciatee, and narratee, figures which appear openly once more to pull together the essentials of the plot.

Now we may move to the second question, the sense in which a film can expand and extend itself. At issue is not the content of the images or sounds, but rather the strategic placement of the elements. What is decisive here is that the four poles are simultaneously in play, thereby permitting an entire series of parallel relations. On the one hand, the enunciator and narrator unite in order to produce the gesture of someone who, having operated in the world of the gaze, now extends an invitation to gaze on this world. And at the same time, they oppose the enunciatee and narratee who designate the gesture of someone, having been led to gaze, who now succeeds in seeing. On the other hand, the enunciator and enunciatee both constitute abstract positions to which the narrator and narratee refer, at a distance, in order to manifest an implicit instance. We thus have the intersection of two fronts which coordinate the multiplication of points of view—the point of view of the one who presides at the film's formation, and of the one who the film addresses; the point of view of the representation, and that of the one represented. This coordination pushes the axis of narrator/narratee to reproduce precisely, but in scale, the axis of enunciator/enunciatee. Or, if one prefers, it makes the axis between enunciator and enunciatee the model for that between narrator and narratee.

Third question: it is true that the four poles form a united and coordinated group, but it is also the case that if we segment the itinerary according to which the film-within-a-film constructs itself, we can see that within each phase, the poles are neither entirely bound nor entirely in alignment. Let us return to our example. In the first part of the sequence (where a voice-over commentary personifies the motivations of the film constructing itself, and at the same time addresses a still faceless, voiceless spectator), the one who takes charge of the field is a narrator who, as a delegate of the enunciator, introduces an enunciatee still without figurativization. What we have is still an arrangement in three terms, linked to one another so as to say, according to the attitude typical of *interpellation*, "*he*—that is, *I*—we address *you* in order to incite you to look at what is shown." By contrast, in the second part of the sequence (where a group of journalists incarnates the destination point of the film, without the guiding "logic" of the film ever becoming concretized in any particular element) it is a narratee who, as the delegate of an enunciatee, manifests that he is put into operation by an enunciator figurativized only in the ineluctable form of the images and sounds of which he is the presupposition. Again we have an arrangement which links three terms, according to the formula of the *subjective configuration*, as if to say, "*he*—that is, *you*—respond to *me* because you see what is shown to you." All this indicates that it will take more than one round to win the game: elements will permutate along the terrain, but only at the end will they occupy their respective positions. Ultimately, the film-within-a-film is a matter of strategy rather

The Spectator's Journey 87

than content, where a proper coordination of actions can guarantee its success.

Let us go now to an example of flashback—the sequence which opens the series of testimonies on Kane. In this sequence the journalist Thompson goes to the Thatcher Foundation to read the diary of the recently deceased press magnate's tutor. Following a dissolve on the Thatcher manuscript, the film presents a visualization of the episodes described in the journal: the mother's act of surrendering her son and fortune to Thatcher, the first Christmas of little Charles far from his family, the beginning of Charles's interest in the daily newspaper *The Inquirer*, the paper's struggle against Thatcher's financial group, and Kane's abandonment of *The Inquirer* due to the crisis of 1929. Thompson closes the diary. He has not found what he searches for: an explanation of the meaning of "Rosebud," the word spoken by Kane on his deathbed.

After our observations of the preceding example, this sequence requires only a brief commentary. And note that our new example also enacts the four basic terms. First there is an enunciator: the force directing *Citizen Kane*. Then comes a narrator: Thatcher, the explicit source of the narrative. Thatcher's very manner of occupying the scene confirms that he is the enunciator incarnate. He appears, in effect, as a monument (with his bust and portrait prominently displayed), as a written text (the handwriting in the diary), and as a personal pronoun (the opening phrase of his diary entry is clearly visible: "*I* first encountered . . ."). In sum, this reality is both present and previously recorded. Simultaneously a sculpted and painted figure, a manuscript and a signature, an equal of the one pulling the strings of the filmic discourse, Thatcher is someone who exists not because of what he is, but because of what he has been.[9] There is also an enunciatee: the point toward which the images and sounds extend. And finally, a narratee: Thompson, reader of the diary and spectator of what the diary relates (confirmed by the fact that Thompson is always framed from behind, a position oriented to the direction of the film spectator's gaze). Moreover, this sequence operates in two states as well. It begins with a subjective configuration: a narratee (the journalist Thompson)—linked to an enunciatee who follows the story—prepares to observe, and will observe, what an enunciator shows him. Now an interpellation is grafted on this situation: a narrator (Thatcher)—in the name of an enunciator, who directs *Citizen Kane*—turns directly toward an enunciatee by putting in view his own writing.

Is this a pure and simple repetition of the preceding case? To answer, we need only examine the way in which the example's elements are organized. The interpellation occurs in the middle of the episode, between the appearance of a character who wants to decipher memories, and the appearance of an account remembered, shown to us at the same time as to him,[10] that is, at the very moment when it is possible to read the manuscript directly before him. After attending to the surface of the film's discourse, if we analyze its deep structure, it is clear that the interpellation is very logically placed at the beginning of the sequence so that Thompson can qualify as the addressee of the manuscript and as the recipient of Thatcher's revelations—precisely within a subjective configuration. "Before" the interpellation, Thompson is a character without a role because, despite his wish to know what happened between Kane and his guardian, he cannot yet access the facts that will "later" become available. In other words, once Thatcher—and ultimately the agent directing *Citizen Kane*—address us directly and invite us to gaze at what is shown,[11] Thompson—and ultimately the spectator as the point of convergence of the film's images and sounds—can see what is shown. Better yet, since we are referring to enunciative roles and not to flesh-and-blood characters, it is at the moment when a narrator and enunciator explicitly call on an enunciatee inciting her to gaze (through interpellation), that the narratee and enunciatee are able to see what the enunciator shows them (using a subjective configuration).[12]

The preceding example, however, presents the opposite case. In our study of the text's surface, we noted first an interpellation and then a subjective configuration, but upon examining the text's deep structures, we discovered that a subjective configuration logically precedes the interpellation. In effect, from and only from the moment when *Citizen Kane*'s director leads a group of journalists (and, at the same time, the viewer) to see what is shown can the agent operating *News on the March* (and with him the one operating *Citizen Kane*) directly confront the viewer—addressee of the images and sounds—and ask her to see and hear what is being presented. In other words, because an enunciator has led a narratee and an enunciatee to see what is shown (due to a subjective configuration) the narrator and enunciator can explicitly suggest an enunciatee, by inviting this enunciatee to gaze (with an interpellation).[13]

If this analysis is correct, it would appear that both the film-within-a-film and the flashback utilize the same components (enunciator, enunciatee, narrator, and narratee) and the same relation among configurations (an alternation between interpellation and the subjective configuration), though ordered differently in each case.[14] In the film-within-a-film, a subjective configuration introduces and controls the interpellation: in our first example, the film seems to say "I am showing these journalists, who occupy your place (subjective configuration), what *News on the March* is showing you in my name (interpellation)." The situation is one in which a capacity to pay attention is realized insofar as to offer a sign of complicity. In a more general manner, it signifies "*I* make both *you* and *him* see someone (subjective configuration) *who*, together with *me*, turns to face *you* in order to make you gaze (interpellation)." There is an exchange of information here that produces a noticeable reduction in the distances separating the different participants. In the flashback, on the contrary, an interpellation introduces and controls the subjective configuration. In our second example, for instance, the film seems to assert: "in *my* name, the banker Thatcher says to *you* (interpellation) what *I* said to the journalist Thompson *for* you (subjective configuration)." Here a direct address to an interlocutor ameliorates the latter's receptivity. Formulated in more general terms, the form of such a sequence signifies: "*he* and *I*—both of us—turn to *you*, asking you to gaze (interpellation) at something that *I* am making both *you* and *him* see (subjective configuration)." Here a contact is initiated which will serve as both the vehicle and guarantee of a successful circulation of information.

If reduced to simple formulas, these two types of construction entail, in one case, an interpellation that unfolds within a subjective configuration, and in the other, a subjective configuration established through an interpellation. They can also be analyzed in terms of the mechanisms of engagement and disengagement essential to the processes involved.[15] In the case of the film-within-a-film, an enunciator first disengages from an enunciatee and narratee to engage a narrator with whom he can then address the enunciatee.[16] This operation signifies that only after projecting a *you* and a corresponding *he* can the *I* designate this *he* as his own alter ego. In terms of the strategy of the gaze, this situation suggests a case in which only after introducing a character who sees can the *I* address the viewer in a confidential fashion.[17] Conversely, in the case of the flashback, an enunciator disengages from a character and immediately reengages this character as its spokesperson, thus transforming the character into a narrator, in order then to disengage an enunciatee and narratee. Perhaps only after being assured of replacement by a *he* does the *I* come to face the *you* and corresponding *he*. In terms of the strategy of the gaze, the situation suggests that only after having introduced a character who gazes, can the *I* elicit us to see.[18]

Mandate and Competence

The parallel formulas outlined above may seem like riddles of the first order. They nonetheless can be quite useful in defining a number of essential questions about film narration. Let us sketch some points that will allow us to approach the heart of the matter.

First of all, these schemas enable the discovery that certain stylistic effects are rooted in an opposition between the "logical" order of the elements involved and their actual order of appearance. This was precisely the case in the preceding examples. The *News on the March* episode, for instance, concludes with a "surprise" to the viewer's expectations of the outcome of the narrative process (here is the classical figure of the "hysteron proteron").[19] In the episode with Thatcher's diary, a "hesitation" on the viewer's part results when, in the midst of a segment, a new level of narration is inserted that constitutes the segment's very premises (a trajectory suggesting a spiral). In both sequences, then, the incorporation of discourse gives a certain "spice" to things, even if the latent structure is still ultimately determinant.

Secondly, our schemas account for the recurrence of a number of elements by linking their appearance to the introduction of a function. Besides the examples cited above, one might add those countershots common in instances of the film-within-a-film that emphasize the presence of spectators supposedly following the spectacle, shots whose purpose is less to define the represented space than to locate a foundation within the representation for the subjective configuration. The same is true of certain fades and dissolves[20] in a flashback which mark a shift backward in the film, and whose goal is less to serve as signs of punctuation than to emphasize the moment of interpellation.[21] Once again, it seems that within the mise-en-scène we can find evidence of a deep structure that explains the development of the narration.

Third, the schemas help decipher certain complex figures that result from the convergence and conjugation of several roles. Consider here the many characters in cases of the film-within-a-film who are both authors and spectators of what happens on the screen,[22] or those characters in the case of flashback who are simultaneously bearers and addressees of a memory. Far from creating confusion between the participants, these characters achieve a perfect fusion between narrator and narratee, with the result that they can appear as true interpreters—that is, as persons who to comprehend a given situation both hear and speak, learn and teach, see as well as gaze. By uniting two functions in one, the film does not abandon its storyline, but rather grasps it that much more closely.

Fourth, the schemas suggest a rather interesting typology of the variety of possible profiles involving three principle axes. When seen in terms of the impact of the different components, it is perhaps useful to distinguish between using the subjective configuration and interpellation as points of departure for a new orientation of the discourse and their appearance as simple insertions. On the one hand, such a distinction yields structures of "impulsion"—that is, when a film introduces a narrator or narratee in order to give over the responsibility of manipulating its own story (as is precisely the case in the film-within-a-film and in the flashback). On the other hand, it may yield structures of "addition," which function when the film manifests specific enunciative roles without constructing a second level of enunciation—this occurs in cases of intertextual borrowings, explicative texts, narration in installments, metaphorical returns to the intrigue or to a scene, etc. Here the text breaks apart and rearticulates itself, but does not produce a "narrative-within-a-narrative." When seen in terms of the order of the different components, it is useful to distinguish between constructions ruled by a subjective configuration and those ruled by an interpellation. In addition to the film-within-a-film, there is the theater-within-a-film, the filmed dream, and in general, any moment in which a discourse incorporated within the film is modeled on its point of reception. In addition to the flashback, these include the flashforward, the deliberate citation, and generally any moment in which a discourse within a film manipulates the mise-en-scène from the point of emission. Finally, in terms of the scope of activity of the various components, it is useful to distinguish between a reported enunciation and an enunciated enunciation.[23] The former includes moments in which a representation traverses another representation—"other," as related to the framing representation, even if it is itself very near to being a representation. Such is the case in the examples of *News on the March* and Thatcher's memoirs: both are distinct from the film *Citizen Kane* while belonging to the same order and literally sharing the same body. Enunciated enunciations, by contrast, include moments in which the representation represents itself, directly unveiling its own "self-construction" and "self-offering," and choosing itself as the true theme of the film. Examples of this kind of self-representation include *mise-en-abîme* constructions where the story told explicitly concerns the act of its own narration. One could certainly extend this typology, but even in its current state it enables an understanding of the ways in which a film defines the various enunciative roles and adapts these to its own specific interests.

Fifth (again, this new category somewhat overlaps the preceding ones), our schemas permit a more thorough delineation of the way a film organizes its processes of emission and reception. Recall the two situations outlined above. In the case of the flashback, the film insists on its "self-construction." It designates a narrator, a character to whom it delegates the power to speak, and displays this individual's actions insofar as the narrator directly addresses a viewer following the intrigue. In the case of the film-within-a-film, the film underlines its availability. It designates a narratee, someone who assumes the role of receiver, and manifests this individual's presence by using her as a filter for what progressively appears. What do these two attitudes have in common? They share the injunction of a double expense: the agent responsible for the production of *Citizen Kane* assigns to a delegate acting within the story—alongside him or facing him—the task of signaling, first, the beginning of the game, and second, its end. In other words, these two structures unveil a double *mandate*. The enunciator "sets in motion" the characters of the narrator and narratee, attributing to them roles that require certain actions. Considering the characters as his own surrogates, the enunciator gives them a precise function. Upon reflection, it becomes clear that the principal consequence of this mandate is precisely to endow a designated character with the means necessary to act—the faculties of speech and hearing, respectively. Above all, the notion of "setting in motion" suggests the rendering of a character appropriate to the action and the endowment of this character with the capacity to perform the assigned role. Consequently, this "setting in motion" permits most importantly a precise access to the rank of narrator and narratee and all the power these roles imply. If one prefers, it allows the installation and elaboration of a subject through a recognition of his or her *competence*.

Our two constructions thus reveal the existence of a mandate, and consequently, the attribution of a competence.[24] The preceding observations concerning the subjective configuration and interpellation suggest the capital importance of certain points of articulation. An analysis of the mechanisms of engagement and disengagement revealed the existence of a network of complicity, whereas the discussion of certain stylistic effects, the recurrence of certain elements and the range of a certain number of solutions indicated how a system can be articulated. It is only now, after gathering all these facts within the more general frame of assigning a task, and especially the enabling of action, that the true bearing of our two examples becomes evident. The examples are certainly quite different: in the case of the flashback, the mandate concerns a demand for information and the competence concerns its management, whereas in that of the film-within-a-film, the mandate demands a deciphering of an event and the competence to perform a "reading." It follows in one case that the film exalts its internal resources, rendering them in a certain fashion responsible for what is re-lived, whereas in the other, the film dramatizes the reception, giving it credit in a certain fashion for what is shown.[25] At the same time, however, the two examples are perfectly complementary. Both involve submitting to the demands of a task (to show, to observe; to say, to hear) and the recognition of the necessity of a certain aptitude (the capacity to perform the task). In either case, there is the demand for an injunction to be given and a predisposition ratified.

This series of actions is indubitably rich with consequences. Once again, it is luminous in the film *Citizen Kane*. In a story constructed from different versions of the same events, it is essential to ask in whose name and by what right each account illustrates or interprets the facts (even if it is discovered that the enunciator's generosity in giving the capacity to speak or hear is only barely apparent and actually turns out to hide profound reluctance). The same type of series can be found in any number of films. Beyond the texts in which they are actualized, the narrative trajectories that we follow on the screen derive from the very logic by which a film constructs and offers itself.

In effect, this series shows the importance of competence: no one can act without the ability to act. Consider particularly the way in which flashbacks, even the most ordinary, bring out the need for a confession, recourse to the one who controls the memory, the privilege of having been a witness, etc., and the manner in which the film-within-a-film insists on the immediate fascination of the one who follows the spectacle, on her tastes, on the importance of her reactions. If an explicit origin or receiver of the information is present, that individual is shown to be capable of acting. It should be added that this faculty is structured as an obligation, an intention, a right, and a capacity to act; one is apt to complete a task when a duty, desire, ability, and know-how are involved.[26] This applies to the narrator and narratee insofar as they are either the bearer or addressee of a narrative encased within the narrative of the film, as well as to the enunciator and enunciatee, abstract instances which govern the film as such. What each case affirms is that "before" anything is done—even before the constitution and self-offering of the text—there is always a modal structure that defines the conditions of realization: that is, a duty, a will, a power, and a know-how without which one could not achieve the task in question. Consequently, the emission and reception acquire substance: from here on, we will remember all that they imply.

Now the series of actions illuminated above also shows that a great amount of work is dedicated to acquiring or attributing the premises of the action. Concerning the flashback, consider how slow memory is to return, and the search for reliable witnesses,[27] or, in the film-within-a-film, think of the rituals which lead a character to see, and the changes this provokes in her.[28] Most of these procedures aim for the acquisition of competence. This conquest, or surrender, can only have a single textual element as a protagonist: we see, then, a true self-nomination, by someone who is both mandatee and mandator. But because it is a question of a game between self and self or a relation among several selves, what counts is the assertion of a field of action. In an operation's development, there is always a moment when one assumes or even receives the ability to act. It is perhaps a moment dissimulated in the hollows of the diegesis, but it is nonetheless quite real. It is a moment that has behind it a competence to some degree acquired. Thus, the making—that is, the text's self-construction and self-offering—appears as a broken and discontinuous trajectory with a certain mobility of positions (anyone can, by turn, be either the addressor or addressee of a competence) and a certain superimposition of levels (a "pragmatic" level which concerns the fact of acting upon things, and a "cognitive" level which determines the conditions of the possibility of acting).[29] The acts of emission and reception expand: after we have unveiled their premises, they are revealed in all their complexity.

Our panorama is now complete, at least provisionally. A mandate that installs and qualifies a subject, a competence that is both a preliminary condition and a participant in the game, procedures of emission and reception that show all their richness: such are the key points brought to light by our analyses. And considered under this angle, the film-within-a-film and the flashback are highly exemplary. Of course, these entail discourses enclosed within other discourses, "second-order" representations, but they also propose a schema of functioning that blankets the film as a whole. In other words, the way in which the life of a narrative is traversed, the moments needed for a voice to arise or for vision to take place, the strategies that weave around the presence of the narrator and narratee, all of this indicates that what counts for the framed text also counts for the framing text—counts in the strongest sense of the term. Our constructions draw a certain privilege in becoming the mirror of a vaster project: organized in a manner that reveals their secrets and puts them forth as emblems, they function as *models* of each film's "self-construction" and "self-offering." Not quite enunciated enunciations, but already more than reported enunciations, we might dub these, *simulated enunciations*.

Let us continue along our path and deepen the above investigation by analyzing a new filmic sequence, one which once again involves an interpellation and a subjective configuration (not superimposed this time but put in perspective, and thus not directly linked to either flashback or a moment of the film-within-a-film). In particular, the sequence presents yet another prominent point, this time in a negative fashion, the admission of indecision.

Performance and Sanction

Photographs fall one after the other, forming a pile upon a desk, seen from the perspective of he who drops them; a voice-over narration says: "No, this is not your ordinary story; no doubt about it." Such is the opening of *Chronicle of a Love Affair* (1950), Michelangelo Antonioni's first feature film.

Let us separate for a moment the scene's verbal and visual components and examine first the voice-over narration: "No, this is not your ordinary story." This commentary initiates the intrigue from outside the space of the scene and immediately signals the presence of a narrator within the film, someone engaged in the task of "presenting" a narrative, of situating or justifying it. However, in this case it is presented within a circumstance of doubt and even of a double incertitude. In effect, the phrase by means of which the narrator introduces himself suggests, "No, this is not my ordinary task." Here the negation carries the representation. In this case, the one placed at a distance is the cinematographic narrator whose voice-over introduces or punctuates neorealist films. Think in particular of Roberto Rossellini's *Paisan* (1946): a quasi-radiophonic presence,[30] the film's voice-over narration functions to filter and objectify narrative events and thus mark a moment of both participation and testimony. It suggests that a *we* is speaking, a subject who has directly experienced a collective event and provides an official version of it,[31] a conglomeration of the experiences of all the protagonists, at the same time a memory and an archive. The motivation for this voice "in the plural" clearly appears to be as follows: behind the voice is a veritable "social mandate"[32] which both controls and guarantees it; this mandate is an invitation which first institutes and qualifies the narrator as guide to the narrative, then as the site of History. The voice that opens *Chronicle of a Love Affair* claims a different status, one opposed to this type of task, this type of responsibility. On the one hand, at issue is a discourse "in the singular." The speaker— the boss of a private detective agency—speaks only on his own behalf and only with respect to a reality that concerns him specifically. This *I* in no way claims direct participation in the events he recounts nor provides a collective testimony; the speaker is content simply to comment confidentially upon what he observes. On the other hand, the events involved concern not a collective destiny but an individual one— involving a couple, at most. The object of investigation is nothing more than a detective's "case," a private and ordinary event, a simple adventure. The fact of being both singular and common clearly indicates that the film's terrain differs from that of neorealism: the story evoked is not History but a simple chronicle[33]—specifically, the chronicle of a love affair. The narrator's task is founded not on a social delegation but something more limited, a personal mandate.

Nevertheless, as we have seen, the hesitation is at least double: "No, this is not your ordinary story" might also mean "No, these conditions are not the ones under which I ordinarily operate." In effect, it lacks the presuppositions necessary for a narration, as is made clear by the sudden interjection of the phrase "no doubt about it." That is, it is missing that consciousness of the need for knowledge that would initiate a story by providing the clue to guide it to the end. What is "doubt" if not an awareness of the insufficiency of one's knowledge, an awareness that would motivate the accumulation of information to solve a mystery? If one paid close attention, this absence of knowledge is an enabling condition of the narration not only because it furnishes the themes of the narration, but still more because it prepares and supports its existence. It is precisely the consciousness of an absence that permits and even requires that one tell about it, as if to respond to a challenge or to conquer the fear of silence. The sudden filling of this void determines the depth of what one wishes and knows how to tell, and makes one directly announce the choices and tools needed to do so. Therefore, a "doubt" is an origin for the motivations and tools that permit the orchestration of a story. It is the background that enables a narrator to play his part. In short, it founds and nourishes a competence. In this sense, the invocation at a film's beginning of an always necessary, but here denied, lack of knowledge corresponds to the recognition of the lack that enables one to act. This lack is precisely what gives value to the obligation and the right to narration, the intention and capacity to tell. The voice that opens *Chronicle of a Love Affair*, recognizing the absence of this lack, exists in a state of the most complete ignorance: beyond having to perform an unaccustomed mandate, it also finds itself incapable of acting.

"No, this is not your ordinary story": yet somehow the story can be told. The simplest way to confront this task is to utilize all the resources of the craft. It is not coincidence that the head of the detective agency announces he has received an important check and that he asks his associate to assemble the elements of the dossier. He approaches the task at hand professionally, obeying a certain number of fixed rules. But there is another way to honor the contract, more subtle than a resort to simple routine. It involves simply acknowledging that one faces a true enigma and behaving not like someone who must tell a story but like someone who knows how to decipher an already existing intrigue. The narrator cedes place to a narratee, to someone who occupies the position of receiver: an exemplary "reader," or "spectator." It is precisely this second possibility which is chosen by *Chronicle of a Love Affair*. Let us take a closer look.

Such an ellipsis—in which the narrator, abandoning his role, is replaced by a narratee—occurs at two different levels. Above all, the narrative changes direction in an entirely characteristic fashion: what had passed for a commentary on (and which was external to) the narrative action swiftly becomes recognizable as the speech of someone who participates in the scene yet is not a true protagonist. In effect, beginning with the film's opening image, another voice is audible, one that asks for specifications and comments upon what has been said. The scene's second shot shows two men in discussion, making it evident that the first offscreen voice, what had seemed initially to be a narrator's commentary, is in fact only a response in a dialogue. We thus convert what had once seemed to control the representation into one of the representation's many constituents—converting an extra- or metadiegetic element into a diegetic one. The narrator becomes an ordinary character, far from the privilege of directing the narrative. The sole evidence of his capacity to incarnate an instance governing the game is in the authority with which he demands action of his partner, another detective at the agency. An alter ego of the enunciator, he holds the game in his hands only to the degree to which he transfers to others the mandate that he had received. Here is an act whose principal consequence is to provoke a behavior directly opposed to his own. In effect, no detective, any more than the one in our story, is trying to tell his own story; instead he tries to find out the story of others. He does not impose, he interrogates. He does not show, he spies. Moreover, the first phrases that he pronounces confirm this disposition. Facing the various photographs of the woman, the detective first asks "Where is she from?" and "What's her name?" Later he remarks, "In that case, you wouldn't say that it's the same." As much in an affirmative mode as in an interrogative one, the detective expresses the obsession characteristic of someone trying to decipher the world—including this textual world. That is, he confronts the problem of the *identity* of what faces him. His attempt to recognize immediately qualifies him as a narratee.

And from here, the detective, an authentic narratee, comes to dominate the entire action. Since he initiates the inquest, it is up to him to signal the actual beginning of the intrigue.[34]

Alongside narrative articulation, there is another manner of exhibiting this change of roles between narrator and narratee. If we consider what occurs at the level of strategies of enunciation, we note that the film's opening establishes a conflict between two opposed structures. The first is determined by speech: we noted above how in resorting to the voice-over, the film chose to operate in the mode of interpellation, displacing its own center of gravity onto the author of the interpellation. In this manner, the film conjugates itself, so to speak, in the first person. The second structure is linked to the image. Analyzing the visual register, the opening shot is a subjective configuration:[35] the scene is seen through a character who literally loans his eyes to the spectator, doubling the latter's position as observer and incarnating her fundamental status. The film, modeled on reception, is then conjugated in the second person. Speech/image, interpellation/subjective configuration, *I/you*: the split that occurs within the first shots of *Chronicle of a Love Affair* is now clear. Thanks to this split, the narrator, the *I* manifest in the voice-over, and the narratee, the *you* that filters the representation, seem to exist in a comfortable state of equilibrium.[36] But this situation has only one time frame: while the use of "first person" will not continue, and while the interpellation will remain an isolated fact, the subjective configuration will indeed return, and with it a representation that is constructed on the axis of *you*. The narratee will immediately gain from this predominance of one structure over the other. He will appear in the film in the guise of all those who play the role of observer within the fiction. And, following the evolution of the configurations which best serve him, the narratee will make himself known in a decisive manner.

Let us consider more closely this victory of the "second person." First, which characters acquire a subjective vision? If one excludes certain purely functional shots, meant to emphasize a fact or detail (as inserts, simple "responses" to other shots: the shot of Mathilde and the letter she writes, that of Enrico Fontana and the report in front of him, or again, those of the head of the detective agency and the photographs that he allows to drop)[37]—if one excludes these three typical passages, one finds true, stylistically marked subjective configurations only with the detective and the couple in love, Paola and Guido. These imply two types of characters: one whose profession is to search for indices, and those who live out an adventure that obliges them to put themselves in question. But—second question—are these subjective visions distinctive? In fact, the three characters listed above possess a rather strange gaze, one that perceives the contour of things without always grasping their profound significance.

Take, for instance, the detective. On the one hand, his inquest leads Paola and Guido once again to cross paths. This circumstance might appear banal, but without it these characters would not have met. It is thus the observer, at the margin of the scene, who throws them into each other's arms. On the other hand, the detective falls into the snare of what interests him. A formal procedure will clearly reveal his position: the subjective shots which involve him are usually semi-subjective, beginning with the object seen and ending by including the seeing subject within the frame, without a solution of continuity. In this kind of construction, the observer is no longer opposed to the observed, as in a shot/countershot structure, but is connected with it, to the point that the two exist literally side by side. This formal procedure recurs at the beginning of the inquest: first, the camera closely frames the interrogated character (the concierge of the lycée, the overseer at the tennis court, etc.); then it moves to include within the frame the individual who interrogates these characters. This is a surprising movement, given that the position of the first character leads one to believe that the second character exactly faces him and that to see this character would require a cut and a new framing. But the movement also clearly underlines that the two characters belong to the same universe, that they inhabit the same world. However, to be too close to something prevents one from understanding it fully. The final report of the detective is in this respect exemplary: his account of the affair—or of the narrative, if one prefers—demonstrates that what had seemed not to be an "ordinary story" was, in fact, little more than a banal romantic triangle—precisely "your ordinary story." At the same time, however, he fails to grasp the true relations or profound nature of the story. The paradox that the detective is led to occurs between two extremes: his furtive gaze produces what he expects to see, yet he fails to look beyond appearances and details, losing himself in an excess of familiarity and failing to achieve the final objective.

Paola and Guido follow a rather similar destiny: their gaze also produces the world they observe, but at the same time deprives this world of signification. On the one hand, analyzing the nature of the link that unites them, the two lovers, in effect, attribute an omnipotence to it; they invest it with their imagination or rather categorize it according to the paradigm of the imaginary. From this point of view, the system of subjective configurations that they utilize becomes very significant. For example, the moment in front of La Scala, when they find one another after many years, they are each framed from the point of view of the other, but in a long or extreme long shot, whereas a medium shot would have been more natural. The distance between the characters, artificially augmented, is psychological rather than physical in nature; it expresses a sentiment more than it represents a space. Likewise, during the charity sale, at the moment of the haute couture runway show, Paola sees Guido, in a subjective shot, dancing with a model, while Guido observes her, but not in a subjective shot. The absence of reciprocity between the two gazes signals a "passionate"[38] movement in the woman—and only in her—and in the occurrence, the apparition of jealousy. In the end, from his hotel room, Guido sees, in a subjective shot, Paola's car approach, here again without a subjective shot in response. This time, the man "suffers," finding in his situation a motif of anguish. But as the gaze of Paola and Guido gives life to the world that surrounds them, they nevertheless fail to correctly evaluate the facts. This is clear in the couple's inability to understand the reasons for the inquest: it is as if the blindness endures, the blindness they displayed when they witnessed, without comprehending, Giovanna's accident before their eyes in the cage of the elevator; the lovers believe that the inquest concerns the death of their friend rather than the conjugal fidelity of Paola. Again, a semi-subjective configuration best expresses the idea that characters can be so taken by what they see as to be unable to understand it fully. When, on the mezzanine of an apartment building that they have entered by chance, Paola declares to Guido that she detests her husband, the camera frames the staircase and elevator from a point of view that could easily be theirs; however a brusque panning movement belies this impression by reintegrating both characters into the image. Rather than existing in juxtaposition, the elevator and couple literally inhabit the same space; and the gaze of the characters, rather than defining the representation, is instead its prisoner.

What lesson might be drawn from this? The gaze, for the detective as well as for Paola and Guido, is revealed to be simultaneously attentive and lacunary, effective and impotent. The three characters see but never succeed in objectifying what they see. They successfully perceive the contour of things—even doing so with real passion—but they can never put them at a distance. In brief, they have the ability "to read" what happens, but they do not transform their "reading" into an autonomous and definitive narrative. Here lies the entire problem: the means for following the events of life very much exist, but not the capacity to completely define them. Confirming what we have already observed, the detective, Paola, and Guido, as perfect narratees, refuse in a sense to accept the tasks of a narrator. Another aspect of the question arises: as perfect narratees, these characters still need very much a supplementary turn in order to truly finish their part in the game. On the one hand, they suffer no lack of resources to assure them a real competence. This is especially clear with regard to the detective, who right away poses the question of the identity of the woman in the photographs—"Where is she from?" "What is her name?" "In that case, you wouldn't say that it's the same." His approach demonstrates the degree to which he feels both obliged and ready, determined and apt, to decipher the puzzle before him. In other words, from the beginning, the detective exhibits a duty and power, a will and knowledge to "read" a situation: he possesses all the qualities necessary to be a competent narrator.[39] Moreover, his questions and observations show how his competence predisposes him. He tries to characterize the woman (by taking an interest in the "type" or "genre" to which she belongs), to extract anything that allows him to identify her (by looking into details of her personal life), and to put in order events relating to her (by reflecting on the relations between her past and present).[40] In concrete terms, he makes clear that in order to accomplish his work, he must define his objectives, focus on them and follow them in their evolution: three spheres of action (corresponding to the recognition of a frame, the identification of a topic, and the organization of an intrigue, respectively)[41] that testify regarding his "aptitude" to understand what is presented to him.

All this concerning the detective applies also to the two lovers. They, too, are endowed with a duty, power, will, and knowledge to "read" the world. They, too, schematize things in order to comprehend them, searching for essences and differentiating components. But they do not, any more than does the detective, "finish" their work: they stop just before taking advantage of the trial in which they have been implicated. It is the reverse side of the coin. The detective, Paola, and Guido need something more in order to validate all that they have noted. They need a *sanction*[42] which would allow and give weight to a certain accomplishment of perception. In the end, their perception has failed, on the one hand because it has been insufficiently verbalized (the detective produces an incomplete account of the facts), and on the other, because it has slipped out of a real consciousness (Paola and Guido suspect the truth but dare not say it). This sanction would have truly aided our characters. Superposing on their interpretation an explicit judgment, positive or negative, it would have furnished the "readers" and their "reading" with precise reference points (a value system) and a point of anchorage (an approbation or condemnation to which to refer). Thus, the sanction would perform the function, for both the detective and for Paola and Guido, of a sort of permit or guarantee. It would evaluate the conformity of their behaviors and the appropriateness of their attitudes[43] by covering them, so to speak (even a disapproval would have been useful for them, because it would have inscribed them among the active participants in the game). In sum, it would have legitimated their presence and their performance by completing a trajectory that began with a specific mandate. But, just as with the mandate, the sanction can only reach those concerned through the intermediary of someone evaluating the action from outside—either another character[44] or themselves, provided that they be invested in a different role, that of judge and no longer that of judged. In other words, the sanction requires, in addition to its own pieces on the chessboard, an arbitrator surveying the game; in addition to subjects who act in a performance, a subject who approves or condemns their action through an epistemic judgment.[45] These are precisely the dimensions absent here. Again, the detective and the couple try to decipher events without knowing how to detach themselves and thus without truly knowing how to manage these events. They adopt a receptive attitude without marking, through perception, the indetermination of things, without identifying a true "source" of speech. They live their experience without being capable of judging it. As a result, they fail to finish their game: they open themselves to the world with their eyes and ears wide open, but remain prisoners of this very attitude. In short, the narratees remain narratees: even if their competence allows them to bring a permanent attention to the events, their inability to put into effect a sanction condemns them to a rather meager harvest, to blind activity, to continual wandering. The narratees remain narratees: proud and firm with regard to their position, yet deprived of the possibility of changing and of integrating into the grand chessboard of enunciative roles.

The diagram implied by *Chronicle of a Love Affair* is clear: this film proposes narrators who are uncertain and receding yet ready to call upon their professionalism, and narratees who are perfectly capable of acting yet incapable of bringing their action to a conclusion. This diagram is curious at first glance since it seems that hesitations and obstacles predominate. It is nevertheless highly symptomatic because it utilizes a certain number of blind spots in order to interrogate the narrative in depth and to propose an eventual line of conduct. A priori, the particular construction of *Chronicle of a Love Affair* forces us to recall what is necessary to a narrative. The one who tells the story and the one who hears it—as they are represented in the text, that is, as symbols of those who concretely manipulate things—must equally confront a mandate which serves as both investiture and qualification. They must acquire a competence assuring them a duty, power, will, and knowledge; they must complete a performance which, depending upon the case, is manifest as a "writing" or "reading"; they must submit to a sanction which will evaluate their work through either approbation or condemnation. These stages punctuate the processes of emission as much as those of reception installed by the text. But the particular construction of *Chronicle of a Love Affair* emphasizes more personal options. If considered in its ensemble, the film seems to advance the hypothesis—perhaps the utopia—of "pure" listening and observation. Faced with a storytelling that appears to be only the result of an ordinary craft (would the cinema exhibit its own nature as machine?), the strongest position is that of the spectator. The narratee claims the most reliable competence. The very absence of evaluation ultimately reinforces this attitude: the attention to the real, without the constraint of having to submit to a judgment, appears free of any finality, no longer measuring itself except in relation to itself in the form of an autarkic exercise. What is lost in certainty—since there is no room for a definitive truth—is gained in availability. "To read" becomes a practice without end, a voyage without destination, open to the provisional and the contingent, an action which benefits from no attestation but which is the sign of fatality and perpetual beginning. It is a strong symbol of the possibility of an in-depth search; the opening of a film (the director's first feature) with perhaps an allegorical weight.[46] "No, this is not your ordinary story": the narration, though necessary, may prove to be difficult, but it is in the reception where the true emotion lies. "No, this is not your ordinary story": we thus open our eyes and ears before the inevitable narrative. We are attentive to what appears: a decor ready to illuminate itself, the meeting of movements and objects, a world . . .

The Lying Image

An excellent example of the development of the moment of vision and hearing, as radical as that of *Chronicle of a Love Affair* but diametrically opposed in form, is without a doubt found in Alfred Hitchcock's *Stage Fright* (1950). In effect, like *Chronicle of a Love Affair* this film treats the spectator's activity itself as a theme of reflection and a narrative pretext; but while the former retains the idea of a diffuse and errant attention, of contact with a text with neither finality nor end, the latter seems to affirm the possibility of a fruitful investigation, of directly productive vision and hearing. We have the same fundamental obsession but with divergent responses. Let us consider *Stage Fright* more closely, and in particular the flashback which opens the film.

An automobile races at top speed through the streets of London. A young woman, Eve Gill, is at the wheel helping her fiancé escape from the police. At Eve's request, the young man relates what has happened to him; his account appears in flashback. He is at his place when Charlotte Inwood, a friend and well-known actress, arrives very upset, her clothes stained with blood. She has just killed her husband during an argument and is now seeking aid. Jonathan calms her and advises her to go to the theater for the evening performance as if nothing has happened. But as her bloodied dress poses a problem, he offers to go to her apartment to get some clean clothes. Though this is risky, Jonathan goes out of love for Charlotte. At Charlotte's, he steps over the husband's body, takes a dress from the wardrobe, and puts the room in disorder to create the impression of a burglary. The maid enters unexpectedly, surprising him, and he flees. Upon returning to his place and allowing Charlotte to change, Jonathan considers the situation in which he has placed himself and imagines that the police, identifying him as the killer, are now searching for him. Indeed, at that moment two police officers ring at the door. Thanks to a ruse, Jonathan escapes and goes to the Academy of Dramatic Art, where he knows that Eve, an aspiring actress, is having an audition. Jonathan asks Eve to hide him for a while in her father's house. And this is why they are attempting to leave London as quickly as possible, avoiding capture by the police.

Such is the flashback that begins *Stage Fright*. One easily discovers here the flashback's characteristic elements: an interpellation introduces a configuration with a subjective tendency (the dissolve accompanying the voice seems to say to the spectator: "Hey, you, are you paying attention to what is being shown you?" and opens an entire series of events, which are presented as if offered to vision and hearing, as if they wanted to be grasped, or even as if they were only there in order to be grasped),[47] a narrator present in the field addresses a narratee (Jonathan tells his adventure in first person[48] to Eve Gill who, with good reason, is anxious to listen). One narration is encased within another, with a "self-construction" and "self-offering" that imitate those of the entire discourse of images and sounds (Jonathan's narrative is only one of the elements composing the larger narrative of *Stage Fright*, but the manner in which the young man stages his own adventure and tells it to Eve likens him to the film's director, who relates things to the spectator). This sequence reproduces the structure and trajectory of our previous examples, except on one point: Jonathan is lying to Eve, and thus the images we are shown are false.

In some ways, this discovery constitutes the central point of *Stage Fright* and has received abundant commentary from critics. The explanations advanced are not always convincing. It is obvious, for example, that to justify the trap held out to Eve, and by implication to the film's viewer, we need to do more than invoke the supposed suggestiveness of an image which enables events without the least proof to pass as true.[49] Nor is it enough to note the actors' performance, an easy metaphor of the superimposition of appearance and reality common to all representation.[50] Rather, the falsification is brought about by means of certain textual procedures: it is the fruit of a split between two principles, one which serves to put in place a delegate of the enunciator, and another which tends to confine him to the role of a simple character within the story. Indeed, this deception takes root in the opposition between the fact of having someone speak in order to reflect the thought of the one managing the whole discourse ("He said such-and-such, and concerning this, I agree"), and the appearance of moments which speak only for themselves, under their own responsibility ("He said such-and-such, and it is he who said it"). Such a switch is common in daily conversation, and is by no means rare in literary works,[51] yet it is relatively unusual in film. Let us observe more closely the unfolding of this operation.

It seems that this flashback allows no doubt to hover over the figure of the narrator. Jonathan tells his own story exactly as the one telling *Stage Fright* would have done. The foundation of this convergence is a tacit mandate above all. The enunciator—scarcely manifest in the opening credits, the ideal place for affirming an *I*—hands the baton (so to speak) to the first character who enters the scene, as if wanting to make the character do his work. The enunciator asks him to take the floor and tell the genesis of the story. There is a parallelism between the different competences. The one who directs the film can do so because he has in hand all the threads of the intrigue.[52] Likewise, Jonathan can evoke what has happened because he has fully lived it. Knowledge of the situation, the fact of controlling it or having lived it, gives anyone holding the position of enunciator or narrator the right and faculty, the obligation and intention, to give his own version of the facts. There is also a resemblance of behaviors: the author of *Stage Fright*,[53] like the author of the confession, presents a carefully ordered narrative (at least in appearance) in the same way, characterized by the same environment and the same characters. Both are involved ultimately in the same endeavor that they accomplish by the same means toward the same goal. Lastly, there is an implicit sanction as well: the one guiding the film substantiates the demonstration of the one telling his own story, either by presenting tangible facts which confirm what is said (in the course of the narrative there will be a confirmation of the crime),[54] or by appropriating and further detailing what is told (during the flashback, we see certain things before Jonathan speaks of them, Charlotte's soiled dress for example, as well as things which Jonathan likely could not tell Eve about, such as the ambiguous way in which he explains his meeting with Charlotte).[55] The author of *Stage Fright* thus aids and abets the author of the confession. The four points of articulation—again, an unquestionably efficacious mandate, a unique competence in phase with a performance, and a punctual sanction—superimpose the trajectory of the enunciator and that of the narrator so that they exist in a state of close solidarity. The narrator is consequently endowed with a legitimacy equal to that of the enunciator and as such also acquires the same credibility. If the narrator can be the substitute and equal of the enunciator, then one can regard him with the same confidence.

Stage Fright, however, precisely through this flashback, pursues an unprecedented path that contradicts our conclusions. Eve is the protagonist of the trajectory. Immediately put in the position of narratee, she valorizes the fact of having been chosen as a confidant; she develops and enlarges her own field of attention to the point of discovering what has not been told to her. But let us follow her in her progress.

First, the young woman herself is given a mandate: the film has charged her with rendering a perceptible listening rather than with exposing facts. Moreover, one of her first lines ("Would it bore you to tell me what happened? I'd like to know") summarizes her assignment very well. She has been asked to give free rein to her curiosity and to assume the role of questioner.

Second, Eve proves that she possesses a competence that here concerns the reading of events more than their presentation in narrative form. The young woman is especially capable of identifying indices, of gathering confidences, following clues, presenting herself as witness; on the other hand, she is less endowed to give her own point of view. We see her first ready to find proof in favor of Jonathan (at risk of personal endangerment) and also ready to take advantage of her father's observations (which cause her to form new suspicions); she is led to trust appearances but is also capable of forcing other characters to reveal themselves. Her specialty is precisely to attend to what is going on around her. At the same time, we see her fail when she changes strategy and invents a story in the first person. Once she disguises herself as the maid Doris, not only does she stop seeing what happens around her because of her thick glasses, but she is instantly unmasked by her mother, who easily recognizes her disguise. And all the while, Hitchcock himself, in one of his habitual "signature" appearances, observes the situation with perplexity. In sum, Eve expresses her best self when she must, wants to, can, and knows how to observe the world and listen to its voices. By contrast, when, as an amateur actress, she adopts a disguise and tries to improvise a scene, she becomes symptomatically blind and destitute.

Third, the young woman also accomplishes actions—not to mention that, in a manner entirely congruent with the preceding observations, she discovers more than she plans. In effect, Eve is constantly searching for something. From the beginning, she searches for a confirmation of Jonathan's statements. She needs this to demonstrate without equivocation, and publicly, what she believes she knows. To accomplish this, the young woman decides to enter directly into the game in every possible manner: she poses as a young woman in need for Commissioner Smith, as a journalist for Nelly, and as Doris, Nelly's cousin, for Charlotte. This multiplication of identities, and proliferation of narratives, is dangerous for Eve. Not only do they force her into a more than suspect ubiquity (during the outdoor party she must succeed in being with Smith and Charlotte at the same time, causing each of them puzzlement), but most importantly, she risks losing all credibility (particularly with Smith, who already suspected her of being an amateur actress when they were first introduced and who believed she was playacting when she declared her love for him). The result of this confusion of roles is that Eve is obliged to change her object of research. She no longer searches for evidence that would exculpate Jonathan but for a verification of her own hypotheses. In short, the young woman feels the need to understand if she has understood well.[56] Now she will again put herself in the position of receiver, but this time with complete consciousness. From here on, she attempts to bring forth tangible proof and no longer to impose her own version of the facts. Then, following her father's counsel, she begins to blackmail Charlotte, thus forcing her to reveal herself. And above all, at the risk of her own life, she isolates herself with Jonathan and makes him confess what has really happened. Eve has favored attention and waiting (on the stage with Charlotte, she simply played the foil; in the theater's basement with Jonathan, she played the perfect confidant) but in return, she has seen the revelation of the truth.

Finally, the young woman is subject to a judgment, except that the verdict brought on her causes a reversal of the one that weighed on Jonathan. The film, in effect, rewards Eve (she withdraws with her new love, Commissioner Smith), and at the same time, it punishes her ex-fiancé (he, as narrator, who should have been the mirror and conscience of the representation, is crushed by the theater curtain, the tool of representation). In the end, the sanction has a double value and acts in an alternate manner.

At this point, Eve's trajectory is complete. Punctuated once again by a mandate, a competence, a performance, and a sanction, the paths it follows are nevertheless entirely different from Jonathan's. Hers is a trajectory that calls for a number of observations. Above all, it progressively contributes to clarifying the nature of the two protagonists. The young man, first appearing as a source of information, lives increasingly within the fiction as the action advances (his destiny is especially linked to Charlotte's, an actress's, even off the stage); whereas Eve, who dreams of being on the stage, discovers as the story unfolds the pleasure of investigation and deciphering (her life becomes especially confused with that of Smith, a professional detective). It is thus easy to recognize within these two characters an example of what the film's very title evokes—the universe of staging. To play a role means either to put on a costume and recite the lines of a text by heart, or to search for oneself through and under the simulacrum. From this point of view, Jonathan and Eve represent nothing other than these two aspects of the theater.[57] It is, however, quite legitimate to find in these two characters a more general polarity: the use of untruth on the one hand, a combination of what appears to be with what is not, and on the other hand, a confrontation with secrets, the conjunction of what is with what does not appear.[58] Jonathan attempts to make what never happened seem real, while Eve must painstakingly assemble facts obvious to no one that are nonetheless real. The young man's effort works precisely through deception, whereas that of the young woman revolves around hidden facts. It is exactly this polarity between a lie and a secret that gives the different trajectories their significance. And it is also this alternative which allows us to catch a glimpse of the grand categories according to which the film operates, the forms of knowledge that relate to one another, and the system of values to which they refer.

At the same time, Eve's trajectory also exemplifies the spectator's condition. It involves not only the assignment of a task, the fitting of a predisposition, and the promise of a reward, but also the fundamental positions of seeing and hearing: the belief in that which is proposed; the will to directly enter the diegesis; the fact of being simultaneously within the scene (on the screen) and in the movie theater, along with the disorientation this ubiquity causes; the alternation between hypotheses and refutations; the fact of being taken in by the action and feeling oneself threatened; the final conquest of comprehension, etc. In this sense, the young woman is the very prototype of the film's addressee. Moreover, Eve shows the terrain upon which she places herself. If, as suggested above, her destiny is to act around a secret, she asks each of her eventual partners to learn to build with what exists but cannot be seen. The correspondence between the work of the spectator and that of discovery and revelation is now obvious.[59] It is a matter of struggling against illusion and silence with the goal of linking essence and appearance, in order that there be full correspondence between what is and what appears to be.

Finally, Eve's trajectory reverses the hierarchy among the enunciative roles. While at the film's beginning the function of guide belongs to the narrator (reinforced at least in appearance by a correspondence with the enunciator), at the end, the narratee is the one who becomes essential in this regard (as an instrument of verification and research). In this optic, one could entirely read *Stage Fright* as an attempt to correct the opening flashback, not so much in its content as in its deep structure. A gaze capable, on its own, of focusing on the objects represented is progressively substituted for a construction which presupposes that an interpellation engenders at least a partial subjective configuration, and therefore, that the point of emission of speech determines its point of reception. It is, if you will, a sort of self-regulating attention. The key moment in this substitution is the moment when Eve understands that she loves Smith upon finding the piano on which he had played. Here the young woman's gaze does not obey exterior directives. Although it once again plays on memory, it no longer depends on the word of a narrator, as in the flashback. On the contrary, in choosing the object of her desire, the gaze manifests the autonomy and mastery of a desiring subject.[60] From this moment on, *Stage Fright* will no longer be ambiguous. The will to reconstruct the facts prevails over the official report, the pleasure of interpretation will take the upper hand over pure and simple declaration. And the narratee (that is, Eve, the one responsible for this new subjective configuration) will be able to render her sphere of action effective.

Here, the one who holds the place of spectator is the strongest. Her victory and the manner in which it is accomplished clearly indicate the difference between *Stage Fright* and *Chronicle of a Love Affair*. Aside from obvious differences of style, referents, and subject matter, there is a profound difference in enunciative apparatus. In Antonioni's film, too, the narratee is substituted for the narrator, but without any confrontation. There, the detective and the two lovers are not preoccupied with dominating the scene when they enter. No problem of precedence arises for them during their progress. In *Stage Fright*, on the contrary, Eve must literally struggle to become the narrative's only reference point. This explains the importance of the sanction administered to the narratee (missing from *Chronicle of a Love Affair*, the sanction is obvious, indeed spectacular, in *Stage Fright*: Jonathan is killed by the fall of the theater curtain and Eve begins a new life). This sanction confirms the idea of a confrontation by distributing rewards and penalties; it identifies who is wrong and who is right by choosing how to end the game. This positive identification attributed to a "reader" thus serves to establish a hierarchy among the different character traits and also to indicate which reconstruction of facts should be believed. Eve's observations emerge magnified and stamped with the seal of authenticity.

"To each his truth."[61] Thus, behind the victory of the narratee is the enunciator who sanctions the action. The one who directs the film, as if wanting to insist on the active function of the one who agrees to receive the images and sounds, recognizes her nature as interlocutor, and associates this individual with the steering of the text. Moreover, this co-responsibility traverses the entirety of *Stage Fright*. In fact, it is Eve who, with an explicit demand in the first sequence, gives Jonathan the mandate to narrate ("Would it bore you to tell me what happened?"). It is again Eve who in a precise report in the last sequence announces the judgment bearing on the young man ("You're crazy"). In short, the narratee is charged with the task of managing the discourse. Aligning the vision and hearing with her own, she becomes a sort of co-author.

"To each his truth." But recall that the narratee's victory has the effect of giving the impression that her version of reality is a faithful reflection. This means that a protocol for reading is progressively put in place throughout the course of the representation: it selects from among the different events, distributes certificates of sincerity or bad faith, verifies and guarantees. In short, it designates the truth of the text. Nevertheless, this very protocol is at first only one version of events among others. It draws its force from being the object of a sanction and thus the result of a transaction between the different partners. As such, beyond indicating what should be accepted or refused, this protocol shows that acceptance and refutation are the result of a precise operation of the text within its very core; beyond signaling the truth of the discourse, it shows that truth *is* a discourse. Eve illuminates well this dual aspect of things: the young woman discovers the secret (what is, but does not appear) as much by *defining* its truth—that is, establishing which appearances correspond to hidden essences—as by *determining* the truth through her maieutic activity, personally giving form

The Spectator's Journey 113

to latent appearances. In other words, Eve acts as narratee through both a *verification* and a *veridiction*.[62]

"To each his truth." This suggests, "It is this way because this is the way it seems legitimate to you," or "It is this way because this is the way the discourse makes it appear to you." Through this short circuit, the co-responsibility of someone attentive, the appearance of critical judgment, and the affirmation of a truth are articulated. One quickly suspects something lacking in this articulation. It is easy to think that being ready to receive confidences and a feeling of self-sufficiency can preclude even more radical stratagems (in this sense, *Chronicle of a Love Affair*'s prudence might be interpreted as a justified discretion, while the self-confidence of *Stage Fright* is almost a provocation of the paradox). We will return to these questions. For the time being though, we shall observe the progressive evolution of the one who occupies the position of spectator, this individual's manner of playing the game, and the weight of her participation. In short, we observe the fecundity of a trajectory. Henceforth, in all aspects, vision and hearing constitute a true treasure.

Verification, Veridiction, and Truth

Let us quickly recapitulate the various trajectories brought out in the analyses of *Citizen Kane, Chronicle of a Love Affair*, and *Stage Fright*. The flashback, the film-within-a-film, and in general, any moment where the film doubles itself, mimicking the process of its own formation and presentation, all display trajectories punctuated by a mandate, the acquisition of a competence, a performance, and finally the evaluation of an action. We witness the installation of a subject, this subject's acceptance of a task, an intention, a right, and capacity, and his or her passage to action and later to judgment. These stages pertain as much to the narrator as to the narratee, although they appear in different forms. In the case of the narrator the mandate functions as an invitation to propose a version of reality, while in that of the narratee it serves as an incitement to observe and hear. In the case of the narrator, competence serves to recover a narrative posture, while for the narratee it concerns a process of attention. The performance in the narrator's case has the status of a rendered account, while in the narratee's it assumes the form of a discovery. Then, in both cases, the sanction can pose as a final assessment, but according to the specificity of each journey. We thus have two parallel trajectories followed by a judgment on their development that pushes them to evaluate themselves in relation to one another. The text appears as a site of confrontation between two simultaneously distinct and specular lines, between the advancement of a proposition and its return toward interpretation, between persuasion and belief. And all of this occurs in a face-to-face encounter sometimes taking the form of a conflict, sometimes of an agreement. This polemico-contractual relation becomes decisive in defining the "truth" of a text. At least at first, the dominant or accepted version of events becomes the measure of reality, and the acceptance or, on the contrary, the refusal of this version establishes what is or is not.[63]

However, a text's "truth" also depends upon a second confrontation. Once a distinction is made between the trajectories of what we can call a subject and an anti-subject, we must distinguish further between the existence of two different levels within each journey. One level involves a push to action (the mandate) and an evaluation of its accomplishment (the sanction), and the other involves a deployment of the faculty to act (the competence) and where it is used (the performance). The first level, which, in a sense, boosts the discourse's "self-construction" and "self-offering," involves the cognitive dimension. The second level, entailing, by contrast, the establishment of a preparation and an action, involves the pragmatic dimension.[64] In the examples we have analyzed thus far, the cognitive level involved a privileged enunciator while the pragmatic level used an alternation between narrators and narratees. In other words, the moment of motivation (in French, *le faire faire*) and of ratification (*l'être être*) appear pertinent to the agent in the wings who directs the film as a whole, whereas the concrete preparation for action (*l'être faire*) as well as its effective realization (*le faire être*) lie in the hands of a character of limited responsibilities. But one could imagine different distributions according to a fixed schema in which each pole is able to accommodate different enunciative roles (figure 3):[65]

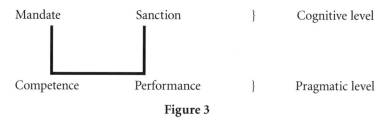

Figure 3

The most interesting cases tend to be, successively, those in which the cognitive level falls into the hands of the enunciatee, those in which the mandate and sanction are guided by a narrator or narratee, and those in which the pragmatic level is taken on by the one who controls the whole film.

The first case—which, remember, assigns the functions of mandatee and judge to the enunciatee rather than to the enunciator—entails a maximum displacement of the text's center of gravity. The very focus of the text's address is offered as the rationale and measure of the narratives that the characters either tell or filter through their gaze. Here the viewing of and listening to a film justify the discourse that is progressively elaborated. A typical example is the "open work"[66] whose interwoven voices and gazes can only be sorted out in reference to the one who later gathers together their traces. The different versions proposed by the text acquire their ultimate cause and motivation in the text's sole recipient. An extreme situation is documentary rushes, whose images lack a pre-determined mise-en-scène, but nonetheless are ready to impart meaning the moment they are "read." Consider cases of fortuitous filming which reveal an unexpected event or cases where a video camera installed in a bank can help solve a possible holdup. The space in which the event plays out is exclusively one of vision and hearing.

In the second case, the mandate and sanction are the concern of a narrator or narratee. Now it is possible to enlarge the domain of the simulated enunciation: a character not only produces or receives a discourse after preparing himself to do so, but proposes himself as the origin and measure of the narratives put into play. Such a character has the capacity to act—and does act—but, more importantly, he is also able to distribute tasks, rather than being limited to receiving the filmic propositions, and is able to give out judgments instead of simply accepting the judgments of someone else. This brings about a form of absolute objectivization of the enunciative frame: the life of a word or image is represented throughout its trajectory, from the moment it is solicited to the moment it is subjected to evaluation. Examples of this include framed flashbacks in which a character moves from simply relating an event to summoning other characters to serve as internal resources to his own discourse, and, generally speaking, any case of a "nested" narrative, in which a story begins only to encounter another story.[67]

Lastly, in the third case, the enunciator or enunciatee directly acts on the cognitive level as much as on the pragmatic. This introduces an apparent coherence among the different moments: the one directing the game or else the one to whom the game is addressed, besides preparing himself and acting accordingly, accepts responsibility and engages in a self-evaluation. From the wings, it is one and the same agent who emits a mandate, endows himself with a competence, enacts a performance, and expresses a sanction. At each instant the text constructs itself and, in doing so, defines its own necessity and appropriateness. The most obvious examples can perhaps be found in narratives based on direct recording.[68] In such cases, hypotheses and memories confided to the characters alone disappear. The narration proceeds exclusively on the basis of its own forces but at the same time behaves as if obeying an agreement made with itself and as if trying to distance its own mode of functioning in order to be able to judge it continually. In sum, the story moves on its own by discovering something absolute within itself ("this is the way things are, I am simply reporting them").

These three cases of course deserve an elaboration as well as a comparison to other possibilities. However, it should be clear that in the case of a substitution of roles, as well as in a multiplication of points of narration or an apparent linearity of narrative, there is always a gap between the cognitive moment and the pragmatic. Even when the text seems to justify itself, as in the third case, there is still a slight but precise line of division between the phase of motivation and judgment and one of realization. Though they may be superimposed, the motivations of the staging (its ideology and legitimacy) and the particular forms that it assumes (its structure and strategy) can always be differentiated. It is precisely the intersection of these two levels—whether slightly intermixed or profoundly diffracted—which enables a text to reveal itself in depth. With all the cleverness and experience of its own process of realization, it is by binding or unbinding the initiating intentions and paradigms of reference that a film brings out its own truth.

Now there is a confrontation between the versions of the subject and the anti-subject and between the pragmatic and the cognitive levels. This double face-to-face allows the text to define its range of choices and solutions, the nature of its own commitments, and the manner in which it wants us to approach them. In short, the text aims to define the appropriate criteria and solutions. Moreover, this face-to-face encounter suggests that when considering the truth *of* a discourse one must think of truth *as* a discourse. This is a truth presented, in effect, as a play on differences among various chess games, as the effect of something said and something received, of a demonstration and an observation, as something to be constructed step by step, a perspicacious mise-en-scène. Again, more than simply verification (where we define what is "true" in a text), a veridiction is also at work (where the "truth" is determined by the text itself).

Nevertheless, within this ensemble of operations the essential pivot remains the point toward which the images and sounds are destined. The contribution this point makes is not limited to a simple act of presence. Insofar as it corresponds to the narratee's tendency to enter into the scene, it reveals something much more profound. Briefly, the importance of the point toward which, ideally, the entire text is addressed is that—by law more than by fact—it is a point of resistance and control: a point of resistance because it can always produce a proposition that would superpose on the proposition of the enunciator and narrator; a point of control because the enunciatee and narratee can always involve themselves in cognitive operations by manipulating the mandates and sanctions. In other words, the film's addressee represents, on the one hand, a necessary confrontation with the text's proposed version of facts (a version constantly waiting for confirmation and completion),[69] while on the other, it serves as instigator and examiner of the entire operation (a "*sub judice*" operation of a sort that the manipulation never becomes persuasion).[70] Ultimately, the film needs a spectator as much because the facts it presents require supplement as because its progression requires continual motivation and reception.

The second point, however, is especially decisive. The narratee, at the level of the diegesis, and the enunciatee, at the level of the global mise-en-scène, are capable of directly controlling a mandate and a sanction. In this context, while perhaps somewhat atypical, the case of the "open work," absolutely inclined toward a *you*, displays the processes present in any text. This permits the narratee and enunciatee to reclaim an active role (promoting their status to that of initiators rather than delegates, judges rather than judged), but it also modifies their profile. The narratee and enunciatee, by becoming signatories of a pact and guarantors of recognition,[71] assume the typical position of addressor rather than that of addressee; by intervening, they qualify as an origin rather than as an end. This is most evident in the sanction. At the very moment when the enunciatee or narratee inscribes the propositions of the enunciator or narrator in their axiological field[72]—and this is exactly what happens in the act of evaluation—they also "hand out" judgment on an aptitude, "decide" on a particular orientation, and "say" whether or not they accept what is proposed to them.

Moreover, when implicated in a sanction, the enunciator and narrator undergo a partial change of identity and become addressees. In effect, the evaluation is always introduced through an interpretation (just as it is followed by a restitution, the mechanism comprising three elements: successively, an interpretation, an evaluation, and a restitution).[73] This means that even before the declaration of a verdict and the attribution of a reward or penalty, an attention is engaged so that the one implicated in the initial phase of judgment behaves like a reader or an observer.

In sum, there is some receptivity in the one who offers her opinion and some appreciation in the one who opens her eyes and ears. We encountered this reversibility of attitudes at the beginning of our analysis, when we saw the subject of the enunciation exposed to division, and the *you* born from the projection of an *I*. We will measure its entire scope now that we have caught the enunciator's transformation from addressor to addressee, and the transformation of the enunciatee from a mere point of observation and hearing to a possible source of images and sounds. A shuffling such as this allows, a posteriori, a specification of the nature of the spectator constructed within the film. After having identified this spectator as a more or less marked presence, and then as a place of experience and knowledge, we now follow her through a trajectory with several stages. Each phase corresponds to a different distribution of elements where the one engaged is progressively assigned tasks. Considered from this angle, the spectator appears as a relatively stratified role whose fundamental function is to punctuate the text's development, to clarify its interstices, and to circumscribe its evolution, but whose attributes are divided among several levels and according to different circumstances. We have already seen this in action during at least three principal moments, first of all as an anti-subject, that is, someone who is able to elaborate a personal version of reality through what is proposed to her; more precisely, it is someone who succeeds in completing the suggestions of the enunciator by considering them a secret to which he has the key, or someone who succeeds in refuting his assertions by disguising them as lies. In short, it is a pragmatic and cognitive operator, either within the scene or from the wings, who filters and restructures the facts of the mise-en-scène. Second, as the protagonist of the interpretation, she allows each one's capacities of observation and hearing to become manifest and thus express themselves; in this sense, it is someone who occupies the same terrain as the enunciator, but only insofar as she illuminates either a will to impose upon the attention of others or an anticipation of what is to come. It is thus an operator who converts intentions (a will to say) into instruction (a duty to perform). Third, as a judge involved in an evaluation—and a restitution—she appraises the different tasks executed by relating them to the relevant original mandates and verifying their appropriateness and conformity. And from here, she pronounces a verdict and distributes rewards and punishments. Concretely, this individual is the "ferryman" of the most well-adapted information; here is an operator responsible for recognizing what is said, in a doubling of operations which guarantees quality.

The spectator designated by the film is thus all this at once: someone presented as a possible counter-proposition, someone who reconstructs the original version of the story, and someone who controls and guarantees something said. We have already seen the first two characteristics; the third completes and motivates them. Considered together, it is because of such aptitudes that the spectator can "close" a representation by redistributing the criteria of truth and relating it to a precise system. Thanks to this plural series of avatars the spectator is able to be the basis of a verification and participate in a veridiction.

Nonetheless, such work by no means exhausts the ensemble of its benefit. Although institutionally the spectator has the last word, something escapes him, or better, escapes the very logic of the game, no matter who the participants might be. The few extracts from the films analyzed above are enough to confirm this. In the flashback of *Stage Fright*, for instance, Eve sees more than what Jonathan tells her yet still does not see what is most important; moreover, Jonathan lets his imagination get the best of him when he mistakenly interprets a harmless ring of the telephone as a sign that the police are pursuing him; soon after, Eve's father warns her not to accept things at face value yet at the same time helps her search for proof which, on the contrary, would exculpate the assassin; later the film inexcusably delays the proof of Jonathan's culpability by handing Inspector Smith information that he could have obtained much earlier, etc. In *Chronicle of a Love Affair*, the detective as well as Paula and Guido also see what is not there, but the couple, in particular, draws no conclusions concerning it. The lovers' constitutional indecision corresponds to the fundamentally random aspect of events, as if their course were entirely capricious. Finally, in *Citizen Kane*, the newsreel *News on the March*, just like Thatcher's diary, shows the sled, "Rosebud," which constitutes Kane's secret, but in a manner never made explicit.[74] Kane also pronounces his last word in the solitude of agony yet everyone is nonetheless aware of it. Lastly, the film's closing sequence shows the burning sled, its name visible, and at the same time suggests that this is not the single piece missing from the puzzle, but that, on the contrary, there is perhaps no mystery at all behind this.[75] Ultimately, all these films, more than it might appear, are full of absent-minded or dissatisfied narratees who let go of the story's thread, and of ridiculed enunciatees who see themselves deprived of a goal. But there are also numerous unconscious narrators who repeat things that have no meaning for them and maladroit enunciators who also make use of these inconsistencies. Considered from this angle, the game's logic truly seems to disappear.

What might one conclude? Let us return momentarily to a concept that so far has functioned in the background, the concept of simulated enunciation. The metalinguistic moments around which our analysis has turned—flashbacks, the film-within-a-film, etc.—have an undeniable utility. On the one hand, they illuminate a film's constitutive mechanisms, its conditions of existence: without leaving the level of the story, they show the work behind the discourse. On the other hand, through an extension which is both a hypothesis and a demand, these moments try to emphasize these indications even during the moment when the film departs from itself and appears on the concrete terrain of interaction; by representing individuals engaged in a face-to-face encounter, they suggest the practical uses of images and sounds. The benefits obtained from this extension of the field are considerable. In effect, a text links up with a context in two principal ways.[76] One is through deictics, which involves a return to the situation in which the discourse occurs. The other is by means of reflexivity, which entails an explanation of the discourse according to its own behavior. Our examples tend to exploit the second solution. By reviewing the instances that inhabit it (where the procedures at work are revealed) and by literally incarnating them (the roles become actual figures, "living" characters), the film, in one movement, reflects on its own forces and destiny. Here simulation functions beneficially. It constitutes an attempt to either render an origin fully present or to completely delimit an end. And the

The Spectator's Journey 121

journey involved—from a mandate to a competence, from a perform-ance to a sanction—illustrates at times the paths that lead a text to be what it is (let us call them the enunciation's lines of force), and at oth-ers, the acts in which it is concretely held (the practices of communi-cation).

It is precisely this double reference and its presentation that exposes the game to uncertainty and indetermination. This strong moment, in its very mode of actualization, reveals a fundamental weakness. What are, in effect, the implications of simulation, and in particular, of a simulation like ours that functions so openly? The restoration in the énoncé of that which constitutes its presupposition and its effects causes confusion between imitator and imitated. In effect, the concen-tration within the scene of what, by nature, is held behind the wings or in front of the screen begins to abolish the very notion of distance; reducing to the pure present that which in itself was, or will be, encour-ages the effacement of punctuation and perspective. Recession and ex-tension are then flattened onto the same surface; memory and foresight are absorbed into the present.[77] Nevertheless the differences—these dif-ferences—become irreducible: an énoncé can exhibit its presupposi-tions but, once these are inscribed within the text, they can claim in turn other presuppositions as a condition of their representation; like-wise, an énoncé can render visible its own effects, but once exposed, they will open a new path to the usage of that which is again proposed. And thus, a "here" and a "beyond," a "before" and an "after" are intrin-sically necessary.

Again, this all applies in the context of enunciation. While the film attempts to say everything it has to say ultimately by joining, as here, the path of reflexivity to that of exemplarity,[78] the constitutive princi-ple of the declaration will nevertheless remain undeclared. The same applies from the point of view of communication. The film tries to see beyond its own limits by representing the various ways in which it might be utilized, but the representation of a behavior can never re-place a concrete interaction. In sum, the simulation approaches the terms of reference, has them converge in its own space, but at the same time sees these terms continually slip away. Here the misunderstand-ings and defeats noted in our examples find their rationale. At the very heart of the text, wanting to stage the origin of the representation as well as its finality, the trajectories characterized by deviations and ob-structions seem inclined to underline motivations of inexpressibility and incompatibility, the inevitability of silence and chance. Perhaps out of prudence, or a desire for clarity so extreme as to integrate to the point of contradiction, the typical itinerary takes shape, all the while signaling its probable unfeasibility.

One can apply this lesson perfectly to processes of vision and hearing. On the one hand, our film examples imply a spectator ready to fill in the gaps of the diegesis, to reexamine what is proposed to her (and eventually to correct it) and ready to anticipate the succession of events (what then gives them a character of necessity). On the other hand, our examples suggest that this spectator who controls the game—sometimes more successfully than others—can nevertheless be led to lose. Mistakes, mirages, and blindness are only symptoms of such a threat.

But above all, we can apply the lesson to what the spectator's actions directly define—the truth of a text. This is where we encounter the function of verification and procedures of veridiction, the display of their decisive aspect, the specification of the game to which the enunciatee and narratee, the enunciator and narrator will adhere. Involved here are simultaneously the disintegration of the limits of the construction, the opening of unforeseen voids, and the emergence of uncertainty. We can do nothing but conclude with questions. Is the "truth" of a text a complete proposition or a mix of predeterminations and chance whose appraisal is possible only through indices? Even more radically, is the "truth" of a text established through the forces of the text itself, or is it something that cannot be reduced to either a skillful manoeuvre or a well-played game?

5 At an Opening

Overview

The systematic examination in the preceding pages of certain of the cinema's most characteristic features—from the look into the camera to subjective configuration, from the flashback to film-within-a-film—has allowed the progressive illumination of the variety of ways in which a film's implied spectator is constructed. The rhythm of this undertaking has perhaps appeared rather obsessional, given the frequent steps backward, the perpetual process of revision, the evident taste for reconsideration and elaboration. Now, however, it is possible to take a different stance and sketch an overview illuminating the paths we have followed and their points of articulation.

Our analyses have revolved around three themes recurrent in film theory: that a film somehow indicates the presence of its spectator, that it assigns this spectator a precise place, and finally, that the spectator must complete a genuine trajectory. These themes, often employed as simple metaphors, actually synthesize rather well the fact that the text is not only the result of a process but is a veritable drill ground. That is, the text is something we can directly interrogate in order to identify the elements in play, their relative importance, and how they interact with one another. What applies to the text's producer also holds for the text's addressee, who function as both the site where the whole ensemble of signs takes form and the site toward which this ensemble is aimed. It appears on the screen, as on a blank page, or canvas: exhibited, modeled, worked upon. This is why we are concerned with the emergence within the film itself of an overarching point of view, beyond that of the film's "self-construction" and "self-offering," a sort of *you* toward which the images and sounds converge. It is also why we have explored the different forms this point of view assumes—actual sample configurations, resulting from a series of judicious interactions with the other components of the process. Finally, it is why we have investigated the operations by means of which such a point of view is asserted—complex strategies, often directly illustrated within the story.

Above all, we find decisive procedures surrounding each point of articulation: our first round of analyses, concerning emergences, allowed an investigation of the process of figurativization by means of which an abstract instance (a film's implicit *you*) becomes manifest within the visual field. The second round of analyses, dealing with forms, enabled a clarification of the processes of aspectualization by which the represented space and time reproduce the model of their ideal destination. And finally, the third and final set of analyses, involving maneuvers, permitted emphasis on the processes of modalization according to which the act of reception proposed by the text expands and connects with a duty, a will, a power, a knowledge, having someone do something, doing something, etc. Moreover, the very existence of such procedures has helped us better to articulate the problem's different aspects. Figurativization, while confirming the embodiment of the "spectatorial" moment, also allows a clear distinction between the purely implicit elements (the enunciatees) and their eventual incarnations in certain characters (the narratees). In much the same way, it enables a distinction between characters who assume, throughout, the function of a point of arrival for the images and sounds (the extra-diegetic narratees) and characters who, while engaged in vision and hearing, do not really represent the point toward which the film reaches (the diegetic narratees). Aspectualization, though it accounts for giving form to space-time, also leads to a juxtaposition of different portraits: the hidden spectator in the objective configuration, a simple witness to what happens; the mobile spectator in the impossible objective configuration, perfectly aligned with the camera; the spectator "in the margin" characteristic of an instance of interpellation, reduced to a sort of "aside"; and the diegetic spectator in the subjective configuration, bearing the traits of one of the protagonists within the fiction. Modalization, finally, while justifying the trajectories that define an act of reception, allows the isolation of certain distinct phases: the assignment of a spectatorial task (a mandate), a predisposition for the task's accomplishment (a competence), a concrete realization of the task (a performance), and finally, an evaluation of the results (a sanction).

Thus our panorama has become progressively enriched. And parallel to this articulation, through degrees, portraits, and phases, the identity of the spectator has grown in complexity. In effect, the point toward which the film claims to aim its address is first manifest through particular, more or less important, more or less explicit appeals (a sign of complicity, a confidential message, a symptomatic gesture). It soon appears in the very layout of the representation (the intersection of a gaze and a scene allows a "reading" of the effects each has upon the other). Finally, it will be told in an exemplary story (the mandate, competence, performance, and sanction constitute a basic narrative schema which, as we have seen, is often illustrated quite literally).

The result has been both a progressive discovery of the various aspects of the film's implied spectator and a recognition of the extent of this spectator's influence. In sum, we have surveyed an array of costumings, while at the same time measuring their impact and basic character. Without question the point of view summoned to gather the images and sounds, the *you* evoked on the screen, has been revealed throughout the course of our research just as it had appeared initially— that is, on one hand, as an antagonist of the *I*, who functions as the game's master, a negative image of the one producing the mise-en-scène, and on the other, as a site where a re-examination of the representation and the represented can occur, a place where the *I* can see itself seeing. But if the spectatorial moment, such as the film circumscribes it, always turns upon this double reality, it is also true that it can evolve as a function of situations, investing in a variety of cinematographic procedures, opening onto an entire range of possibilities. In short, it can develop its own motivations and strategies. Thus, the themes identified earlier—that the text opens itself to a spectator's *presence*, that it gives to this spectator a well-defined *place* and requires that this spectator accomplish a true *journey*—no longer appear as simple metaphors but rather as parameters that enable an appreciation of the film's "self-offering" to vision and hearing. They are, if you will, "units of measure" to be added to those previously proposed in other domains, for example by Dubois (distance, transparency, and tension),[1] by Benveniste,[2] by Genette,[3] etc.

We have an outline here of the frame in which we have conducted our research, without omitting its foundations and limits. It is important to recall that our analyses have always relied upon the concept of enunciation as a point of anchorage: a gesture which gives life to a film as such, a moment when cinematic virtuality converts into concrete realization, enunciation has been the basis of each of our reflections. Everything else has necessarily followed. It is precisely in enunciation that the film's "self-construction" and "self-offering" enter into play. It is in enunciation that a subject is unveiled (someone appropriates a language), and that individuals articulate relations among themselves (the appropriation of language introduces a distinction between an *I*, a *you*, a *he*, or a *she*).[4] In this sense, the construction of a discourse and assertion of a destination—or, if one prefers, the deployment of a mise-en-scène and advancement of a proposition—are two actions that are truly of a pair.[5] No analysis of the spectator can begin until that moment when the film literally takes form. Filling the screen with its presence, this surface soon offers itself to eyes and ears charged with perceiving the images and sounds.

Such premises, however, are somewhat paradoxical in relation to the theme of our research. The *you* that is constituted in the very construction of the filmic discourse is, in effect, the prisoner of a double constraint. On the one hand, it is clearly distinct from what is represented: it is one of the representation's principles of organization, one of its fundamental coordinates. Indeed, this implied *you* constitutes one of the measures of the representation. And yet, it continually attempts to become part of what, in fact, one would expect it to master. This occurs not only because the gaze which carries the *you* is always and exclusively revealed within the diegesis, but also because such a gaze readily becomes a form of action, a moment in the diegesis, a gesture represented in the behavior of a character. Ultimately, what should in itself be simply a presupposition comes to share the space of its own posture, either because it is reflected there or because it traverses it. Nonetheless, this *you* affirmed by the film can foresee something that ultimately escapes the film, that is, the capture of the images and sounds by a flesh-and-blood human being. In the end, the target toward which the filmic discourse aims, and which it directly posits through the very fact of its own existence, lies outside its scope. Existing beyond the screen, the target is much more than a simple expectation. Left as a mere enunciative role, this *you* will never become that which would make it complete, a body.

And so, by its very status, a film's destination can be expected to work with two limits: on the one hand, the limit separating a presupposition from a position, an enunciation from an énoncé, and on the other, the limit separating a should-be reality from a factual one, enunciation from communication. Moreover, it is not a coincidence that in the course of our analysis we have sometimes attended to the merging of commentary into narrative, in asserting the representation's "natu-ralness" and "transparency," and sometimes to the intervention of a radical offscreen space, in separating the eye and the view. As a result, the subject we have called the enunciatee, that serves as the pivot for the film's "self-offering" to vision and hearing, finds its field of action per-petually threatened. Situated between an overbearing presence, some-thing so close that it both reveals and masks, and a dangerous absence, something so far that it is out of control and whose anchorage is left to chance, the enunciatee can work only at the margin of the process. Its existence is qualitatively residual.

This is especially true if one considers the kind of relation that an enunciatee holds with its own correspondent, the enunciator. In ef-fect, the enunciator places the enunciatee at the very moment that it is placed itself, thanks to a division that allows the construction of an anti-subject. In order to objectify itself as well as its manner of acting, it shows up each time that it searches to see itself seeing and thus dis-cover itself through the eyes of an other.[6] It is not by chance that we began with interpellation—that is, with a moment when the *I*, turning outward, tries to pass to the other side of the screen and interact with someone who is certainly facing it, but who also seems to be respond-ing to an implicit invitation; the moment when the one controlling the process creates his own interlocutor, in a gesture of complete self-assertion. Likewise, it is not by chance that we conclude with a discus-sion of the sanction—that is, the moment when the enunciator faces different versions of the facts and compares them with his or her own, a moment when the one controlling the process appropriates the énoncé and all its conditions of existence, but only after submitting to a judg-ment like anyone else. These two stages clearly display the reversible and complementary aspects of the enunciative roles: it is only in the face-to-face encounter that subjects can constitute themselves as such. This causes the film's internal addressee, the *you* who underlies the im-ages and sounds, to work not only at the text's margins, but at the in-terior of a clearly differential structure. The *you* appears as someone in hiding.

Marginality and difference: these characteristics that we have so in-sisted upon, and which seem to confirm a sort of weakness or *fading* of the film's implied spectator, are indicators of strength as well, as we will soon see.

An Interface

In examining the development of the film's internal address, we spoke of a kind of double limit, one involving a slight demarcation that separates and nullifies, but at the same time makes contact and allows a passage. In effect, the "self-offering" of the images and sounds is always both an element represented in one fashion or another and a measure of the representation, just as it is both a textual coordinate and the indication of its eventual usage. The expanse of this sort of no-man's-land then develops parallel to other more peopled zones. That is, the *you* posited by the film—a *you* constantly threatened by the disappearance of its own space—characteristically functions as a place of mediation between a text's content and the use made of such a content, between a staged universe and its destiny, between a diegesis and its reception. Appearing on both sides, this *you* can observe them both simultaneously and measure each in relation to the other. In other words, because it is implicated on both borders, straddling the two different spaces, this *you* can function as a point of articulation between the ensemble of a text's meanings and its frame of interaction. It operates, if you will, between a semantic structure (into which it runs the risk of being utterly absorbed) and a relational structure (which the *you* itself puts in motion even at the risk of seeing it slip away).[7] Consider here that the *you* posited by the film, as with any other enunciative element, serves as an actual *interface* between the world represented on the screen and the world in which the screen is nothing but one object among many.

An interface then—using this term literally, we are dealing with a device that allows a particular coordination of the functions of two machines: on one hand, the organization of the signifieds, and on the other, the dynamics of their reception. We have here both a filter and an extension: something which puts in perspective the universe of discourse with a system of instructions, and a system of instructions with the concrete space of reading, allowing a passage from the former to the latter and vice versa. Moreover, this is a real passage rather than a simple juxtaposition, as a number of analyses that fail to acknowledge the operation's complexity might suggest. There are, for example, investigations of a film's outcome or spectatorial effect that posit a communication between what is represented and the recipient of the representation that is so direct and precise, it becomes impossible to grasp the potential problems involved.[8] Consider also naive utilizations of notions of identification and projection in which what is seen and the one who sees are thought to be superimposed by a spontaneous automatism, as it were.[9] The same tendency toward simplification is evident even in far more elaborate works, such as Sorlin's idea of the visible,[10] Odin's notion of institution,[11] or Metz's concept of the apparatus, all of which propose that the confrontation between content and the reality outside the text occurs always between two partners.[12] All the same, these works advance the hypothesis—or at least acknowledge the necessity—of a "translation" from one fact to another; the analysis of the enunciative components attempted here subscribes to this perspective and attempts to bring out all its consequences. By virtue of this fact, facing two realities whose interconnection is not obvious—signifieds on the one hand, and behaviors on the other—our analysis must insist on the existence of a space expressly destined to be a space of mediation. It proposes a double confrontation where one alone has proven insufficient.

Hence an interface. Both punctuating what is told and preparing entry into the field of the one who will be told, this component entails a specific weakness: it can lose itself and become absorbed in pure representation just as it can lose the one who appropriates the representation. Nevertheless, its capacity to orient the images and sounds by constantly accompanying their appearance, its capacity to anticipate the point of arrival by somehow prefiguring it, and particularly its capacity to do both of these at the same time, compensate for the ambiguity of the interface. Its capacities transform a weakness into a genuine strength.

It is on the positive character of the interface that I would like to conclude, indicating, however briefly, two possible directions of research. The first concerns *interpretation*. We underlined at the beginning of our work an opposition between an interpretive model and a generative one, choosing the second as our point of departure. Though it may seem odd to salvage now the very model that we had set aside initially, the conclusions we have come to thus far justify such a decision. In effect, the idea of a mediation allows an in-depth examination of the relations between the film and the moment of its "reading," both because it exposes the fact that there is a spectator within the gaps of the images and sounds who evolves simultaneously with them, and because it enables the hypotheses advanced by the text to achieve a realization, attaches them to a concrete space, and submits them to a personal, even unique verification. In other words, for at least two reasons, the presence of an interface legitimizes and gives substance to the problem of reappropriation that the film encounters. First of all, this presence is a reminder that each text, in its gesture of self-offering, undertakes a precise task. It orients itself toward an interlocutor, moves toward a future, in short, constructs its own approach toward its other. This involves not only an indication of its own limits, but again, an attempt to exceed these limits. Secondly, the interface also satisfies a demand. By situating itself between the énoncé and the act of communication, between the figurativization of the enunciative roles and the intervention of actual bodies, it allows the first engagement, as marked in the generative model, to find an outlet. Certainly the space it proposes is still marked by separation. It is an unattainable out-of-field that opens up before the one who interpellates. In the subjective configuration, this space is the counterfield separating the eye from what it sees. In the flashback, it is the space of the unseen and unheard which comes back to the narratee. But the space proposed by the interface is also marked by its practicability and richness. As proposed above, it is the space of both a support and a reserve. And in this way, it is a space in which the orientations of the initial project are made concrete. Placing itself before a new perspective, the project, once formulated, finds its own conclusion and adapts itself to new interactions. From this point of view, the text's other, ungraspable by definition, constitutes an essential point of meeting. It is, if you will, a home in which to dwell (the hypothetical *you* becomes a factual *you*) and a surface from which to spring (once seized, the *you* can become *I*).

This double maneuver by the interface fulfills all the conditions of an interpretive approach. On the one hand, the text can be approached from its interior: on the basis of what is represented, one can bring out the text's instructions, the signs which punctuate it, in short, the keys with which it is endowed.[13] On the other hand, the text can be confronted from the exterior: by recognizing its efforts to transcend its limits, we can confront the text in the space which opens before it, an inexhaustible and fleeting space, but also a place of rest (the body as support), of nutrition (the body as reserve), and of anchorage as much as departure. It is entirely possible to accomplish these two trajectories—from inside to outside, and vice versa—in perfect synchrony; in effect, they are perfectly complementary. Moreover, the function of any interface is to ensure a double transitivity. What we get then is a reappropriation of the text that disallows any removals as well as any abusive additions. It is both a search for a mythic center, and the projection of signifieds onto signs which in fact are empty; any idea of plenitude is opposed by the weight of alterity, and any idea of silence by the weight of the word. This is a reappropriation that knows how to make the discourse's self-reflexiveness interact with the world of life, concrete action and all that determines it, through purely symbolic strategies. All this occurs as a result of inevitably provisional meetings, made cautiously, and under precise control.[14] It is designed to obtain a true articulation of the film's construction with its lines of force—and also of the theoretical frame at work here, with its own tangents and out-of-field.[15]

The second path introduced by the notion of interface relates directly to the first. In theorizing how a text offers itself to a spectator hidden within its lines, our research has attempted to bring out a film's "conditions of visibility." We have tried to describe the general mechanisms whereby images and sounds appear as realities already endowed with a destination. And here, our use of a number of examples has been quite revealing. The recall of a given film or sequence has served above all to clarify principles of functioning. Whether a concrete analysis serves to stimulate the discussion or ultimately to confirm the initial hypothesis, what emerges are still fundamental procedures, both common and widely applicable. However, we might have chosen a different approach. Rather than concentrating on the functioning of the text as such, we could have beheld it in its singularity; rather than delineating its typical features we could have emphasized its distinctiveness. To do this would simply involve focusing on a given film's awareness that it acts within a precise time and space, analyzing how the film integrates the idea that the spectator is after all part of a specific public, and taking note of the address foreseen in light of the address realized. In short, it would mean systematically superimposing the effective spectator upon the ideal spectator, verifying what is already effective in the former, and the ideal qualities residing in the latter. Moreover, it is the very idea of an interface that permits such an operation. It proves that this is not a simple operation of addition or alternation, but rather the logical continuation of a single journey. Beyond the conditions of visibility of a film, what emerges here is a *history of vision* in which the cinema has played a crucial role.

A history such as this would allow us to better articulate our corpus. Of course, all of the examples cited above belong, at times rather provocatively so,[16] to an ensemble often designated as the "narrative/representational/industrial" cinema.[17] They all tend to tell a story, represent "real" life, and adhere to the logic of commercial cinema. At the same time, however, this ensemble, which comprises a variety of relatively distinct domains, is by no means a unified whole, separate from avant-garde cinema, scientific-industrial cinema, amateur cinema, and so on.[18] Here an analysis of vision might help us to delineate the contours of the ensemble, which has been—and remains—dominant. It would reveal the internal articulations of these films as well as their rivalries with alternative stylistic systems, the different projects which guide them, and the dynamics of change within. In short, such an analysis would measure the validity of a general schema as well as the restrictions specific to each cinematographic domain. And by coordinating with an analysis of visual culture, such an analysis could avoid the pitfalls of a cinema history conceived as a simple succession of names and facts or as an extention of critical discourse.[19] These two types of analysis are not contradictory. Indeed, they share the same fundamental principles.[20]

Interpretation and a history of vision: we conclude with these two proposals; with an opening rather than a closure—on the threshold of two new domains—we part company.

Glossary of Terms

Anaphora/Cataphora: In a two-shot sequence, when what is seen precedes the seeing subject, the construction is anaphoral; when the seeing subject precedes what is seen, the construction is cataphoral.

Anti-subject: The role of the enunciatee, in its intention to complete the suggestions of the enunciator.

Aspectualization: The process by which an ideal eye receives, then modulates what is received in order to define what is represented according to its own attitudes and goals. Through aspectualization, the represented space and time will reproduce the model of their ideal destination. Aspectualization occurs at four levels: **dimension, order, limits,** and **status**:

> **Dimension**: What is represented is perceived either as a whole, or fragmented, depending on the scale of the shot (panoramic versus close-up, for example).
>
> **Order**: This level determines the presence or absence of focalization within a scene as either centered or dispersed.
>
> **Limits**: Limits define the framed reality as complete (a portion of the world is represented and appears as a self-sufficient scene) or incomplete (cutting and framing render obvious the offscreen space, which is not included).
>
> **Status**: Here a representation can be approached either directly (with the gaze seizing the scene as an already fully formed object) or indirectly (where it is seized at the same moment as its constitutive gesture and thus is filtered through the motivations, conditions, and objectives which have presided over it).

Blind spot: During enunciation, the space where the potentiality of vision is annulled; for example, the zone of suspension between the gaze in interpellation and the offscreen space it attempts to see but cannot see, or the gap in the subjective configuration between what the character and spectator see and what is not shown to them.

Cinematographic enunciation: The traces within a cinematic discourse of the act generating that discourse. Cinematographic enunciation is an appropriation of the cinema's expressive possibilities, giving body and consistency to a film; according to Benveniste, it is "the setting to work of language through an individual act of utilization." This is the act of uttering a message; the way in which a content is articulated.

Commentary: See **enunciated enunciation**.

Communication versus Enunciation: Communication is a process of interacting between individuals, which involves the Sender and the Receiver as concrete bodies. The enunciation is the linguistic process, which turns a language into a discourse, and involves the Sender and the Receiver as an abstract Origin and Destination.

Competence: The knowledge required to relate the story; a modality of narrational authority. Those responsible for telling or hearing a story are endowed with the duty, desire, ability, and know-how to carry out their mandate.

Contract: The biunique relation between the two poles of the enunciation: both the enunciator and the enunciatee cooperate to construct meaning; the former is an interpreter by being also a judge, and the latter has an active role as well.

Coordinates: See **ego-hic-nunc**.

Decoder: Includes concepts such as receptor, addressee, decipherer, critic, etc.

Deixis (deictics): In grammar, the function of pointing out; direct indication such as the personal pronoun as demonstrative of the person. **Deictics** are elements that refer to the domain of the narrative and to its spatio-temporal coordinates.

Diegesis (diegetic): The narrative or story-line; the posited events and characters of a narrative; the signified of narrative content; the characters and actions taken in themselves without reference to the way they are presented by the discourse; the fictive world of the film.

Ego-hic-nunc: Refers to the articulation of a film's **coordinates**; the who, where, and when from which a text's various elements are organized; what semioticians call a "syncretism."

Énoncé: The enunciated; any result of the enunciation; the utterance itself, which may refer to the film, sequence, shot, etc.

Enunciated enunciation: Parallel to the enunciative énoncé, this is a message or text which bears the explicit trace of the speaker; a mode of address in which the speaker is unambiguously inscribed as the source of the message; moments when the representation represents itself, revealing its constitutive elements. This can appear in the form of commentary.

Enunciatee: The implied receiver of the message as opposed to its sender; the film's implicit "you"; a target fixed by the énoncé as the ideal addressee; an ideal spectatorial point of view, hence an abstract instance implied by the film, but nonetheless available to connect with the body of a genuine spectator.

Enunciation: See **cinematographic enunciation**.

Enunciative énoncé: An énoncé which traverses and refers to its enunciation, acknowledging the gesture that constitutes it, identifying or mimicking the paths and mechanisms of its enunciation.

Enunciative Roles: The four figures involved in the enunciative act: enunciator, enunciatee, narrator, narratee.

Enunciative Traces: Indicators that refer to the enunciative act.

Enunciator: The film's implicit "I"; the primary discourse activity lying outside the diegesis and flowing from the medium itself; an abstract instance of "narrating" implied by the film; the one in charge of directing the enunciation toward its destination; the narrational presence that can validate or sanction one or another character's vision in the film.

Enuncive énoncé: An énoncé concerned only with its own "contents" rather than its origin or mechanisms; Benveniste's "histoire," a message that does not bear the stamp of a speaker. The events seem to narrate themselves.

Figurativization: A process by means of which an abstract instance, such as the film's implicit *you*, becomes manifest in the visual field; the enunciator and enunciatee become figurativized as a narrator and narratee, etc., or any trace which refers to or recalls the presence of a presupposition within the text.

Filmology: An early attempt at an organized academic study of film, filmology developed around the Sorbonne in Paris just after WWII. Gilbert Cohen-Seat founded *La Revue Internationale de Filmologie*, which from 1946 well into the '60s published sociological and psychological approaches to the medium.

Hermeneutics: The field and method of interpretation, originating with biblical exegesis in the Middle Ages and then being revived in the nineteenth century as a science of reading literary texts. Hermeneutics has in our day been most associated with philosophers Hans-Georg Gadamer and Paul Ricoeur.

Hysteron-Proteron: A trope in which that which should come last is put first; the technique of arranging things or positioning them in the reverse of their natural or rational order. In cinema this can take place on many levels: use of reverse motion; editing a sequence in reverse cause/effect order; or optical printing.

Illocutionary/Perlocutionary: Illocution is the act of saying something, in the form of an argument, entreaty, etc., about the kind of performance a discourse represents (i.e., does it inform, promise, command, greet?) beyond what its vocabulary and grammar may state or represent, while a perlocutionary act involves that which a discourse achieves, in addition or in opposition to what it states (i.e., does it convince, or warn, or ridicule?). Beyond the illocutionary act of communicating an intention, the perlocutionary act produces an effect.

Impossible objective view: A configuration that, due to incongruous camera angles, colors, etc., does not allow the view to be attributed to any human character. Here the work of the technical apparatus is obvious, and the film's self-construction and self-offering are made explicit by the camera blatantly presenting its own functioning; the enunciator is figurativized in the camera itself: "What you see, is thanks to me." This configuration involves total *seeing*, metadiscursive *knowing*, and absolute *believing*.

Interlocutor: A person who takes part in a dialogue, a mediator; the spectator, for example, as someone that the film can address and who can be expected to respond accordingly. An interlocutor is the actant on either end of a communication instance; e.g., sender/receiver, enunciator/enunciatee, speaker/hearer.

Interpellation: The recognition by the film of someone outside the text to whom the film makes a direct appeal, "hailing" this "you" in the form of an aside; the enunciator, in the form of a narrator, a voice-over, titles, or the like, that directly addresses the spectator. Addressing an offscreen space that can never be made visible, interpellation can be considered a gaze without effect.

Locutor: One who speaks in conformity with the rules of grammar and on the basis of a given lexicon.

Mandate: The designation of the enunciative agent as the one responsible for relating the narrative; the moment when the enunciator sets the characters in motion, attributing to them roles that require certain actions; the assigning of a task (to show, to observe; to say, to hear).

Metalanguage: A language used to talk about language, and which puts forth terms for analyzing or describing a language. Metalanguage or metadiscourse in the cinema is manifest when, for example, a screen appears within the frame of a scene and thus refers to the screen on which the movie is projected; moments when the film uses devices which point out the constructive devices of film, as if to say, "This is for you; it comes from the cinema; that is, from me."

Mise-en-abîme: A reflexive strategy; an infinite regress of mirror reflections that denotes the filmic process by which a scene or sequence plays out in miniature the processes of the text as a whole.

Narratee: The figurativization of the film's enunciatee; at the surface of the text, in the guise of a character, the one to whom the film's images and sounds are directed; as a protagonist in the film, an explicit "you."

Narrative: The recounting of two or more events that are logically connected, occur over time, and are linked by a consistent subject into a whole; cf. **receding enunciation**.

Narratology: The study of storytelling, including the two main branches of enunciation theory and the syntax of plots and characters.

Narrator: The figurativization of the film's enunciator. While the final enunciator remains hidden, the narrator at the surface of the text, in the guise of a character, purports to direct the images and sounds; as a protagonist in the film, the narrator is an explicit "I."

Objective view: In this configuration, a scene is presented "anonymously"; the enunciator and enunciatee are not figurativized in any way; the nature of the film's construction and availability are hidden; "neutral" writing, adhering to either a theatrical or realist conception of mise-en-scène where all elements are clearly placed, but without anyone's gaze determining their placement; "I gaze at something and make you gaze, too." This configuration involves exhaustive *seeing*, diegetic *knowing*, and solid *believing*.

Open work: Opposed to a discourse that is logically closed and admits little ambiguity, an open work is a text that requires a "you" to invent the means of its interpretation. We are dealing with an open text when various interwoven voices and gazes can only be sorted out in reference to the spectator who gathers these elements together and invents strategies for decoding them. See Umberto Eco for more on this topic.

Operators: See **point of view**.

Performance: The concrete realization of a mandated task. This generally takes the form of a "writing," that is, an account rendered, or a "reading" of the text, the discovery of facts; this adds strategy to the narrative schema, occurring at the pragmatic level.

Phenomenology: A branch of philosophy associated with the first half of the twentieth century concerned with describing experience while ignoring (bracketing) questions about its ontology. Phenomenology deals with appearances rather than things, aiming to elide the duality of Western metaphysics between subject and object; it claims to describe the interaction of the subject (including the body and the intending or "interested" mind) with phenomena whose status it does not at first try to disentangle from the subject. Edmund Husserl is usually listed as the father of phenomenology, although Maurice Merleau-Ponty has had far more impact on phenomenological aesthetics and linguistics, including much work in cinema studies.

Point of view: The gaze which forms the scene, corresponding to either the camera's location during filming, or the ideal position of an observer witnessing what is projected on the screen; the site where the point through which one shows, the point from which one observes, and the point which is seen converge. These points involve logical **operators** corresponding respectively to the enunciator, the enunciatee, and the discourse through which these operate. The configurations of point of view also serve as **operators of context**, elements which anchor the flux of images and sounds to a single point, designating and determining the environment in which a text or textual fragment will be placed. Variance in point

Glossary of Terms 139

of view will influence the levels of the scopic activity (*seeing*), the cognitive process (*knowing*), and the degree of faith (*believing*).

Pragmatics: Opposed to syntactics and phonology, both of which examine a language's possibility and production of meaning, pragmatics is that branch of linguistics concerned with what transpires in and around a text and its reception; a field of research concerned with the constantly interactive relation between text and context.

Receding enunciation: Enunciation which does not attempt to enter the scene, but remains undetected and invisible in the wings, leaving the stage filled only by the narrative.

Reported enunciation: In linguistics this involves a speaker quoting another speaker; in film it involves the enunciation of a representation that traverses another representation; for example, the enunciation of a film-within-a-film or flashback sequence.

Reporter: The figurativization of the Sender, which structures the film's proposal, and works as a data bank for the film.

Sanction: Authorization to establish the facts of the fictional world over and above any false reports about that fictional world or its inhabitants. The enunciator may transfer this role to an internal character (i.e., a narrator) but in order for this to occur, the competence, performance, and mandate of the narrator must be present and be judged by an arbitrator outside the action, generally another character, in the form of an approbation or condemnation, occurring at the cognitive level.

Self-construction: A film's implicit functioning and make-up; the origin of the film's point of view. In Italian: *il "farsi."* In French: *le "se faire."*

Self-offering: A film's implicit availability to vision and hearing; the destination of the film's point of view. In Italian: *il "darsi."* In French: *le "se donner."*

Semiotics: The general science of signs, originating in the philosophy of Charles Sanders Peirce and in the linguistics of Ferdinand de Saussure. Semiotics of cinema was systematically pursued from the mid-1960s, especially in the writings of Christian Metz, Gianfranco Bettetini, and Umberto Eco.

Semi-subjective configuration: A frame that starts from the seen object to include the diegetic viewer. The spectator thus sees as if standing beside the diegetic viewer.

Shifters: Indicators of person or time or place that can be identified only by the instance of discourse that contains them. Personal pronouns (I, you), for instance, shift reference depending on who speaks them. Adverbs like "here" and "now" and demonstratives like "this" shift their meaning depending on the situation in which they are used.

Simulated enunciation: Metalinguistic moments such as the film-within-a-film and flashback, beyond the reported enunciation. This is an enunciation which serves as an emblem or model of each film's "self-construction" and "self-offering."

Subjective view: A scene structured so that we see a character who gazes, and then see what is seen through that character's eyes; here, the character figurativizes the enunciatee. We, along with the character, see only what we are shown, with the sense that the course has been decided in advance: "I gaze, and make you gaze at the one who gazes; I am making him see what I make you see; you and he see what I show you." Thus, the viewer in the subjective configuration produces a *gaze without intention*.

Symbolization: A level of figurativization which may involve elements such as mirrors, eyes, and/or windows as metaphors for the forces behind the text.

Text: Any finite organized discourse intended to realize communication. The filmic text designates the construction of moving images and sounds as an intended object, with a complex organization; the word "text" links films to literary works and to semiotics, a science based in linguistics.

Unreliable narrator: The figurativization that seems to speak in the name of the enunciator, but lies. In the end, the film will deny its version.

Veridiction: The process whereby the text itself determines its "truth"; where the "truth" is a discourse within the text.

Verification: The process of defining what is "true" in a text.

Notes

1. In Search of the Spectator

1. For a survey of the theoretical writings of the period see G. Aristarco, *Storia delle theoriche del film* (Turin: Einaudi, 1951, 1963). An interesting study of the Italian context can be found in G.-P. Brunetta, *Storia del cinema italiano, 1895–1945* (Rome: Editori Riuniti, 1979).

2. H. Munsterberg, *The Photoplay: A Psychological Study* (New York: D. Appleton and Co., 1916).

3. B. Eichenbaum, "Problèmes de la cinéstylistiques," *Cahiers du cinéma*, n. 220–21 (May–June 1970). The concept had repercussions for psycholinguistics and a substantial diffusion among the formalists. For an account of the intellectual historical context, see R. Levaco, "Eichenbaum, Inner Speech and Film Stylistics," *Screen*, v. 4, n. 15 (1974–1975); P. Willemen, "Eichenbaum's Concept of Internal Speech in the Cinema," ibid.; and E. Garroni, "Linguaggio verbale e componenti non-verbali nel messaggio filmico-televisivo," *Filmcritica*, n. 279–80, 1977. Consider also Sergei Eisenstein's fundamental contribution. Beginning with the notion of "attraction" and later those of "ecstasy" and "inner speech," Eisenstein theorized a cinema whose functioning crucially involved the spectator. On this point see P. Montani, "Introduzione," in S. M. Eisenstein, *Nonindifferent Nature* (Cambridge: Cambridge University Press, 1994).

4. W. Benjamin, "The Work of Art in the Age of Mechanical Reproduction," in *Illuminations*, trans. H. Zohn (New York: Schocken, 1968).

5. E. Morin, *Le cinéma ou l'homme imaginaire* (Paris: Minuit, 1956). Parallel to Morin were interventions of a more specifically psychoanalytic character in which an analogy between film and dream involved a parallel between a film's operations and those of the spectator. Noteworthy among these interventions, very frequent during the 1940s and '50s, were those of C. Musatti.

6. See F. Casetti, *Teorie del cinema 1945–1990* (Milan: Bompiani, 1993), pp. 16ff.

7. Concerning filmology, see the work published in *Revue internationale de filmologie* (1947–1961), and the collection *L'univers filmique* (Paris: Flammarion, 1953).

8. Given the impossibility of citing here a complete bibliography, see

the discussion in F. Casetti, *Teorie del cinema 1945–1990*, particularly chapters 7–10.

9. The term "decoder" aims to include concepts often taken as synonymous, such as receptor, decipherer, critic, etc.

10. The term "interlocutor" aims to encompass the concepts of allocutee, communicative partner, etc.

11. Debate on these two hypotheses during this period was often considered linked to two linguistic dimensions (*langue* versus *parole*) or, in certain respects, characterized by two directions in semiotic research (the semiotics of communication and the semiotics of signification). It is difficult not to recognize their fundamental solidarity.

12. Concepts like "open work" or "feedback" are not sufficient to make up for the lacunae of this approach. By underlining the exceptional character of irresolution, the function performed by blank spaces, the programming of response (in a word, by reducing the dynamic relation between communicative partners to a mechanism), such concepts fail to account for the systematic and normal aspects of cooperation between sender and receiver.

13. See especially J.-L. Baudry, "Ecriture, fiction, idéologie," *Tel Quel, théorie d'ensemble* (Paris: Seuil, 1968).

14. Exemplary in this regard is Barthes's *S/Z*, trans. R. Howard (New York: Hill and Wang, 1974).

15. For an overview centering on the aesthetics of reception, see A. Rothe, "Le rôle du lecteur dans la critique allemande contemporaine," *Littérature*, n. 32 (1978).

16. W. C. Booth, *The Rhetoric of Fiction* (Chicago: University of Chicago Press, 1961); W. Iser, *The Implied Reader* (Baltimore: Johns Hopkins University Press, 1974); M. Corti, *Principi della comunicazione letteraria* (Milan: Bompiani, 1976); S. Chatman, *Story and Discourse* (Ithaca: Cornell University Press, 1978).

17. I. Lotman, "Tekst i struktura auditorii," in *Trudy po znakovym sistemam* (Tartu: 1977).

18. See especially G. Prince, "Introduction à l'étude du narrative," *Poétique*, n. 14 (1973), revised and reprinted in *Narratology* (Berlin and New York: Mouton, 1982).

19. C. Metz, *Language and Cinema* (The Hague: Mouton, 1974).

20. This does not necessarily entail the return of an impressionistic kind of analysis. See, for instance, *Language and Cinema*, pp. 121ff. Recall that in the same text Metz characterizes semiology's "reading of the film" as an enterprise that aims "to understand how one understands a film"—that is, as a sort of "metareading."

21. R. Bellour, *L'analyse du film* (Paris: Albatros, 1979).

22. A quite interesting survey of problems relative to the notion of the

reader can be found in M. Nøjgaard, "Le lecteur et la critique: quelques contributions récentes à l'étude de l'instance de la réception littéraire," *Degrées*, n. 21 (1980).

23. U. Eco, *The Role of the Reader* (Bloomington: Indiana University Press, 1979); G. Bettetini, *Tempo del senso* (Milan: Bompiani, 1979); concerning the cinema, see J.-P. Simon, *Le filmique et le comique* (Paris: Albatros, 1979); D. Dayan, *Western Graffiti* (Paris: Clancier-Guenaud, 1983); E. Branigan, *Point of View in the Cinema* (New York: Mouton, 1984); R. Odin, "Pour une sémio-pragmatique du cinéma," *Iris*, n. 1 (1983); C. Metz, *The Imaginary Signifier* (Bloomington: Indiana University Press, 1982).

24. An extensive examination of this notion can be found in Eco, *The Role of the Reader* and in Eco, "L'antiporfirio," in *Sugli specchi e altri saggi* (Milan: Bompiani, 1985). For a comparison between this concept and that of the lexical, see C. Castelfranchi, *Una Mente enciclopedica* (Rome: IP/CNR, 1974).

25. For a critique of the notion of code, see O. Ducrot, *Dire et ne pas dire* (Paris: Hermann, 1972). Particularly regarding the cinema, one can find a critique of the notion of code and a defense of the concept of rule in G. Bentele, "Regel und Code in der Filmsemiotik" (presented at the Second Congress of the AISS, Vienna, 1979, not published).

26. The term "competence" is here used in a sense broader than Chomsky's. See A.-J. Greimas and J. Courtès, *Semiotics and Language: An Analytical Dictionary*, trans. L. Crist et al. (Bloomington: Indiana University Press, 1982); and Greimas, *Du sens II* (Paris: Seuil, 1983).

27. On the concept of the text and its importance to film semiotics, see F. Casetti, "Le texte du film," in J. Aumont and J.-L. Leutrat, eds., *Théorie du film* (Paris: Albatros, 1980).

28. It is often through reference to this distance that models of interpersonal communication and mass communication have been opposed. Such a distance also provides the foundation for conditions believed to be naturally linked to mass communication—alienation, derealization, the loss of civic responsibility, passivity, and so on. For a critical survey of these themes, see G. Bettetini, *La conversazione audiovisiva* (Milan: Bompiani, 1984).

29. An essential analysis of this phenomenon has been available since H. Munsterberg, *The Photoplay*. Recall also the debate within textual analysis concerning the "flow" of film or on the "film still." See R. Bellour, *L'analyse du film*.

30. There are numerous studies that explore in depth the spectator's participation in the narration rather than his or her internal construction. Examples can be found among the selections in D. Château, A. Gardies, and F. Jost, *Cinémas de la modernité* (Paris: Klincksieck, 1981).

31. On this theme, see the always pertinent formulations in E. Morin, *Le Cinéma ou l'homme imaginaire*, and their elaboration in specifically semiotic terms in N. Browne, "The-Spectator-in-the-Text: The Rhetoric of *Stagecoach*," *Film Quarterly*, v. 29, n. 2 (1975–1976), and R. Odin, "L'entrée du spectateur dans le film de fiction," in J. Aumont and J.-L. Leutrat, eds., *Théorie du film*.

32. Given the impossibility of providing here a complete list, one reference must suffice: M. Lagny, M.-C. Ropars, and P. Sorlin, "Analyse filmique d'un ensemble extensible: les films français des années 30," in J. Aumont and J.-L. Leutrat, *Théorie du film*. This article attempts to define how a character can become a subject of the narration (and within the narration).

33. See C. Metz, *The Imaginary Signifier*.

34. See E. Morin, *Le cinéma et l'homme imaginaire*.

35. This involves a self-offering inherent in the text's very being, thus anterior to any metalinguistic procedure (such as conserving the sound of the clap boards, showing the cinematic apparatus, etc.) and present even at moments when the filmic "écriture" operates at "ground zero" (the classical cinema's transparency)—a self-offering in many respects close to the exhibitionism discussed by Metz in "Histoire/discourse" in *The Imaginary Signifier*.

36. See the very interesting suggestions in S. Worth, "Cognitive Aspects of Sequence in Visual Communication," *Audio-visual Communication Review*, v. 16, n. 2 (1968), and D. Bordwell, *Narration in the Fiction Film* (Madison: University of Wisconsin Press, 1986).

37. For an introduction to this question, see F. Casetti, "Les genres cinématographiques: quelques problèmes de méthode," *Ça cinéma*, n. 18 (1979). A notion parallel to that of genre, also interpretable in terms of pragmatics and with a clear impact on the spectator's comprehension, is that of the "cinematographic institution" as defined in the recent work of R. Odin.

38. Consider in particular the phenomena associated with "focalization" in F. Jost, *L'oeil-caméra* (Lyon: P.U.L., 1987).

39. Such is the case with the offscreen or temporal ellipsis analyzed in F. Casetti, "I bordi dell'immagine," *Versus*, n. 29 (1981).

40. This remark does not always imply a theory of reflection. Moreover, a simple mirror play is not enough to activate the spectator's identification or to lead him or her to construct the cinematographic signifier, as Metz explains in *The Imaginary Signifier*.

41. Structural semiotics, by identifying the spectator as a decoder, effectively concedes the analysis of the spectator to psychology and sociology.

42. *Translator's note*: In the Italian this is termed: il *"darsi"* del testo. In French: le *"se donner"* du texte.

43. *Translator's note*: In Italian: *il "farsi" del discurso*. In French: *le "se faire" du discours*.

44. Although in Benveniste subjectivity is founded within language, it becomes actual only through a relation to the extra-linguistic. See his "On Subjectivity in Language," in *Problems in General Linguistics*, trans. M. Meek (Coral Gables, Florida: University of Miami, 1971). Concerning the problem of subjectivity in language, see also C. Kerbrat-Orecchioni, *L'énonciation: de la subjectivité dans le langage* (Paris: Armand Colin, 1980). The issue of subjectivity provided the more or less direct reference point for many of the "political" and "theoretical" interventions of mid-1970s film criticism. See, for instance, the work of J.-L. Comolli, T. de Lauretis, S. Heath, and C. Johnston.

45. Concerning this double determination, see A.-J. Greimas and J. Courtès, *Semiotics and Language*, pp. 369ff. Similar observations about the cinema, elaborated within a different research context, can be found in C. Metz, *The Imaginary Signifier*.

46. See here Oswald Ducrot, "Enonciation," in *Encyclopædia Universalis*, supplement (France: 1980), pp. 529–532.

47. On this point, see R. Odin, "Pour une sémio-pragmatique du cinéma."

48. It should be noted that Eco's interpretive approach takes particular account of mediations: his "model reader" is both a strategy imposed by the text and the hypothetical medium of an effective reading. The most "extreme" examples of the interpretive approach draw on "reception theory" to reconstruct the historically successive readings of a text. See, for example, H.-R. Jauss, *Toward an Aesthetics of Reception*, trans. T. Bahti (Minneapolis: University of Minnesota, 1982).

49. For a synoptic view, see G. Leech, *Principles of Pragmatics* (London and New York: Longman, 1983). A historical outline of the central debates can be found in B. Schlieben-Lange, *Linguistische Pragmatik* (Stuttgart, Berlin, and Köln: Kohlhammer, 1975). Regarding the fundamental distinction between illocutionary pragmatics and enunciative pragmatics (our project belongs to the latter), see P. Pugliatti, *Lo Sguardo nel racconto* (Bologna, Zanichelli, 1985). Lastly, see A.-J. Greimas and E. Landowski, "Pragmatique et sémiotique," *Documents*, v. 5, n. 50 (1983).

2. The Figure of the Spectator

1. Consider here both exhortations to political mobilization in propaganda films as well as expository intertitles with messages like "ten years later . . ."

2. Among the many works dedicated to this theme that began appear-

ing in the 1970s, see in particular, P. Bonitzer, "Les deux regards," *Cahiers du cinéma*, n. 275 (1977), and J.-P. Simon, "Les signes et leur maître," *Ça cinéma*, n. 9 (1976), both of which center on an analysis of the gaze. For another illuminating formulation of the problem, see M. Vernet, "Le regard à la caméra: figure de l'absence," *Iris*, v. 1, n. 2 (1983).

3. A less direct form of interpellation has been dubbed "designation," in which "here-it-is" is always a "here-it-is-for-you." See J.-P. Simon, "Référence et désignation: notes sur la déixis cinématographique," in *AAVV*.

4. Concerning the musical, see J. Collins, "Vers une définition d'une matrice de la comedie musicale: la place du spectateur dans la machine textuelle," *Ça cinéma*, n. 161 (1979). On the comedy, see J.-P. Simon, *Le filmique et le comique* (Paris: Albatros, 1979).

5. On home movies, see R. Odin, "Rhétorique du film de famille," in *Rhétoriques sémiotiques* (Paris: U.G.E., 1979).

6. Concerning the look into the camera in television, see F. Casetti, L. Lumbelli, and M. Wolf, "Indagine su alcune di genere televisivo," *Richerche sulla comunicazione*, n. 2 (1980), and n. 3 (1981), and E. Veron, "Il est là, je le vois, il me parle," *Communications*, n. 38 (1983).

7. The concept of enunciation has already been applied in the context of the cinema. Besides the writings by J. Collins, R. Odin, and J.-P. Simon already cited, see G. Bettetini, *Tempo del senso* and *La conversazione audiovisiva*; N. Browne, "Rhétorique du texte spéculaire"; J. Bergstrom, "Enunciation & sexual difference," *Camera Obscura* 3–4 (1979); F. Casetti, "Le texte du film," in J. Aumont and J.-L. Leutrat, *Théorie du film* (Paris: Albatros, 1980); F. Jost, *L'oeil-caméra*; and, of course, *Communications*, n. 38 (1983), a special issue on enunciation in the cinema.

8. I refer here explicitly to Benveniste, and in particular to his definition of "enunciation" as "the setting to work of language through an individual act of utilization." See his "The Formal Apparatus of Enunciation," in *Problems in General Linguistics*, trans. M. Meek (Coral Gables, Florida: University of Miami Press, 1971).

9. One can find important discussions of the pertinence of the term "langue" in designating this ensemble of virtualities, that is, as a finished and stable system, in E. Garroni, *Progetto di semiotica* (Bari: Laterza, 1972), and C. Metz, *Language and Cinema*. If the two terms join here it is simply because when cinema is defined as a reserve of signs and formalizable procedures, rather than considered as a realized discourse, it involves a new level of abstraction comparable to langue.

10. Concerning these two uses of the term, see A.-J. Greimas and J. Courtès, *Semiotics and Language*.

11. We will use the term "énoncé" to designate any unit of discursive actualization: a shot, a sequence, an entire film, and so on. Such an extension

of the term is justified given the absence of a film critical terminology capable of distinguishing, for example, between an "empirical" unity and a "theoretical" one, between unities of different sizes, and so on.

12. To directly approach the topic of enunciation would involve studying it as a "mode of production" of the énoncé and not, as we are attempting here in the frame of a semio-pragmatic approach, as a "condition of its existence" or a "rule of constitution." Such a direct approach could be undertaken only at the cost of changing the object of analysis.

13. It is clearly a question of a paradoxical presence but one whose opposite can be neither eluded nor reduced. In fact, the indirect presence in the énoncé of the subject of the enunciation is not, properly speaking, an absence, as Bettetini and J.-P. Simon propose in the texts cited above. "Absence" signifies either the disappearance of a presence (which is not the case since the presence will nevertheless make itself felt) or a momentary vacancy by a presence (again, not the case since this implies no possibility of return). Thus I prefer to continue to speak of presence, but of a *deferred* presence, where the subject of the enunciation exists in a displaced fashion. It is in the énoncé (where it is unable to be the subject of the *enunciation*) rather than in the enunciation (of which it is nevertheless the *subject*). The example of a letter, sent and then received, gives a good idea of what is at issue.

14. For the time being we will define point of view rather largely as the sign of a linguistic operation. Someone gazed in a certain way, and in gazing, delimited the image which we now have before our eyes. This will endow the concept with some of the characteristics which Genette attributes to the voice as an indicator of subjectivity. See G. Genette, *Figures III* (Paris: Seuil, 1972). Also on the notion of point of view, see S. Chatman, *Story and Discourse* (Ithaca and London: Cornell University Press, 1978); C. Segre, "Punto di vista e polifonia nell'analisi narratologica," in his *Teatro e romanzo* (Turin: Einaudi, 1984); S. Volpe, *L'Occhio del narratore* (Palermo: Quaderni del circolo semiologico siciliano, 1984); and especially P. Pugliatti, *Lo Sguardo nel racconto* (Bologna: Zanichelli, 1985), which provides a thorough account of the debate concerning the concept of point of view and which gives an exhaustive bibliography. Concerning the cinema more specifically, see E. Branigan, *Point of View in the Cinema*.

15. See A.-J. Greimas and J. Courtès, *Semiotics and Language*.

16. Metz expresses doubts concerning the importance of the level of enunciation in film in "Histoire/discours," in his *The Imaginary Signifier*. For a systematic study of the marks of enunciation in film particularly attentive to technical traces see G. Bettetini, *Tempo del senso*. For another account dealing with technical traces, although from a different perspective, see G. Tinazzi, *La Copia originale* (Venice: Marsilio, 1983).

17. In this sense, "communicative dynamics" like those of the cinematic rhèmes and thèmes studied by M. Colin in *Langue, film, discours* (Paris: Klincksieck, 1985) would be expected to originate in the process of enunciation.

18. In speaking of "stages," "paths," and later a "journey" or "trajectory," I do not wish to imply a "genetic" model of enunciation. What is suggested here, which goes from the simple to the complex, serves to organize a description of facts and not to represent them in a "realist" fashion. This does not exclude an acceptance of Greimas's claim that a filmic discourse can involve different levels of constitution. The point is simply that the stages in question are best understood as the steps of a staircase rather than as successive phases of a linear development.

19. Concerning the difference between "enunciative" and "enuncive" and the notion of the "enunciated enunciation," which we will define more broadly, see A.-J. Greimas and J. Courtès, *Semiotics and Language.*

20. The two binarisms, which derive from Benveniste and Weinrich, respectively, are analyzed and applied in J.-P. Simon, *Le Filmique et le comique.* See also, on the first dualism, C. Metz, *The Imaginary Signifier*, and on the second, G. Bettetini, *Tempo del senso.*

21. Concerning the superimposition of narrative and commentary see the excellent account in G. Bettetini, *Tempo del senso.*

22. Our exploration of the notions of "body" and "role" will involve an elaboration of the distinction between the "concrete speaking subject" and the "locutor enunciator," and the distinction between the "concrete auditor" and the "addressee within the enunciation" proposed in O. Ducrot, "Enonciation," in *Encyclopædia Universalis*, supplement (France, 1980), pp. 529–32. It will also entail a consideration of the distinction between "empirical author" and "implicit author" and that between "empirical reader" and "implicit reader" in S. Chatman, *Story and Discourse.* We find in U. Eco, *The Role of the Reader*, a comparison essential to our research. On the one hand, the notion of a model reader designates both the reading process defined by the text and the most average of the various possible readings (two levels of abstraction in relation to a concrete act), and on the other hand, the model reader is joined by an *empirical reader*, who is intended to specify the point at which an actual, individual interpretation occurs. For an essential reflection on the relation between body and role, see C. Segre, "Contribution to the Semiotics of Theater," *Poetics Today*, n. 3 (1), 1980. Here the relation between a text's internal and external "I" yields a very interesting typology.

23. The same holds even with a sui generis reverse shot, common in this genre of films, in which the auditors of the radio broadcast are visible.

24. See C. Musser, *The Emergence of Cinema: The American Screen to 1907* (Berkeley and Los Angeles: University of California Press, 1990), p. 354.

25. For an outline of the cinema's (co)textual dimension, see F. Jost, "La sémiologie du cinéma remise en cause par l'analyse textuelle," in *Regards sur la sémiologie contemporaine* (St. Etienne: Cierec, 1977). For a revision of the notion of a transtextual dimension, see the elaboration of the concept of "topos" in M. Vernet, "Strade per l'analisi," *Carte semiotiche*, n. 1 (1985). On the institutional dimension, consider the recent work of R. Odin, such as his "Pour une sémio-pragmatique du cinéma," *Iris*, n. 1 (1983).

26. In effect, each fragment can establish its own context, just as it can serve as a point of intersection between several "contexts." On the issue of a tension between "fragments" and ensemble, see the discussions of Warburg's "l'Atalante" and Holbein's "Ambassadors," in O. Calabrese, *La Macchina della pittura*, p. 7 ff. and p. 53.

27. On the distinctions between appropriation, grammaticality, and congruence, see F. Casetti, "Le texte du film."

28. Concerning this aspect of the musical, see J. Collins, "Vers une définition . . . ," op. cit.; and for its applicability to film comedy, see J.-P. Simon, *Le filmique et le comique.*

29. An example which well reflects this process, and which is commented upon by the film itself in a tone simultaneously critical and poetic, is the look into the camera by a young Persian woman in B. Bertolucci's documentary *La Via del petrolio* (1965–66).

30. We specify again that the fragment does not simply submit to its environment, it chooses it and models it: our extract from *Wind from the East* will provide an example.

31. In this context the history of film realism is entirely exemplary. The "reality effect" has been linked to different and relatively mutable textual practices, in which the dimension of commentary sometimes prevails, sometimes cedes place to certain elements. Consider, for example, indications of the camera's presence which serve as much to explain the "figuration" of the frame as to reabsorb it. On this point see the quite interesting reflections in G. Bettetini, *Produzione del senso e messa in scena* (Milan: Bompiani, 1975).

32. The same could be said of the extracts from *Bitter Rice* and *The King of Marvin Gardens.* Likewise placed at the films' margins, at the opening, the interpellations are still under the influence of the titles and credits, and thus more linked to them than to the narrative proper. Both cases also involve precise intertextual considerations: in the case of *Bitter Rice* there is an invocation of the neorealist practice of opening the film with a voiceover which establishes the event's historical coordinates (as in Rosselini's *Paisan* [1946]), whereas in the other film, an allusion is made to television news and the talk-show.

33. See J.-R. Ross's thesis concerning executive hyperphrases, discussed

in B. Schlieben-Lange, *Linguistische Pragmatik* (Stuttgart, Berlin, and Köln: Kohlhammer, 1975).

34. On the concepts of narrator and narratee, see S. Chatman, *Story and Discourse*. The two concepts are taken up and redefined in A.-J. Greimas and J. Courtès, *Semiotics and Language*, pp. 242ff.

35. Concerning these oppositions, see, for example, J.-F. Lyotard, *Discours, Figure* (Paris: Klincksieck, 1971), whose concept of the "figural" reactivated debate in the early 1970s; J. Aumont, "Le point de vue," *Communications*, n. 38 (1983); and F. Jost, "Narration(s): en deça et au-delà," *Communications*, n. 38.

36. Consider here the "*cinéma d'essai*," which was among Godard's projects during this period.

37. This distinction is proposed in G. Genette, *Figures III*.

38. This world does not preexist the gaze that shapes it, but it can nonetheless use this gaze to present itself as if it had autonomy. In other words, this world is only ever a *possible* world.

39. Once again, the example entails an explicit interpellation.

40. This differs from *The Magnificent Ambersons*, in which Welles never actually appears.

41. Note that François Reichenbach is present both as operator and actor.

42. The terminology here is loosely adapted from G. Genette, *Figures III* (Paris: Editions du Seuil, 1969).

43. This basic situation allows a reexamination of the quite relevant problem of the "fraudulent narrator." See S. Chatman, *Story and Discourse*.

44. Concerning these concepts, see A.-J. Greimas and J. Courtès, *Semiotics and Language*.

45. The term here acquires a Bakhtinian sense. See M. Bakhtin, *Esthétique et théorie du roman* (Paris: Gallimard, 1978).

46. It is impossible here not to mention the complementarity, underlined in C. Metz, *The Imaginary Signifier*, between a primary identification with the gaze of the camera (that is, with either the enunciator or enunciatee), and a secondary identification with that of a character (a narrator or narratee).

47. In addition to these few functions, we should mention others, like the frequent anticipation in the credits of the film's style, and of figures that metaphorically illustrate its intrigue.

48. For us, the letter "K," beyond being the hero's intitial, can be understood as a coded allusion to Welles. Both the letters "K" and "W" are constituted by means of a conjunction of two acute angles; a simple rotation would turn one into the other.

49. Another, equally exemplary credit sequence is that of Alain Resnais's

Providence (1977), in which a lengthy camera movement penetrates the interior of the villa named in the film's title.

50. See here the analysis of the frame in painting and of the stage in theater in I. Lotman's "Valore modellizzante dei concetti di *fine* e *inizio*," in I. Lotman and B. Upenskij, *Tipologia della cultura* (Milan: Bompiani, 1975), pp. 140ff. On film credits, see S. Raffaelli, "Il titolo e il film," in *Retorica e poetica* (Padua: Liviana, 1979), and of course, A. Gardies, "La forme générique, histoire d'une figure révélatrice," *Annales de l'Université d'Abidjan*, n. 14 (1981), and A. Costa, *Sapere vedere il cinema* (Milan: Bompiani, 1985), pp. 145–55.

51. And all the other characteristics which make them into communicating subjects.

52. Consider here the difference between the notion of the subject as it is presented in Greimas's writings (e.g., *Semiotics and Language*) and as it is elaborated in research on the act of language in works like J. L. Austin, *How to Do Things with Words* (London: Oxford University Press, 1962). In the first case, a linguistic process models the world, whereas in the second, a subject situated within the world performs a linguistic act.

53. Here Goffman's work on the concept of the "self," its construction, exhibition, etc., could usefully inform a specifically semiotic study.

54. It is clear, beyond Welles's intentions, that the mystery of Kane is not resolved by the concluding view of the sled. The metonymic displacement which the attentive spectator can perform—from the sled to the lost childhood, and in particular to the mother, or to the irrecuperable childhood, and to Susan Alexander (upon whom Kane imposed an old dream of becoming a singer, a dream bequeathed, moreover, by the mother whose wealth Kane inherited)—this displacement fails to enable a discovery of any of the pieces missing from the puzzle. At the risk of ceding to fashion, can we not conclude that Kane's mystery is that of *absence*?

55. The term "competence" is here used in the Greimasian sense. See A.-J. Greimas and J. Courtès, *Semiotics and Language*, and A.-J. Greimas, *Du Sens II*. This concept will be elaborated in chapter 4.

56. The analysis of the body as a semiotic object has been developed considerably. See, for example, P. Magli, *Corpo e linguaggio* (Milan: Espresso Strumenti, 1980), in which I have a contribution. Here, the body in itself, apart from a consideration of its expressivity, constitutes a semiotic object.

57. It appears next to the name of director of photography, Gregg Toland. In the titles at the beginning, Welles's name is paired with that of the production company: "A Mercury Production / by Orson Welles /// *Citizen Kane*.

58. Limit cases would include the dream—where there is no deliberate attempt to communicate, and "natural" signs that are not enunciated by any

human agent. However, in the dream there is still an involuntary communication or a sort of counter-communication, and with the "natural" signs, interpretation could potentially provide the signs of enunciated significations.

59. We limit ourselves here to three points. The first involves a clarification: in defining enunciation we have insisted on the double nature of the relation between the process of mediation and the linguistic act. It now becomes clear, in light of the above division of the field, that enunciation as such must be considered above all as a process of mediation and that enunciation insofar as it is linked to communication, or becomes communication, must be understood as a linguistic act. The second point concerns specifying terminology: the variety of elements designating acts of speaking and hearing which occur within the text can in fact be understood to refer to something constructed outside of it. Consider the notions of the "implicit author" and "implicit reader" which presuppose the existence of a real author and reader. Here the recourse to the concepts of enunciator and enunciatee allows, on the one hand, an acknowledgment of an itinerary founded on the enunciation and, on the other, a clarification of the way in which the text's "self-construction" and "self-offering" are already well-defined at the text's interior. The third point concerns an elaboration yet to be undertaken: Goffman, with his notion of "format," has begun elaborating a typology of modes of textual production and reception (see E. Goffman, "Footing," *Semiotica*, n. 25). In taking into account the "responsibility" on the part of the subjects of communication when confronted with a text, this typology relates, in isomorphic fashion, to what we have attempted here concerning enunciative roles.

60. This concept is given a more formal meaning here than in Van Djik, for example, who defines it as an ensemble of contextually determined "socio-psychological factors" rather than as an "abstract system." See T.-A. Van Djik, "Pragmatics and Poetics," in T.-A. Van Djik, ed., *Pragmatics of Language and Literature* (Amsterdam: North Holland, 1976), p. 29.

61. In this sense, but only in this sense, is it proper to speak of calculating the *utilization* of language.

62. For an entirely different approach, this double aspect of the notion of representation is examined by V. Melchiorre, "Sul concetto di rappresentazione," *Comunicazioni sociali*, n. 2 (1979).

3. The Place of the Spectator

1. The subjects put in play by the enunciation could be equated with what Greimas refers to as actants (or, in some cases, actantial roles).

2. The term "cinema" is here used in the specialized sense of the "cinematographic language" elaborated in C. Metz, *Language and Cinema*.

3. Starting from the gaze/scene dualism, see the excellent essay by N. Brown, "The Spectator in the Text: The Rhetoric of *Stagecoach*."

4. The expression "point of view," uniting the "point" that derives from the placement of the gaze and the "view" that derives from the gaze's effect or content, favors such a polysemy.

5. See the notion of a "tangential receiver," proposed in G. Nencioni, "Parlato, parlato-scritto, parlato-recitato," *Strumenti critici*, n. 29 (1976).

6. See, for example, R. May, *Il Linguaggio del film* (Milan: Poligono, 1947).

7. Is it possible that there be no enunciatee, or that the enunciatee be unable to see? This can occur when the image is suppressed (as when there is an introduction of black leader, an interruption of the projection, etc.) or when something escapes the scope of the point of view (an irrecuperable offscreen, etc.). Still, when conditions like these occur, the viewer waits for an enunciatee to appear. And so we could say that even if the enunciatee *always* gazes, he or she does not always see—this point we will take up later on.

8. It is perhaps preferable to speak here of metadiscourse rather than metalanguage.

9. Similarly, the author of a literary work can merge into a character or into the writing and serve as both the cause and theme of his or her text.

10. Concerning this point, see the excellent schematization proposed in C. Segre, *Teatro e romanzo: due tipi de comunicazione letteraria* (Turin: Einaudi, 1984).

11. A case where the two components figure within the same shot might entail, for example, along with a representation of that character's supposed visual field, the presence of a character's feet or hands within the frame, the noise of footsteps or breathing, and so on (that is, elements which refer metonymically to the seeing subject).

12. Here the order of the two shots and their essential elements are variable. In a construction involving two shots, when the seeing subject precedes what is seen, it is a cataphoral construction, while in the reverse situation, you have an anaphoral construction.

13. And as a consequence, a narratee is introduced.

14. An example is *The Lady in the Lake* (1946), directed by Robert Montgomery.

15. For a theoretical contribution on this point, see G. Mammucari, *La Soggettivazione nel film* (Rome: Smeriglio, 1951). On the theme of subjectivity, see J. Mitry, *The Aesthetics and Psychology of the Cinema* (Bloomington:

Indiana University Press, 1997); C. Metz, *Essais sur la signification au cinéma II* (Paris: Klincksieck, 1972); E. Branigan, "Formal Permutations of the Point-of-View Shot," *Screen*, v. 16, n. 3 (1975); and E. Branigan, *Point of View in the Cinema* (New York: Mouton, 1984).

16. These four cases might be understood as syntactical structures offering several possibilities. In each case, there is the *obligation* that the first element be followed by a second in the defined form. (For example, in the "objective view," the second element must occupy the same frontal axis as the first without becoming an "unreal objective view," and in a "subjective view," the second element must indicate the origin of the character's gaze without appearing to be "objective," and so on.) In other cases, an *interdiction* prevents a certain succession of elements (for example, instances of interpellation forbid that a look into the camera be followed by a countershot suggesting a "subjective view"). These are only a few examples of a regime that could be studied in much greater detail.

17. On this issue, explored primarily by philosophers, see V. Melchiorre, *L'imaginazione simbolica* (Bologne: Il Mulino, 1972).

18. The inspiration here is Greimas's "square." See, for instance, A.-J. Greimas and J. Courtès, *Semiotics and Language.*

19. Concerning the operations suggested by the square, see, again, A.-J. Greimas and J. Courtès, *Semiotics and Language.*

20. One might dub these indicators of context "indicators of the frame." On this point, consult G. Bateson, *Steps to an Ecology of Mind* (New York: Chandler Publishing Co., 1971), and also the observations in U. Eco, *The Role of the Reader.*

21. We have intentionally cited the shots analyzed by André Bazin in "William Wyler, or the Jansenist of Directing," in *What is Cinema?* (Berkeley: University of California Press, 1974). Even though, strictly speaking, the filming of Homer's marriage does not involve a frontal composition, nor does Herbert Marshall's death use deep focus, we cite these shots to indicate the necessity of rethinking Bazin's analysis from a semio-pragmatic perspective. And likely, we could have cited other passages that are just as significant, if not more so. In *The Best Years of Our Lives* alone, think of the shots of the ex-servicemen's arrival in the city, showing streets and houses through the taxi window, the close-up in the restaurant of the pianist behind whom Homer and Butch's arrival is faintly visible, the domestic scene at Al's, and the many scenes featuring open doors that provide a view of adjacent spaces.

22. Concerning this point, see the analysis by Bazin cited above.

23. Certain gazes have a clear value as spatial vectors but still do not constitute explicit marks of enunciation. For a definition of the spatial vector,

see U. Eco, *A Theory of Semiotics* (Bloomington: Indiana University Press, 1976).

24. The tension faced by each textual fragment between either submitting to a context or, in contrast, creating one, is resolved here in favor of the latter.

25. *Translator's note*: This term was used by Michel Carrouges in his book, *Les Machines célibataires* (Paris: Arcanes, 1954), in regard to the work of certain writers and artists, including Franz Kafka, Marcel Duchamp, Raymond Roussel.

26. Rather than the color red constituting a spectacle in itself, its presence and spectacular aspect are an effect of cinematographic technique.

27. After gazing into the camera, each character ends up occupying a space other than the one from which he or she had gazed. This pattern is always made clear, particularly in the case of the actors who play principal roles.

28. If such a saturation could occur, then we would have a case of a subjective configuration.

29. Concerning the differences between enunciation and communication, see the section from chapter 2, "To Enunciate, To Communicate."

30. One cannot fail to see a parallel here with the propaganda-oriented documentary, whose configuration of address is typically the voice-over rather than the look into the camera.

31. This involves abandoning the view of the roofs, whose subjectivity is uncertain. Note also that the backward zoom shot which marks the first gaze seems deviant given that Scott remains immobile, suspended from the gutter. Beyond providing a visual actualization of the expression "averting one's eyes," this zoom serves to reinforce an emotive register that, in a subjective configuration, is just as essential as the perceptual register. See the following paragraph on this topic.

32. There are also auditory forms of point of view, as when the soundtrack reveals noises or voices while the image shows the ear that perceives them. Subjectivity can thus be auditory. Although the topic is rarely studied, it merits attention.

33. In this third section, the film shows something that Scott does not yet know—that Judy and Madeleine are the same person. This disparity in knowledge introduces a demarcation between enunciatee and narratee. It gives the enunciatee an advantage by establishing a distance with respect to his or her surrogate within the diegesis. In practical terms, the film renders Scott's hallucination obvious to the spectator, even though this hallucination is also the spectator's.

34. This excludes, of course, the distinction proposed in the previous note.

35. Examples would include Scott's dreams.

36. On the concept of aspectualization, see A.-J. Greimas and J. Courtès, *Semiotics and Language*. The notion of perspective has been introduced into discourse theory by Gérard Genette in *Figures III*. His position differs from that proposed here in that it sets the notion of perspective to oppose that of distance, considering the former a code rather than an aspect. See also C. Segre, *Semiotica filologica* (Turin: Einaudi, 1979), pp. 137ff.; and, of course, O. Calabrese, *La Macchina della pittura* (Bari: Laterza, 1985), pp. 264ff.

37. Concerning focalization, an ample bibliography can be found in P. Pugliatti, *Lo Sguardo nel racconto*. On the use of the concept with respect to the cinema, consult the definition and bibliography in J. Collet et al., *Lectures du film* (Paris: Albatros, 1980). Among recent contributions, see especially F. Jost, *L'oeil-caméra* (Lyon: P.U.L., 1987).

38. For a discussion of the notion of the out-of-field and of temporal ellipsis as an operation on the implicit realm, see F. Casetti, "I bordi dell'immagine," *Versus*, n. 29 (1981).

39. In E. Dagrada, *Strategia testuale et soggettiva* (Bologne: Mimeo, 1982), there is a discussion of the pragmatic aspect of the "conditions of felicity" necessary for the elaboration of textual configurations. Here we invoke syntactic rules which suggest a predicate-complement structure, but which are interpretable in terms of pragmatics.

40. The reference here is to perceptual activity in general. Although subjectivity is perhaps most common in visual form, it can also be conveyed by means of sound.

41. Concerning the terms *agent, patient*, etc., and the general project of a case grammar of the cinema, see M. Colin, *Langue, film, discours*; and F. Casetti, "Le texte du film."

42. There must be chronological coincidence in relation to the visual axis. On this point, see E. Dagrada, *Strategia testuale*. Recall that a slight offsetting of the visual axis, apparent, for example, when a camera movement ends by including within the visual field characters who were expected to remain observers (including them totally, not simply feet and hands which they themselves would be capable of seeing) gives way to what one might call, following J. Mitry, a "semi-subjective shot." See Mitry, *The Esthetics and Psychology of the Cinema*.

43. The actual order of the shots can vary.

44. This mark of reflexivity is clearly illuminated by the suppression of the patient, relegated to a radical out-of-field. At the level of discursive effects, there is a certain symmetry between the two configurations. Concerning the subjective configuration, it is as if the film itself sees what it shows. With respect to interpellation, it is as if the film itself shows what it sees.

45. Thus we have here a negative prescription. The film must not conjugate itself with either the first or second person. We might cite, for a stylistic equivalent, the "impersonality" of the realist novelists.

46. A different elaboration of these three levels can be found in S. Chatman, *Story and Discourse* (Ithaca: Cornell University Press, 1978). For a more developed version of the first two levels, see S. Volpe, *L'Occhio del narrator* (Palermo: Quaderni del Circolo Semiologico Siciliano, 1985). For useful suggestions concerning the third level, see A.-J. Greimas, *Du sens II*.

47. *Moonfleet* (1955); *The Woman in the Window* (1944); *Doctor Mabuse, the Gambler* (Germany, 1922; remade in 1933 and 1960, also in Germany).

48. These shots supposedly correspond to the monster's vision. In the horror genre, aside from obvious subjective shots, there are many shots that seem subjective and whose function is to maintain suspense.

49. Rather than the subjective configuration, it might be best to speak of procedures of subjectivization.

50. One might propose that interpellation figurativizes only the enunciator, whereas the subjective configuration figurativizes only the enunciatee.

51. Consider, for instance, *Lady in the Lake* (1946), directed by Robert Montgomery.

52. This includes both real or supposed "property" (immobile goods that have been claimed but not recognized) and also metaphorical qualities (the woman conquered but not possessed).

53. In this sense, the subjective configuration that accompanies Francisco's hysterical crisis is symptomatic. It is an explicitly hallucinatory subjective configuration in contrast to which the film offers a sort of "reality principle."

54. For an analysis of *El* that explores the same issues, see P. Lipari, El *di Luis Buñuel e il problema dello sguardo nel cinema* (Milan: Mimeo, 1981).

55. The countershot of Francisco responds as much to her gaze as to the shot in which her eyes are closed.

56. Here we will not delve more deeply into the degree of diegeticization of this narrator and narratee.

57. These themes are developed with respect to the notion of a Buñuelian "écriture" in the excellent G. Tinazzi, *Il Cinema di Luis Buñuel* (Messina: Palumbo, 1973).

58. The same is true of the *I*.

59. One might also describe this in terms of a change in focalization: from a perspective through a character to one that originates beyond the action.

60. Consider here the discussion of the various components of enunciation in chapter 2, in the section "Cinematographic Enunciation."

61. An examination of this structure can be found in V. Melchiorre,

L'Immaginazione simbolica, and in *Metacritica dell'eros* (Milan: Vita et Pensiero, 1977); likewise, for a Sartrian approach to this issue, see P. Magli, "Sotto quello sguardo," in *Strategie di manipolazione*, ed. C. Sibona (Ravenna: Longo, 1981).

62. Again, the two elements might figure in the same shot, as when there is a metonymic reference to the seeing subject (hands, feet, the sound of breathing, etc.).

63. Concerning this double possibility of judgment, see E. Dagrada, "Strategia testuale e soggetiva in *Spellbound*," art. cit.

64. *The Milky Way* (France/Italy, 1969); *That Obscure Object of Desire* (France/Spain, 1971).

4. The Spectator's Journey

1. For a remarkable analysis of the film's first sequence, one that takes a different approach from ours, see M. Marie, "La séquence/le film," in R. Bellour, ed., *Le cinéma américain II* (Paris: Flammarion, 1980), pp. 27–44.

2. The first title, which announces "the latest news," signifies the sequence's status as a documentary, while the second, "Necrology," indicates the focus on someone deceased.

3. The lines are from the opening of Coleridge's "Kubla Khan."

4. The terms "discourse" and "story" refer to a distinction posited by Benveniste between the "opacity" of the work occurring at the level of the signifier and the "transparency" of the narrative.

5. That is, in relation to the one who announces "Necrology" and the other titles (all of which, moreover, are in the past tense).

6. The opposition between "public" and "private" will remain central to the film given that the latter is constructed as a series of (public) testimonies gathered ultimately to explain an incomprehensible (private) utterance. More generally, the titles within *News on the March* seem to have an introductory and thematic function. An exception perhaps is the title "I am, have been, and will be only one thing: an American," signed by Charles Foster Kane. This title openly contradicts the statements of Thatcher and the labor leader and repeats verbatim a phrase spoken by Kane in the newsreel footage. As Michel Marie rightly notes, the phrase perhaps amounts to nothing but a tautological repetition of the film's title, *Citizen Kane*.

7. A new field emerges, opposed to the preceding one, yet falling short of a true countershot.

8. Here, "world" is intended to refer not to an "empirical reality" but to a "discursive universe."

9. A claim basic to much film theory is that a film exists fundamentally in the present tense. See, for instance, the critical survey of this idea and the proposal for a new analytical approach in G. Bettetini, *Tempo del senso*. Nevertheless, a necessary result of speaking of film in the context of enunciation is the introduction of a notion of absence—an absence defined in terms not of an absolute lack of origin but of an obliteration of origin. This absence functions not as a simple "non-being" but as an inevitable "being-no-longer" (or, prospectively, as a "being-to-come"). Hence, we speak of the subjects of enunciation in the past tense. These subjects testify to a finished action, one that serves as a presupposition of their operations, even when the operations appear to occur openly. (Likewise, one could speak of enunciatees in the future tense, their traces indicating actions yet to come.) In short, from the point of view of enunciation, the filmic present appears to be a genuine illusion, a simple "presentness effect."

10. That is, the interpellation seems to happen between two moments, or movements, which constitute a subjective configuration.

11. Like an address on a letter, we have here an interpellation that allows the addressee to receive information provided by the sender. Indeed, Thatcher's diary might be understood to be a kind of "open letter." Concerning the letter as genre, see the important analysis in P. Violi, "L'intimità dell'assenza: forme della scrittura epistolare," *Carte semiotiche*, n. 0 (1984).

12. Let us take a moment to recapitulate and schematize the above. The episode featuring Thatcher's diary can be described as follows: "The journalist Thompson prepares to read" / "the statements in Thatcher's diary are addressed to the viewer" / "this viewer is the journalist Thompson." This suggests the following formulation of the flashback's structure: "We, he and I, address you, in order to lead you to gaze (second segment; interpellation) / at something that I will make both you and him see (first and third segment; subjective configuration)." This signifies that the elements put in play are, respectively: (enunciator and narrator) plus enunciatee / and then enunciator plus (narratee and enunciatee).

13. Let us again recapitulate and synthesize. The *News on the March* episode could be described in this way: "A voice addressed to the spectator shows this spectator images / the spectators on the screen have seen what has been shown and have understood what has been said." This description suggests that the basic structure of the film-within-a-film is as follows: "you and him, I will make you see something (second segment; subjective configuration) / this, together with me, is addressed to you with the aim of making you gaze (first segment; interpellation)." This signifies that the elements occur in a logical order: enunciator plus (narratee and enunciatee) / then (enunciator and narrator) plus enunciatee.

14. These evidently occur in a logical rather than chronological order.

15. On the concepts of engagement and disengagement, see A.-J. Greimas and J. Courtès, *Semiotics and Language.*

16. Note once again that the terms "first" and "then" designate a logical rather than temporal succession.

17. One could schematize the process of the film-within-a-film in the following manner: an enunciator disengages a narratee and an enunciatee, then engages a narrator. This schematization corresponds to the following strategy of the gaze: institution of a gaze, affirmation of an act of seeing, affirmation of a gaze.

18. We can schematize the process of the flashback thus: an enunciator engages a narrator, then disengages a narratee plus an enunciatee. This suggests the following strategy of the gaze: affirmation of a gaze, affirmation of an act of seeing.

19. This figure has been elaborated with reference to the work of Dziga Vertov in A. Michelson, "L'homme à la caméra," *Revue d'esthétique*, ns. 2/4 (1973), especially pp. 305ff.

20. Consider here the various optical effects common in the classical cinema. (A typical example is a transition from one shot to the next by means of movement upon a liquid-like surface.)

21. As in the case of the subjective configuration, this eagerness to enact the interpellation might indicate that here the articulation of time and space depends on an articulation of subjects.

22. The same holds for the group of journalists, who are simultaneously spectators and authors of *News on the March.*

23. Concerning this distinction, see A.-J. Greimas and J. Courtès, *Semiotics and Language.*

24. For a discussion of these two concepts and their relations, see A.-J. Greimas, *Du sens II.*

25. If we were to interpret these procedures psychoanalytically, we might conclude that, in the first case, the film manifests a "neurosis" concerning its capacity to speak (in introducing a narrator, it signals its desire of being heard only when it is certain of its capacity to speak), whereas in the second case, the film displays a "neurosis" concerning its own reception (by manifesting the presence of a narratee, it seems to want to complete its own "self-construction" only when certain of its own "self-offering").

26. On the modal structure of competence, see A.-J. Greimas, *Du sens II.*

27. Examples include the flashbacks in *Citizen Kane* and, most strikingly, in *The Enforcer* (1951).

28. The use of a film during the trial in Lang's *Fury* (1936) is in this respect exemplary.

29. The terms "pragmatic" and "cognitive" are here used in a specialized fashion. See A.-J. Greimas and J. Courtès, *Semiotics and Language.*

30. One finds a theorization *ante litteram,* at least for certain of these aspects, in R. Arnheim, *Radio* (London: Faber and Faber, 1936).

31. This story, though, is one "seen from below." It is a "history of the people" rather than a "history of the historians."

32. The theme of the "social mandate" is abundantly present in neorealist thought. See, for instance, the texts collected in *Sul Neorealismo: testi e documenti, 1939–1955* (Pesaro: Mostra Internazionale del Nuovo Cinema, 1974). I am clearly using the term "mandate" in a more directly semiotic sense—that is, to refer to the moment of a discursive subject's investiture and qualification. On this point, see A.-J. Greimas, *Du sens II.*

33. In the neorealist debate the binarism chronicle/history served to distinguish between two opposed tendencies within the neorealist movement. On this point, see G. Aristarco's editorial "Dal neorealismo al realismo," in *Cinema Nuovo,* n. 53 (1955), in which the author proclaims the need "to pass from chronicle to history, from documentary, anecdotal, denunciative cinema to a critical cinema." Antonioni's "chronicle" is clearly not the type that Aristarco had denounced.

34. Concerning the importance of the detective as narratee in the police film, see F. Casetti, "Il sapere del telefilm," in F. Casetti, ed., *Un'altra volta ancora: strategie di comunicazione e forme di sapere del telefilm americano in Italia* (Rome: Eri, 1984); and M. Vernet, *Narrateur, personnage et spectateur dans le film de fiction* (Paris: EHESS, doctoral thesis).

35. Of course, it will later become clear that this is a subjective configuration—the object seen can be juxtaposed to the seeing subject.

36. Note that during this opening sequence, the roles of narrator and narratee cohabit within the same character, the chief detective. Subsequently, the film will dissolve this cohabitation and attribute the role of narratee to distinct characters.

37. Note that the subjective configuration featuring the chief detective includes imprecisions. In the first shot, the one showing the falling pictures, it appears that someone's *left* hand is allowing the pictures to fall. However, in the second shot where the man appears with the photographs, the photos are held in the *right* hand, indicating that the framing is displaced in relation to the detective's own eyes. It will become evident three shots later that the framing represents the gaze of the associate, who stands next to the boss.

38. The term "passionate" is here used in the sense proposed in A.-J. Greimas, *Du sens II;* see also the special issue "Sémiotique des passions," *Bulletin,* v. 2, n. 9 (1979).

39. Again, a competence born from the mandate that invests the character and qualifies him or her as a narratee.

40. The cited phrases of the detective indicate, respectively, these three preoccupations.

41. On these three domains of competence and performance, see F. Casetti, "Il sapere del telefilm."

42. On the notion of the sanction, see A.-J. Greimas and J. Courtès, *Semiotics and Language*, p. 320; and *Bulletin*, v. 5, n. 21 (1982).

43. To the degree that it refers to behaviors (doing), the sanction could be called *pragmatic*; insofar as it refers to attitudes (being), it could be labelled *cognitive*. See A.-J. Greimas and J. Courtès, *Semiotics and Language*.

44. Here, a possible sanctioning subject would be Paola's husband (he is the source of all the mandates). It is no coincidence that he dies just before being able to intervene in the course of events.

45. Again, the epistemological judgment can bear upon either the action as such or the agent as motor of the action—that is, upon either "doing" or "being."

46. Consider the notion of a "disorienting, deterritorializing vision" introduced apropos of Antonioni by L. Cuccu in *La visione come problema* (Rome: Bulzoni, 1973), and that of an "uncrossable territory" advanced in L. Quaresima, "Da *Cronaca di un amore* a *Amore in città*: Antonioni e il neorealismo" in *Michelangelo Antonioni: identification di un autore* (Parma: Pratiche, 1983). These concepts seem not only to confirm our hypothesis but to authorize its extension to much of Antonioni's oeuvre.

47. The nature of this subjective configuration merits a precise description. In *Citizen Kane*, it was clear from the beginning that events were filtered through Thompson's eyes, due mainly to the shot that shows Thatcher's diary from Thompson's point of view. In contrast, at the beginning of *Stage Fright* the filter supplied by Eve is less evident. Jonathan's voice, an interpellating voice, dominates, and the images seem directly to translate what he says. Precisely because the images translate this voice, it enters into the game while in its phase of "self-offering," literally in a state of transition. This is why we spoke of a configuration with a subjective "tendency." Indeed, it may be appropriate here to use the term "subjectification" rather than "subjective configuration."

48. His narrative begins with the phrase "I was in the kitchen . . ." which is followed by a close-up of Jonathan.

49. This has been proposed by certain French critics, notably François Truffaut in *Hitchcock* (New York: Simon & Schuster, 1967).

50. This is done in the excellent analysis by K. Thompson in "The Duplicitous Text: An Analysis *of Stage Fright*," in *Breaking the Glass Armor*.

51. See the analysis of the unexpected narrator in S. Chatman, *Story and Discourse*.

52. He even masters the ellipses of the narrative: he knows how not to know.

53. The term here obviously refers to Hitchcock not as director but as "signature."

54. This decidedly confirms the facts, but in a manner different from which they were produced.

55. Insofar as the situation involves a configuration with subjective tendencies on the part of Eve in response to Jonathan, we might conclude that the ambiguous manner of expression is due to the young woman imagining the behavior of her fiancé's friend, as a function of what he does not tell her, but also does not prevent her from thinking.

56. Her father had already warned of the risks and confusions that can be created by a mise-en-scène: "All this has the air of a fascinating role for a future actress. . . . We have an intrigue, interesting characters and even costumes. Unfortunately, in life one must confront reality."

57. As early as the flashback, Jonathan basically attempts "to present an image" of himself, while Eve attempts to "take part" in the events.

58. On these themes, see A.-J. Greimas and J. Courtès, *Semiotics and Language*, pp. 417ff, where they are related to the general question of veridiction. A fine analysis of secrecy in the domain of the visual can be found in O. Calabrese, *La Macchina della pittura*, p. 157ff.

59. On "reading" as "illumination" see the interesting remarks in E. Dagrada, "Strategia testuale e soggettiva in *Spellbound.*"

60. On "object relation," punctually enacted in the piano sequence, its formulation in general terms, and its properly Hitchcockian applications, see the analysis in R. Bellour, *L'analyse du film.*

61. *A chacun sa vérité* is the French title of Pirandello's play *Così è, se vi pare.*

62. This opposition is developed in A.-J. Greimas, *Du sens II.*

63. Here we can see the roots of a reduction from the true to the acceptable, a reduction that will constitute the theme of the following pages. For an analysis of the same phenomenon in the domain of the audiovisual, see G. Bettetini, *L'Occhio in vendita* (Venice: Marsilio, 1985).

64. See A.-J. Greimas, *Du sens II.*

65. *Translator's note:* In the French, each of the four corners of the schema are followed by what translates roughly to: the Mandate (*le faire faire*—having someone do something), the Sanction (*l'être être*—being able to be), the Competence (*l'être faire*—being able to do), and the Performance (*le faire être*—making into being).

66. *Translator's note:* Reference to U. Eco's *Opera aperta.*

67. This holds even in the flashback from *Stage Fright.* Included within the story Jonathan tells Eve is the story that he says was told to him. An ex-

traordinary example of the proliferation of flashbacks remains, of course, *Sorry, Wrong Number* (1948), directed by Anatole Litvak.

68. For example, in descriptive texts or in those of "direct recording" (as a literary genre).

69. U. Eco, in *The Role of the Reader*, proposes a conception of the text as a "lazy machine" that waits for its reader to cooperate by both filling in the gaps and correcting the programmed equivocations and misunderstandings.

70. See A.-J. Greimas, *Du sens II* and *Bulletin*, n. 21 (1982).

71. On the equivalence between mandate-contract and sanction-recognition, see L. Panier, "Remarques de grammaire narrative," *Bulletin*, n. 21 (1982).

72. In L. Panier, art. cit.

73. The sanction thus concerns three elements: the object, what the object has become subsequent to transformation, and the conversion of the subject into an operator.

74. Recall, however, that the non-focalization within the narrative of objects of knowledge is one of the stylistic (and ideological) keys of *Citizen Kane*, as André Bazin fully recognized.

75. The puzzle in question is like the one that Susan Alexander obsessively assembles in Xanadu, a puzzle that becomes a metaphor for the loss of meaning the film presents. Recall that at the film's end, Thompson (even speaking of a puzzle!) explains the word Rosebud as "something Kane had not obtained or had lost." This remark alludes less to the sled than to a horizon encompassing the ineffable.

76. The term "context" is used here in the sense elaborated in chapter 2—that is, as both the frame of the enunciation and as a linguistic and extra-linguistic enviroment.

77. See M. Perniola, *La società dei simulacri* (Bologna: Cappelli, 1980).

78. One might consider simulated enunciation as equivalent to a clever compromise between the enunciated enunciation and the displaced enunciation, in that it strives for both the "honesty" of the first and the "prudence" of the second.

5. At an Opening

1. J. Dubois, ed., *Dictionnaire de linguistique* (Paris: Larousse, 193), pp. 319–320.

2. E. Benveniste, "L'appareil formel de l'énonciation."

3. G. Genette, *Figures III*.

4. E. Benveniste, "L'appareil formel de l'énonciation."

5. For Greimas, actorialization is precisely among the procedures of discursivization. See A.-J. Greimas and J. Courtès, *Semiotics and Language*.

6. Essential here is obviously a reading of the pages dedicated to this theme in J.-P. Sartre, *Being and Nothingness*, trans. H. Barnes (New York: Washington Square Press, 1956).

7. Apropos of the relational structure that emerges and becomes essential in the act of language, see, for instance, G. Bateson, *Steps to an Ecology of Mind*.

8. For a critique of this type of approach and a review of alternatives, see M. Wolf, *Teorie delle comunicazione di massa* (Milan: Bompiani, 1985).

9. Even Edgar Morin's excellent *Le cinéma ou l'homme imaginaire* falls into this problem.

10. P. Sorlin, *Sociologie du cinéma* (Paris: Aubier Montaigne, 1977).

11. R. Odin, "Pour une sémio-pragmatique du cinéma."

12. See C. Metz, *The Imaginary Signifier*.

13. Consider here the notion of the "textual knot," or *nodo testuale*, proposed in U. Eco, *The Role of the Reader*.

14. On the requirement of a hermeneutic "weakness," see especially M. Ferraris, "Invecchiamento della'scuola del sospetto," in G. Vattimo and P.-A. Rovatti, eds., *Il Pensiero debole* (Milan: Feltrinelli, 1983), and *La Svolta testuale* (Pavie, CLUEP, 1984).

15. I attempted to accomplish this articulation of the theoretical fields in F. Casetti, ed., *Un'altra volta ancora. Strategie di comunicazione e forme di sapere nel telefilm americano in Italia*.

16. Godard's *Wind from the East* or Welles's *F for Fake* are peculiar films, to say the least.

17. See C. Eizykman, *La jouissance cinéma* (Paris: U.G.E., 1976).

18. Roger Odin has undertaken a systematic investigation of these different cinemas.

19. G.-P. Brunetta, in *Storia del cinema italiano* (Rome: Editori Riuniti, 1979–1982) attempts—successfully, in my view—to find solutions to this problem.

20. By its precision and conscious opposition to film history as a succession of facts, such a history of vision would be compatible with a "geography of vision" like that proposed by O. Calabrese, in the introduction to *La Macchina della pittura*.

Index

absence: of knowledge, 98–99; of spectator, 2
addition, 92
address, 30; modes of, 15; to spectator, 23
addressee, 60, 66, 82, 118–19; identity of, 24; as witness, 74
addressor, 118–19
alterity, 132
Althusser, Louis, 6
L'Analyse du film (Bellour), 6
anaphora, 51, 134
Anglo-American theory, xvii
anonymous space, 55, 63
anti-subject, 65, 115, 134
Antonioni, Michelangelo, 97
apparatus, cinematic, 4, 8–9, 10, 79, 130; function of "you" and, 80; omnipotence of, 50; spectator's identification with, 57; transparency of, 146n35
appropriateness, 28, 30, 43
appropriation, 19, 20
aspectualization, 64–65, 70, 73, 134
audio-visual discourse, 54, 55
Aumont, Jacques, xii
author, 19, 33, 79, 92, 108

Babes on Broadway, 57–60
Barthes, Roland, 6
believing, 66–74, 138
Bellour, Raymond, xi, 6
Benjamin, Walter, 2
Benveniste, 11, 126, 147n44, 148n8
Berkeley, Busby, 57
The Best Years of Our Lives, 54, 57, 156n21
Bettetini, Gianfranco, 7, 140, 161n9
Bitter Rice, 16, 151n32
blind spot, 105, 134
body, 22, 40–44, 127, 131, 150n22
Booth, Wayne, 6

Bordwell, David, xi
Branigan, Edward, xi
Buñuel, Luis, 73, 83

camera movements, 20, 24, 56, 57, 158n42; in *El,* 74–75; in *Fury,* 67, 69, 72
cataphora, 51, 134
Château, Dominique, xii
Chatman, Seymour, xii, 6
Chronicle of a Love Affair, 97–106, 112, 114, 120–21
cinema. *See* film
cinéma vérité, 34
circuit of speech, 4
citation, 65, 92
Citizen Kane, 39–42, 113, 121, 153n54, 164n47, 166n74; mandate and competence in, 91–94; simulated enunciation in, 84–90
codes, 7, 145n25
cognitive level, 96, 115–17
commentary, 22, 28–29, 87, 99; narrative and, 36, 38
communication, 17, 22, 122, 127, 131, 145n28; enunciation and, 39–44, 136; linearity of, 5
Communications (journal), xi, xii
competence, 7, 42, 114, 115, 117, 122; in *Chronicle of a Love Affair,* 105; defined, 125, 136; mandate and, 91–96; in *Stage Fright,* 108, 109
confession, 95, 108
configurations, enunciative, 60, 66, 68–69, 70–71, 156n16
confrontation, process of, 22, 30, 40, 44, 113, 115, 130
context, 27–30, 43
coordinates, filmic, 40, 55, 74, 75
coordination, narration and, 37
credits, 86, 108
criticism, 1–2

in *Citizen Kane*, 88–92, 93, 95, 96, 161n12; in *Stage Fright*, 106–109, 112, 120, 165n67
flashforward, 92
Fury, 67–73

game, film text as: arbitrator of, 104; disappearing logic of, 121; enunciation and, 24; geography of the visible and, 63; initiation of, 19; plan of, 10; representation and, 40; spectator as participant in, 11–12; types of gaze in, 48–49; unveiling of, 17
Gardies, André, xi
Gaudreault, André, xi, xii
gaze, 9, 19, 32, 35, 44, 64; into the camera, 17, 23, 25–27, 28–30, 44, 58, 59–60, 124, 151n29; in *Chronicle of a Love Affair*, 101–103; of desiring subject, 112; in *El*, 75–80; engagement and disengagement, 90–91, 94; filmic construction and, 54–63; four types of, 45–50; in *Fury*, 71–72; reciprocity and, 102; without effect or intention, 51–54. *See also* seeing
generative methodology, 12–13, 130
Genette, Gérard, xii, 126
gesture, 35
Godard, Jean-Luc, 25
Gone with the Wind, 56–57
The Great Train Robbery, 25–26, 27, 29–30
Greimas, A.-J., 13

Hamburger, Käte, xii
hearing, 111, 116, 123
hermeneutics, 6, 137
"he/she/it" (third person), 46–48, 52, 53, 86, 90–91, 127. *See also* point of view
histoire, 22
Hitchcock, Alfred, 61, 106, 109
hysteron-proteron, 91, 137

ideal spectator, 48, 55, 132
ideal subject, 12
identity, deciphering and, 99
ideology, critique of, xvii
"I" (first person), 48, 51–53, 55, 64, 119, 127; in *Chronicle of a Love Affair*, 100; in *Citizen Kane*, 86, 90–91; as master of the game, 126; parameters of representation and, 76; self-offering and, 65; in *Stage Fright*, 108. *See also* point of view
The Imaginary Signifier (Metz), 152n46
implied reader, 6, 11
impossible objective configuration/ view, 54, 70, 73, 76; anonymous space of, 63; defined, 51, 137–38; in *Gone with the Wind*, 56, 57
impulsion, 92
informational point of view, 70
infradiegetic narration, 35, 38
interfaces, 129–33
interlocutor, 5, 16, 144n10; defined, 138; text and, 10–14
interpellation, 17, 23, 29, 54, 94, 96; in *Babes on Broadway*, 58–61; in *Bitter Rice*, 16, 151n32; in *Chronicle of a Love Affair*, 100; in *Citizen Kane*, 88–89, 90, 91, 92; as configuration, 73; defined, 138; form and taboo, 25–27; in *Fury*, 8; by gaze, 31; "good" and "bad," 32; implied marginal spectator of, 63, 66, 125, 128; indirect, 148n3; in *The Kid from Spain*, 47–48; in *The King of Marvin Gardens*, 16, 151n32; in *The Magnificent Ambersons*, 33; as partial seeing, 70–71; in *Stage Fright*, 107; typical attitude of, 87; verification and, 44; in *Wind from the East*, 27
interpretation, 130, 133
interpretive methodology, 12–13, 130
intertext, 28
intertitles, 147n1
intradiegetic knowing, 71
intradiegetic narration, 38
irony, 30
Iser, Wolfgang, 6

Jost, François, xi, xii
judging, 104, 116

The Kid from Spain, 45–51
The King of Marvin Gardens, 16, 151n32
knowing, 66–74, 70, 71, 138
Kuntzel, Thierry, xi

Lang, Fritz, 67, 72
language: conversion into discourse, 18, 46; subjectivity in, 10
Language and Cinema (Metz), 6, 144n20
langue, 148n9
Lector in fabula (Eco), 7
linguistics, 15
The Little Foxes, 54
locutor, 11–12
look. *See* gaze
Lotman, Yuri, 6
lying image, 106–14

The Magnificent Ambersons, 33–34, 35
mandate, 114–18, 122, 163n32; in *Chronicle of a Love Affair*, 99; competence and, 91–96; defined, 125, 138; in *The Kid from Spain*, 47; in *Stage Fright*, 108, 109
McCarey, Leo, 45
memory, 112
message, film as, 8
metacinema. *See* film-within-a-film
metadiegetic narration, 35, 38
metadiscursive knowing, 70, 71
metonymy, 31, 36, 68
metteur-en-scène, 6
Metz, Christian, 6, 130, 140, 144n20
The Milky Way, 83
mimesis, 21
mise-en-abîme, 93, 138
mise-en-scène, 29, 37, 57, 118, 126, 127; in *Citizen Kane*, 42; defining barriers of, 59; documentaries and, 116; gaze and, 27; manipulation of, 92, 119; representation and, 44; risks and confusions of, 165n56; "second" point of view in, 35–36; theatrical concept of, 54
montage, 31, 58
Moonfleet, 72
Morin, Edgar, 2, 143n5
Munsterberg, Hugo, 2, 145n29
musical accompaniment, 39

narratee, 33–38, 53, 86, 87; defined, 138; extradiegetic, 125; judging and, 104–105; mandate of, 109

narrative closure, 8
narratives/narration, 22, 24, 26, 83; addressees in, 11; in *Chronicle of a Love Affair*, 97–100, 105–106; in *Citizen Kane*, 88, 91; commentary and, 36, 38; complicity with, 27, 29–30, 49; defined, 138; within diegesis, 48; extradiegetic, 35, 38; in installments, 92; multiple, 110; "nested," 107, 116; organization of, 32; voice-over, 20, 44, 45, 85, 86, 96–97
narratologists/narratology, 6, 138
narrators, 33–38, 53, 87; credibility of, 108; defined, 138–39; qualities of, 103; unconscious, 121
neorealism, 97, 163n33
neutral space, 66
neutral writing, 54
News on the March, in *Citizen Kane*, 84–86, 89, 90, 91, 93, 121, 160n6, 161n13

objective configuration/view, 50, 56, 70, 73, 76, 156n16; defined, 139; documentaries and, 74
Odin, Roger, xii, 130
offscreen space, 17, 24, 65
offscreen voices, 26, 99
open work, 116, 139, 144n12

Paisan, 97, 151n32
Peirce, Charles Sanders, 140
perception, 13, 68, 71
perceptive point of view, 70
performance, 110, 117, 122; defined, 125; sanction and, 96–106; status of, 114, 115
personification, 46
phenomenology, 6, 139
plan américain, 67
point of view, 32, 46, 48, 56, 61, 73; complexity of, 66–71; defined, 139–40, 149n14; multiple, 87; types of, 70. *See also* "he/she/it" (third person); "I" (first person); "you" (second person)
pornography, 72
Porter, Edwin S., 25
pragmatic level, 96, 115–17
pragmatics, 15, 140

presence, 118; in narration, 33; of spectator, 2

prohibitions. *See* taboos

prologues, 39, 41

psychoanalysis, xvii, 4, 143n5, 162n25

psychology, 4, 146n41

"pure cinema," 31–32

Rafelson, Bob, 16

reading, 103–104, 105, 113, 116, 126, 130

reality, 2, 40; appearance and, 107; framing of, 64–65; reproduction of, 83; symbolic dimension and, 10–14

"reality effect," 151n31

receding enunciation, 21

reception, 11, 60, 75, 81, 93, 96

referents, 1

reflexivity, 121, 122, 158n44

repetitions, 51

representation, 62, 66, 80; appearance and reality, 107; conquest of, 29; doubled, 84; enunciation and, 22; "naturalness" of, 128; "second-order," 96; spectator and, 7

revelation, 68

roles, 22, 40–44, 45, 150n22; in *Citizen Kane*, 89; in *El*, 77; enunciative, 137; exchange of, 100, 117; place and, 66–67

Rossellini, Roberto, 97

sanction, 114, 116, 118, 122, 128; defined, 125, 140; performance and, 96–106; in *Stage Fright*, 108, 110, 112–13

Saussure, Ferdinand de, 140

scene, gaze and, 47, 64, 66, 126

science, xiv–xv

scopic activity/drive, 9, 70

seeing, 66–74, 70, 78, 87, 111, 138. *See also* gaze

self-construction/self-offering of filmic text, 20, 65, 124, 129, 146n35, 154n59; in *Babes on Broadway*, 59; in *Citizen Kane*, 34, 38, 85, 162n25; defined, 140; in *El*, 77, 78, 81, 82, 83; elements revealing, 33; enunciated enunciations and, 93; enunciatee and, 128; enuncia-

tion and, 126–27; gaze and, 64; in *Gone with the Wind*, 56; images and sounds in, 68; interfaces and, 131; montage and, 31; point of view and, 46, 70, 73; simulated enunciations and, 96; spectator's trajectories and, 115; in *Stage Fright*, 107; in *Vertigo*, 63

semiotics, xvii, xviii, 4, 13, 15, 140, 146n41; symbolic dimension and concrete reality, 10–14; theorization of spectator, 5–10

semi-subjective configuration/view, 102, 140

shot/countershot, 75, 77, 79, 101

signifieds, 7, 132

signifiers, 7, 13

signs, 7, 13, 40, 43, 132

Simon, Jean-Paul, xii

simulation, 121–22

sociology, 4, 15, 146n41

spectator(s): constructed by film, 14; as "critic," 62; as decoder and interlocutor, 5–10; direct gaze into camera and, 26; in film theory, 1–5; geography of, 63–66; hidden, 18, 66; influence of, 126; mobile, 66; participation in narration, 145n30; position of, 69, 73, 124; presence of, 124; seeing and hearing, 111; trajectory of, 84–124; virtual, 16

spectatorship, 4

spectator-to-be, 1

Stage Fright, 106–14, 120, 164n47

storytelling. *See* narratives/narration

structuralism, 5

subjective configuration/view, 52–53, 92, 94, 96, 124, 125, 156n16; in *Citizen Kane*, 87, 89, 90, 164n47; defined, 141; in *El*, 74–83; emotional effect of, 72; "false," 67–69; in *Fury*, 73; in *The Kid from Spain*, 49, 50; in *Stage Fright*, 164n47; in *Vertigo*, 61

subjectivity, 10, 11, 19, 74, 147n44; camera movements and, 72; construction of, 68; logical subjects, 46; subjugation and, 52

subordination, narration and, 37

substitution, 8, 51

suspense, 8

syntax, 68
"systematic" investigations, 3

taboos, 25, 28, 29
Tel Quel (journal), 6
television, xii, 72, 148n6
Tempo del senso (Bettetini), 7, 161n9
Terrenoire, Jean-Paul, xii
text: audio-visual discourse and, 54;
  author's intervention in, 21–22; configurations in, 73; deep structure of,
  89; defined, 141; film as, 8; interiority
  and exteriority, 12, 14–15, 39, 40, 82;
  interlocutor and, 9–10; meaning of,
  15; self-offering of, 96; as site of confrontation, 115
That Obscure Object of Desire, 83
theater space, 58, 59
thematization, 20
titles, 85, 86
topology, 63, 66
tracking shots, 77
traveling shots, 77
truth, of text, 115, 123

Un chien andalou, 76

veridiction, 114–23, 141
verification, 69, 112, 114–23, 131, 141
Vernet, Marx, xi
Veron, Eliseo, xii

Vertigo, 61–63
virtuality, 86
vision, 116, 123, 133, 167n20
voices, 32, 35, 44
voyeurism, 4, 20, 72

"we," spectator as, 97
Welles, Orson, 33, 35, 39, 42, 152n40,
  152n48
Wind from the East, 25, 26–27, 29–30,
  31, 32
witnesses: in *El*, 74; enunciatees as, 47;
  outside diegesis, 75; spectators as, 55,
  63, 66, 125; in *Stage Fright*, 109
The Woman in the Window, 72
work, film as, 8
writing, 105
Wyler, William, 54

"you" (second person), 45, 46, 51–53,
  65, 82, 119; as aim of discourse, 64; as
  antagonist and prolongation of "I,"
  73, 126; in *Babes on Broadway*, 60; in
  Chronicle of a Love Affair, 100; implicit, 125; in *The Kid from Spain*, 48;
  as mediation, 129; parameters of representation and, 76, 127; in strategy
  of the gaze, 90–91; true scopic subject
  and, 55. *See also* point of view

zero mark, enunciation and, 63, 146n35

FRANCESCO CASETTI, Professor of Cinema and Television at the Catholic University of Milan, is the author of *Film Theories 1945–1990*. He is also a visiting professor at the University of Paris III and at the University of Iowa.

NELL ANDREW is a doctoral student in the Department of Art History at the University of Chicago.

CHARLES O'BRIEN is Assistant Professor of Film Studies at Carleton University in Canada. He has published articles on film historiography and on relations between film theory and film practice. He is now completing a book on sound cinema in France.